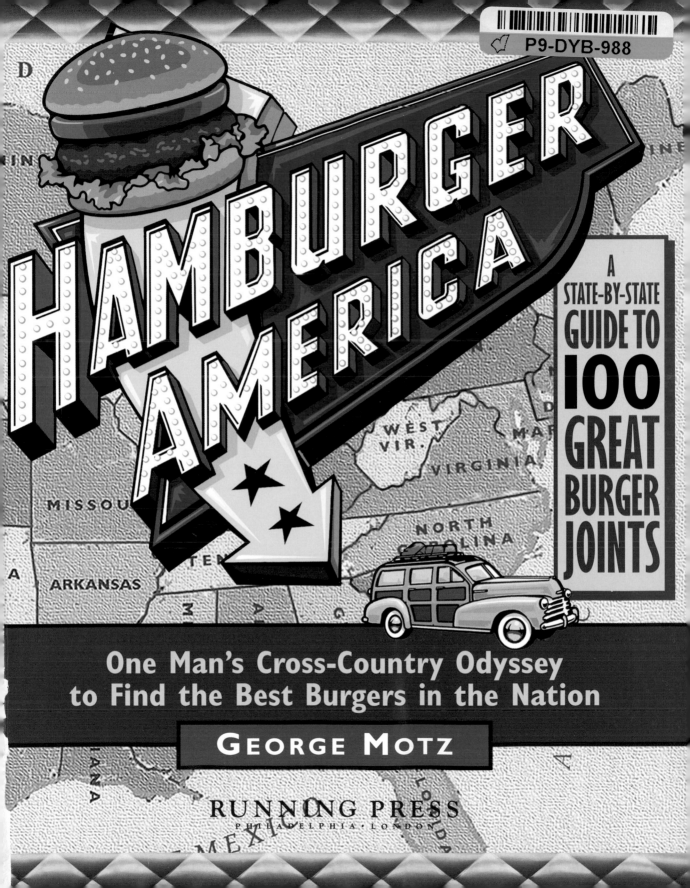

HAMBURGER AMERICA

A STATE-BY-STATE GUIDE TO 100 GREAT BURGER JOINTS

One Man's Cross-Country Odyssey to Find the Best Burgers in the Nation

GEORGE MOTZ

RUNNING PRESS
PHILADELPHIA · LONDON

© 2008 by George Motz
All rights reserved under the Pan-American
and International Copyright Conventions
Printed in China

*This book may not be reproduced in whole or in part, in
any form or by any means, electronic or mechanical,
including photocopying, recording, or by any information
storage and retrieval system now known or hereafter
invented, without written permission from the publisher.*

9   8   7   6   5   4   3   2
Digit on the right indicates the number of this printing

Library of Congress Control Number: 2007940489

ISBN 978-0-7624-3102-1

Illustrations by David McMaken

Book design by Matthew Goodman
Edited by Jennifer Kasius
Typography: Gill Sans.

All color photography by George Motz except
page 21: Photo by Dan Appel
page 25: Photo by Jim Shea
Back cover author photo: Kacy Jahanbini

This book may be ordered by mail from the publisher.
Please include $2.50 for postage and handling.
But try your bookstore first!

Running Press Book Publishers
2300 Chestnut Street
Philadelphia, PA 19103-4371

Visit us on the web!
www.runningpress.com

**To anyone
who appreciates
a good burger, and to my
vegetarian wife, Casey**

CONTENTS

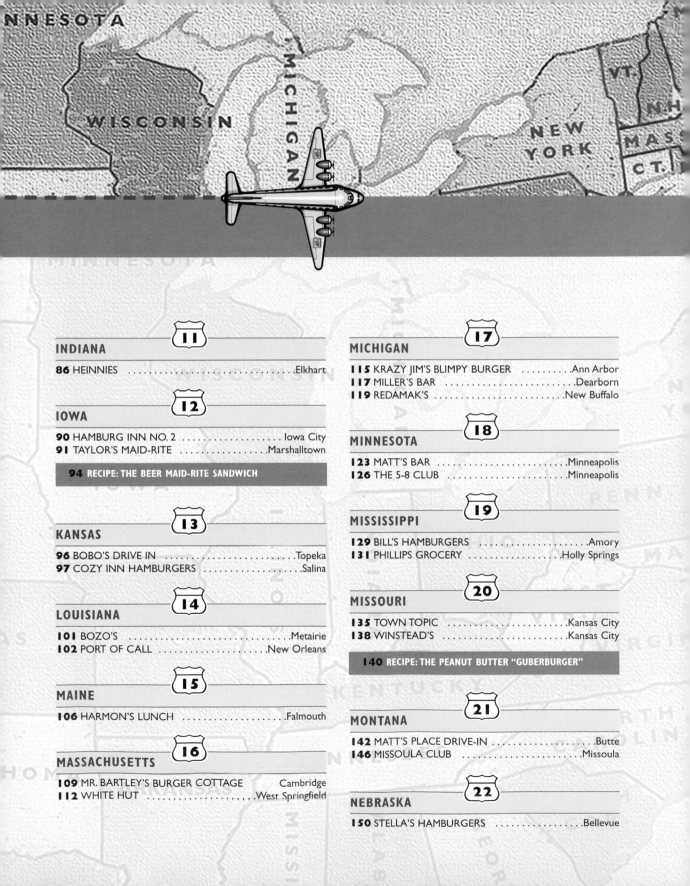

CONTENTS

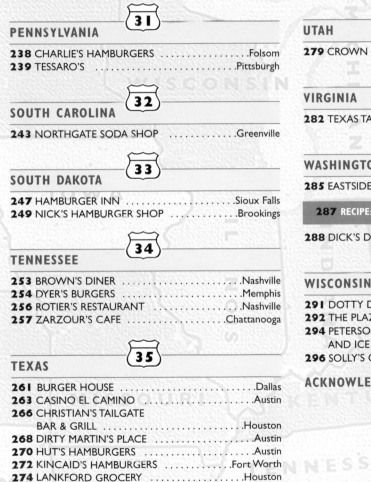

FOREWORD

There is no delicate way to put this: George Motz is nuts. Who in his right mind would spend years traveling the country, clogging his arteries, parting with his hard-earned money, and suffering culinary indignities and belt-busting insults, all in pursuit of the perfect burger, something even he admits might not exist? And he has done all that and more, often in the company of his lovely wife, Casey Benjamin, who happens to be a . . . vegetarian.

I first met George when he came to Chicago to visit that subterranean tavern know as the Billy Goat. Being a New Yorker, he knew little of the legend of this venerable spot; I don't think he realized that the *Saturday Night Live* "cheezborger, cheezborger" skits were inspired by this place and its shouting Greek "chefs"; and he'd never heard of Mike Royko and the other journalists who called the place home.

There have been, by my rough calculation, 4,540,762 burgers served at the Billy Goat since it opened on Hubbard Street in 1964, but none was more significant than the one grilled at 12:14 p.m. on April 19, 2003, and consumed seconds later by George.

Between bites of another Billy Goat burger some months later, George recalled that momentous day, saying, "I had never heard of the place, but most people in the burger world kept saying, 'The Goat has got to be in there.' The first time I came for a visit, I had a hard time even finding it. I was lost for a while, just wandering the bowels of Chicago . . ."

The Goat's burgers are griddled, but Motz has eaten them deep-fried, steamed, broiled, baked, and raw; eaten them on buns, rolls, and bread; eaten

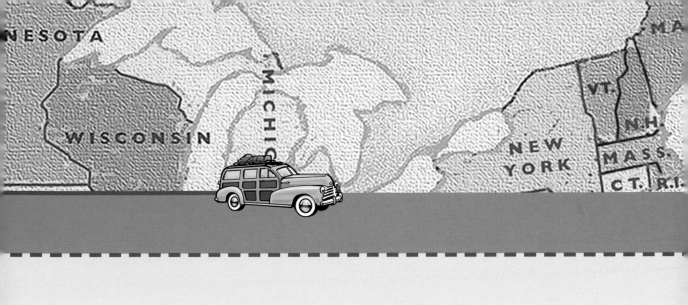

them plain and covered with butter, bacon, chili, peanut butter, pimentos, pastrami, and almost any other topping that can be concocted by a cook's imagination and whatever might be lying around the kitchen.

He did this initially to create the film *Hamburger America*. The documentary gained a robust cult following. It made George proud but it did not make him stop. Rather, the film became the inspiration for and foundation of this book, for George's search for the best hamburgers in the country.

The great television journalist Charles Kuralt once observed, "You can find your way across this country using burger joints the way a navigator uses stars." And George set out to prove him right.

What you hold in your hands is the labor of his travels—a gathering of meat, if you will, but also a celebration of burgers and the people who make them.

Yes, George Motz is nuts.

As nutty as Columbus, or Lewis and Clark, but in his quest to find the best burgers in America, George has found something more important. He has discovered, in the mom-and-pop grills and out-of-the-way diners, an America that most of us probably thought had already vanished, a country of individuality and inventiveness, of people willing to rage, rage against the homogenizing of the land. You should enjoy that as much as what arrives on your plate. It's not just about the meat but the people you will meet.

Rick Kogan,
Chicago Tribune

INTRODUCTION

I know what you're thinking. Isn't a vote for the best burger in America based on an arbitrary, albeit personal, assessment? You are absolutely right. Calvin Trillin once said, "Anyone who doesn't think their hometown has the best hamburger place in the world is a sissy." (Trillin is from Kansas City and, incidentally, his hometown burger Winstead's is in this book.) So maybe you do know where to find the best burger. I've done the research though, and these 100 are among some of the best in America. I repeat, *some* of the best. I'm only human, but I know hamburgers. One hundred was a number I believed could accurately represent a cross section of what this country has to offer. It was also the number of burgers I felt I could handle consuming in the two years it took to visit all of these restaurants. There's a good chance your favorite spot is not in this book but that does not necessarily mean their burger is no good. By my guesstimation, there are well over 10,000 burger joints in America. I'm sure there are spots that I missed, that there are perfectly cooked burgers out there that meet all of my criteria and would look great in my hand and melt in my mouth. But alas, those I missed will have to wait for the next edition of this book. Nothing personal.

That brings me to an integral part of this introduction—the criteria. To make the list, the burger had to be made from fresh ground beef (chuck, sirloin, rump—something good from a cow) and never frozen. Meat ground that day was a bonus, and in the case of Joe's Cable Car in San Francisco,

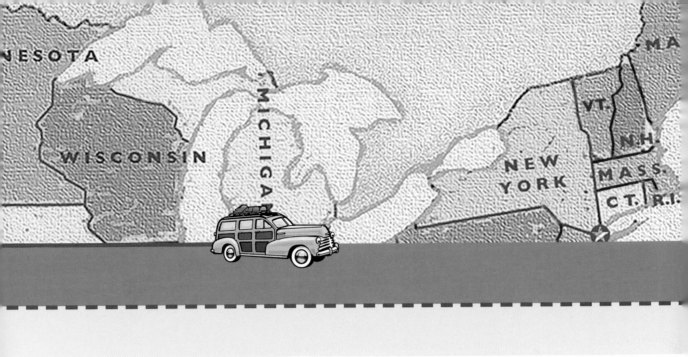

ground right in front of me. And in most cases age, provenance, and historical context played a factor in deciding what was most relevant for this book. For example, White Manna in New Jersey makes a great hamburger, has been around for over seven decades, AND is a historically significant burger joint. Louis' Lunch in New Haven may or may not have "invented" the hamburger, but it's safe to say that it is, without argument, the oldest continually operating burger joint in America (at well over 100 years), run by the same family for four generations, and they still make a tasty hamburger. And naturally, the burger had to excite and satisfy this expert's taste buds. Many of the burgers in this book fall into the under $5 category and I avoided most of the supersized 47-pound burgers and bloated over-the-top wallet-busters—bigger is not always better and Kobe beef should be enjoyed in Japan as a steak. Furthermore, I chose places you'd want to visit, and should, before the wrecking ball comes down and replaces all of these wonderful bits of Americana with a Wal-Mart parking lot, or worse, a McDonald's. In 2007 we almost lost the home of the peanut butter–slathered "Guberburger," The Wheel Inn of Sedalia, Missouri, to highway expansion. The next victim could be just around the corner.

Please don't try to be a hero (or a martyr) and eat all of the burgers in this book back to back. During my research, even I, scarfing up to five burgers a day (not recommended), sought out the hotels with exercise equipment so that I might be alive today to bring you this book. My doctors

laughed when I told them of my quest to write the Great American Hamburger Book, but then took my expanding waistline seriously, as should you. Embrace moderation.

The real reason for writing this guide was to bring to the table the vast importance of the all-American burger joint and shine a light on this nation's favorite food. I can't tell you how many people chuckled when I told them what I was working on. Was I the only person in America who saw a deeper meaning to the hamburger? Or is the burger so omnipresent that we forget it's even there? I knew my mission was true when a hotel desk clerk in Eau Claire, Wisconsin, asked what brought me to town. "I'm writing a book about hamburgers," I told him. "Hamburgers! Huh? Really? Wow, hamburgers, hmmm . . ." and he trailed off, giggling. He was dumfounded. All I could say was, "Hey, someone has to do it."

My other motive for making this guide was to make sure that the next generation of burger lovers has a starting point for saving the all-American hamburger. The way to do this is to patronize as many of these restaurants as possible. Looking into the not-so-distant future I see the McDonald's hamburger as a reference point for many as to what an American burger should look and taste like. This is not a good thing. A real American hamburger is so much more.

Go forth into America—Hamburger America that is—and meet real people and eat real burgers. Across the nation, regional uniqueness

abounds. You'll learn about the steamed cheeseburger of central Connecticut, the fried-onion burgers indigenous to Oklahoma, and the Pacific Northwest's beloved Goop Sauce. Meet some of the hardest-working Americans you'll ever come across, whose commitment to great burgers will astound you. Meet Bill Sianis of the Billy Goat in Chicago, who attended architecture school but upon graduation chose to help out his dad's enormously successful hamburger business instead. Or Bob Hall of Sid's Diner in El Reno, Oklahoma, who left an executive job at Exxon to flip burgers at his nephew's new burger venture. You'll also meet one of my favorite burger icons, Charles Collins of the timeless Apple Pan in Los Angeles. Charles has been working at this beloved burger counter for over 50 years, a life dedicated to your burger enjoyment.

This book is for you, the burger aficionado. It is also for those who truly appreciate the preservation of a part of America that is threatened by the homogenization of the eating experience in this country. A visit to any one of these burger counters and restaurants instead of the ubiquitous uberchain is a step in the right direction. Tell them all I said hi, and PLEASE, no ketchup . . . use mustard!

George Motz,
Brooklyn, NY 2007

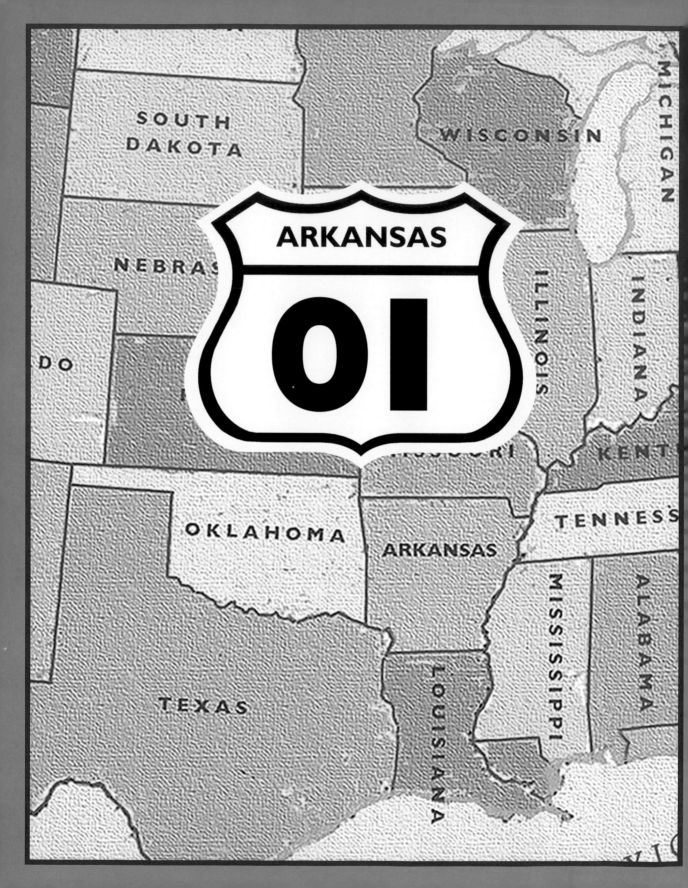

COTHAM'S MERCANTILE

5301 HIGHWAY 161
SCOTT, AR 72142
501-961-9284
WWW.COTHAMS.COM
MON–THURS 11 AM–2 PM
FRI & SAT 11 AM–8 PM

There's really only one reason to go to Cotham's—for their Famous Hubcap Burger, so famous that you knew that already. What you may not know is that the Hubcap is made with over a pound of meat. You read that correctly; 17 ounces of fresh ground beef is cooked on a flattop griddle and served on a bun that resembles a small throw cushion. But aside from its frightening proportions, the Hubcap makes a tasty meal. I had no problem finishing one.

Cotham's (pronounced *cot-hams*) is a restaurant that in a previous life served as the local grocery and dry goods store. The place contains the standard country store antiques and collectables that give it a lived-in feel. Original wood and glass cases are still in place, only now they house vintage food boxes, snuff canisters, and some truly bizarre tonics for curing "the chills and malaria."

For all of the attention Cotham's has received nationally, it is still a local place at heart. The restaurant is a major tourist destination, but conversations can still be overheard that start with sentences like, "What church do you go to?" Cotham's is only a few minutes from downtown Little Rock but from the view out the front window you'd think you were in the middle of nowhere. The scene looks straight out of *The Wizard of Oz*—long, telephone pole–lined dirt roads leading out to dusty cotton and soybean fields. There's even a working chicken coop right next door to the restaurant.

In 1999 a new location opened in down-

town Little Rock. Be aware, though, that both locations are open only for lunch during the week (for three hours) and only the original Scott location is open on Saturdays.

The Hubcap comes with mayo, green-leaf lettuce, tomato, onion, and pickles and at $9.00 is a bargain. If the prospect of hefting this Frisbee-sized burger to your lips sounds daunting, ask for the children's Lug Nut Burger (get it?) which is much smaller and adds ketchup. But you really need to set your sights on the hefty Hubcap.

President Clinton was no stranger to Cotham's during his time as governor of Arkansas. The old country store made a nice backdrop when the press followed him out to Scott to get a burger. "He loves the Hubcap," waitress Danielle told me. Now that the Clintons live in New York, frequent trips to Cotham's maybe a bit difficult.

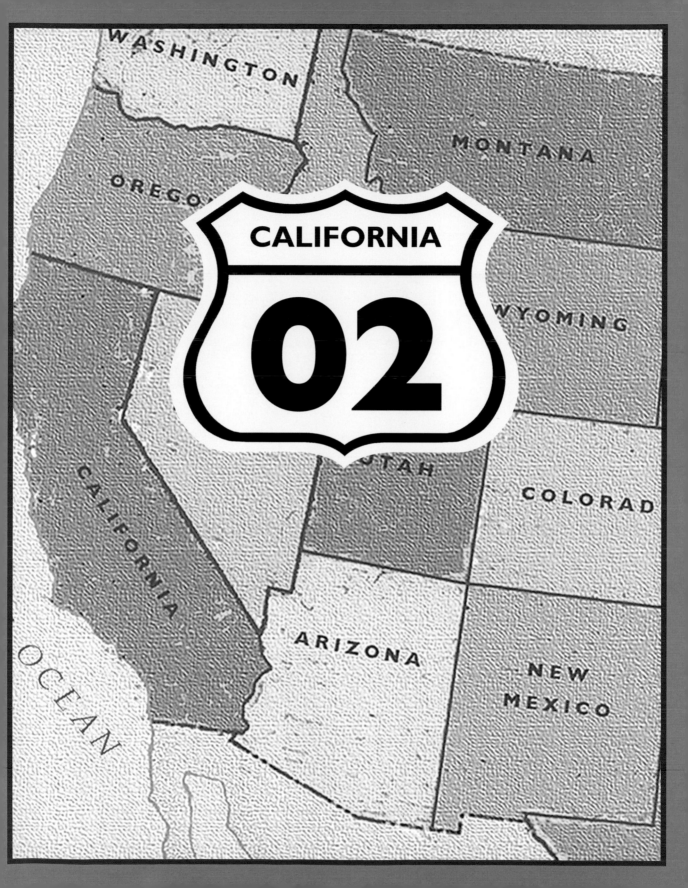

THE APPLE PAN

10801 W. PICO BLVD
LOS ANGELES, CA 90064
310-475-3585
TUES–THURS 11 AM–MIDNIGHT
FRI & SAT 11 AM–1 AM
CLOSED MONDAY

The Apple Pan may serve the best burgers in America. I say *may* only because I don't like playing favorites, but believe me, if there were a definitive burger in America this would be it. The synthesis of flavors and textures in their burgers is second to none, and the presentation is entirely Californian with its waxed paper wrapping. And the atmosphere of the place is pure nostalgia, not the kind that is manufactured, but real and enduring. They may serve the best burgers in America because in the 15 years that I have been going there nothing has changed—the burger I ate in the early '90s is exactly the same as the one I ate last week.

The Apple Pan looks completely out of place on Pico Boulevard in the neighborhood of West Los Angeles. The small white-shingled burger cottage is directly across the street from the towering behemoth Westwood Pavilion Mall. All of Westwood has built up around the tiny burger spot but the Apple Pan remains. Where the four-story mall stands was once a pony ride field. If you look directly at the Apple Pan and block out all of the surrounding urban chaos you will be transported to a burger shack on a quiet country road somewhere in rural America.

Clark Gable used to visit regularly when he was working down the street at Paramount. Jack Nicholson and Barbra Streisand are regulars, as are many other Hollywood stars looking for a late-night burger fix.

The interior looks the same as it did on opening day in 1947 with its scotch plaid wallpaper and now worn terrazzo floor. A horseshoe counter with 26 red leather stools and two clunky old mechanical cash registers surrounds an efficient short-order kitchen. The counter- and grillmen all wear crisp white shirts and paper hats and take your order the minute your pants hit the stool. If you ask for fries, out comes a paper plate and the *thwock-thwock* of a counterman pouring ketchup for you. Ask for milk and you'll receive a metal cup holder with a paper insert. It's almost as if someone forgot to tell them the '50s were over. I hope no one does.

The burger menu consists of only two choices—the Steakburger and the Hickory Burger. Both start as fresh ground beef that is formed into quarter-pound patties in the restaurant daily. "We'll patty up to a thousand a day," Sunny Sherman, the owner and granddaughter of the man who started the restaurant told me. The most popular burger at the Apple Pan is the Hickory Burger. What separates this burger from most is a proprietary, tangy hickory sauce that goes on the burger, along with pickles, mayo, and a sizable wedge of crisp iceberg lettuce (no tomato). All of this (and a slice of Tillamook cheddar if desired) is placed on a toasted white squishy bun and served the way most burgers are in Southern California—wrapped in waxed paper, no plate. The Steakburger replaces the hickory sauce with a sweet relish.

Iceberg lettuce on a burger is an LA tradition, but no burger I've met takes this condiment so seriously. "We only use the middle layers of the head, not the core or outside," grillman Lupe told me. "Just the crisp part." A prep chef slices perfect chunks of the crisp lettuce—one head of iceberg can yield only seven to eight chunks. That's a lot of heads of lettuce when you are cranking out up to a thousand burgers a day.

The result of biting into this pile of textures and flavors is pure bliss. The softness of the bun, the tang of the sauce, the warmth of the griddled beef, and the snap of the lettuce and pickle synthesize in that first bite like no other. It's nearly a perfect burger experience.

Walking into the Apple Pan at peak times can be daunting. There's no real order to who sits where. The trick is to position yourself behind someone who looks like they are finishing (look for half-eaten pie). If you are alone, the wait is minimal. For groups of ten—forget it.

Ellen and Allan Baker opened the Apple Pan in 1947. Allan had succeeded with another venture across town called King's Kitchen. From King's he brought the Steakburger. With the Apple Pan he introduced the Hickory Burger.

Allan built the Apple Pan as a business to retire on and had not planned to work there but did anyway. He hired Joe Kelly, his caddy from his golf days in Chicago, to be the general manager. In 1973, when Joe fell ill, Charles Collins took his job. Charles celebrated his fiftieth year of employment at the Apple Pan in 2007, but he is not alone. Many of the countermen have been donning paper caps and serving up burgers and pie for decades. Today the Bakers' daughter and granddaughter, Martha Gamble and Sunny Sherman, own the Apple Pan. They are committed to keeping the Los Angeles landmark as vibrant as it has been for 60 years.

The timeless quality of old Los Angeles is a draw that is hard to ignore. The Apple Pan does its part to remind us of what can endure in this town of disposable careers and an ever-changing cityscape. But there's no need to rush down to the Apple Pan. It'll be there forever.

The Hickory Burger

Four Questions for filmmaker Todd Field on the Apple Pan

Not much had changed at the Apple Pan until I walked in the West LA burger counter one day in 2005. To my dismay, the red plastic cup holders with the cone-shaped paper inserts I had come to associate with burger greatness had been replaced by gaudy Styrofoam cups. When I asked Roberto the counterman what had happened, all he could tell me was that they were "all gone and we couldn't find any more." According to third-generation owner Sunny Sherman, they were pilfered over the years as keepsakes and the manufacturer had discontinued the holders.

So here I am, the annoying guy asking what happened to the cups as if they were as important as the burger. Well they are, actually. They're part of what I call the "Whole Burger Experience," which includes the taste of the burger, the environment in which you are enjoying that burger, and the people you are eating with. These are all very important components to creating the perfect burger moment. It's easy to have a perfect burger moment at the Apple Pan, but on that day in 2005, the Styrofoam cup holding my milk was clouding that moment. Was I the only one who noticed or even cared about the change in drinking apparatus? Apparently not.

About six months later, I sat at my usual seat on the far right side of the horseshoe counter by the pie window, and upon ordering milk was greeted with a vintage metal Dixie cup holder. It seemed that the Apple Pan had recovered some of its mojo.

I asked Sunny where the holders had come from and she told me, "A guy in the film business, Todd, delivered them to us!" Todd, she would later discover, was not just a regular; he's the Oscar-nominated director Todd Field of the Hollywood films *In The Bedroom*, and *Little Children*. I was curious about what made Mr. Field hunt for this lost slice of Americana.

GM: What possessed you to find and deliver those cup holders?

TF: When I was a boy my mother read to me Virginia Lee Burton's *The Little House*. It is the story of a family who builds a fine little house that can never be sold for "gold or silver." The surrounding countryside changes, skyscrapers go up, but the house remains on its foundation. For me, *The Apple Pan* is the living manifestation of that idea. The Baker family has become part of *our* family history. I took my son there after his first haircut—after his first Little League game. Magic happens around that place. I received one of the most extraordinary phone calls of my life inside those wooden doors, right out of the blue from Stanley Kubrick. And although my family hasn't lived in Los Angeles for years, whenever we do find ourselves there for any reason, we head straight for The Apple Pan. Last year I was completing a film in Los Angeles and entered those doors, took a seat on the left side of the horseshoe counter, as is my custom, and ordered my meal. But when the Coca-Cola arrived it was in a Styrofoam cup! "What's this?" I asked Roberto, the counterman. "They quit making the paper cups," he said. The next day I contacted a restaurant supply house and found out that the paper cups were still manufactured and available. I returned to the Apple Pan and gave Roberto the information. "No, not the paper cups—the paper cup *holders*. They don't make them anymore." He explained that many people had walked off with the things as souvenirs, and that Martha, the owner, was heartbroken. "That makes two of us," I told him. Over the next few weeks I hunted everywhere for the holders. I tracked them down through prop houses, soda counters in small-town pharmacies, and of course, eBay. They turned up in places like Kentucky, Missouri, Quebec, and Texas. As the boxes arrived at my office I would make delivery pit stops at the Apple Pan on my way in to work. When the number of holders exceeded 50 (there are 24 seats) they began to use them in full rotation. Martha's daughter Sunny called to inform me that Styrofoam was officially and permanently retired.

GM: Do you believe the cup holders make for a better dining experience at the Apple Pan?

TF: Yes. They are as much a part of the place as the wooden ceiling fans and the Tillamook cheddar that adorns their famous Hickory Burger.

GM: Do you plan on supplying more if they run out?

TF: It seems I'll have to. Just today I spoke with the manager and he said they were running low again. People keep stealing them.

GM: What do you order when you go to the Apple Pan?

TF: Allan Baker's Hickory Burger, fries, Coca-Cola, and once in a great while a slice of Roma Grover Baker's wonderful apple pie.

Photo courtesy of Dan Appel

HODAD'S

5010 NEWPORT AVENUE
OCEAN BEACH, CA 92107
619-224-4623
SUN–THURS 11 AM–9 PM
FRI & SAT 11 AM–10 PM

Hodad's is exactly what you are looking for in a Southern California burger destination—an open-air restaurant serving enormous, tasty, no-frills burgers wrapped in waxed paper just steps from the beach. The atmosphere is inviting, with its license-plate-covered walls, the front end of a '66 VW Microbus that serves as a two-person booth, a public water bowl for dogs outside, and a sign reading "No shoes, no shirt . . . no problem!"

There are basically three burgers to order here: the Mini, the Single, and the Double. Single burgers start as a one-third pound patty. A Double involves two patties, and after adding cheese, lettuce, tomato, onion, mayo, bacon, and so on, becomes very large. The bacon served at Hodad's is out of this world. Longtime employee Benny invited me into the kitchen to show me how the bacon is prepared. Fortunately for the sake of keeping proprietary secrets safe, I didn't really follow the process. It involved large amounts of special, uncooked bacon in a sieve sitting over a pot of boiling water. At some point this *bacon boil* is transferred to the grill, cooked to crispy, and married to your burger. The taste is truly unique and adds an intense smokiness to the burger experience. I also got a glimpse of the decades-old cast-iron grill. Needless to say, I can see where a Hodad burger gets its flavor.

The restaurant doesn't grind their own beef anymore, though tattooed ten-year employee J.R. told me, "We get a delivery of fresh patties every morning." And don't miss the fries. They are enormous, battered slices of potato that resemble the popular "Jo-Jo," a deep-fried, Mid western truck stop spud specialty.

Like a surprising number of hamburger stands in America, Hodad's has moved locations three times, but all within a few blocks. It is owned by Michael Hardin, whose parents built the first stand in the sand next to the lifeguard tower in 1969. "This location has been great for us," he said of the newer central Ocean Beach spot. "We have crowds all year, even in winter."

Michael is a true, tattoo-covered, Ocean Beach local. He even has the local surfer's code

"1502" tattooed across his back, which in surfer vernacular refers to Ocean Beach. You can see Michael driving around town regularly in his customized, chopped VW Microbus, a great-looking, shortened bus with about six feet missing from its center. "We'll drive it into the O.B. parades unregistered," Michael told me laughing, "and the guys will do donuts and throw fries out the window."

Hodad's still accepts license plate donations, and if you submit a custom plate your meal is free. You really have never seen a collection of plates quite this extensive.

What is a "hodad"? A person who hangs out at the beach and pretends to be a surfer. Hodad or not, I would suggesting eating here *after* surfing, not before . . .

IRV'S BURGER

8289 SANTA MONICA BLVD
WEST HOLLYWOOD, CA 90046
323-650-2456
WWW.IRVSBURGERS.COM
MON–FRI 7:30 AM–8 PM
SAT 8 AM–7 PM
CLOSED SUNDAY

Irv's was saved, thank God, and Sonia Hong was responsible. When I found a worn leather stool at the ramshackle burger spot 10 feet from the traffic on Santa Monica Boulevard, my first impression was that Sonia

was not an Irv. "I am NEW Irv" she said and let out a chuckle. Korean-Americans Sonia and her brother Sean bought the business, with every penny they had, in 2000 from Irving Gendis, who had flipped burgers there from 1978 to 2000.

Before it was Irv's, the tiny stand on old Route 66 opened as Queen's Burgers in 1948. Typical of post World War II burger ventures along the "Mother Road," Irv's remains as an icon of a quickly vanishing component of the early automobile age in Southern California. Over the decades, many Hollywood stars and musicians became regulars, including Jim Morrison and Janis Joplin, cementing the popularity of this burger destination. Irv's also made a great backdrop for the inner sleeve of Linda Ronstadt's *Living in the USA*. Open the record album and you'll see a nighttime snapshot, two feet wide, taken in 1978 at Irv's, with

Photo courtesy of Jim Shea

Linda grabs a bag of chips at Irv's in 1978

Linda and her band posing.

The most significant event in Irv's nearly 60 years in operation was a day in 2005 when Starbuck's West Coast nemesis Peet's Coffee tried to push Sonia off her little slice of prime real estate in West Hollywood. The regulars were appalled, the neighborhood was empowered, and cute little Sonia was not going down without a fight. The locals petitioned Peet's. "We were on the news and received thousands of letters," Sonia told me. The mission to save Irv's became a public issue. Sonia set up multiple meetings at city hall, and after a year of fighting, Los Angeles County declared Irv's a historical monument.

The burger at Irv's is a California classic: tucked into waxed paper, on a soft, toasted white bun, and served on a paper plate. A wad of fresh ground beef is slapped on the tiny griddle and smashed HARD with a bacon weight once. Somehow Sonia, or whoever is at the grill, manages to whack the ball of meat with just the right amount of force to create the perfect-sized patty.

Usually three people are hard at work at Irv's, including Mama, Sonia's mother. In all of the craziness that goes on inside the little shack Sonia still has time to write personalized messages on everyone's paper plate. On my last visit she drew, down to the color, the shirt I was wearing and included the message, "Just for George." She positions the burger on the plate so that both the burger and the art can be admired simultaneously. I believe the shirt drawings are her way of matching the burger to the customer—one of the more unique methods of order managment.

When asked what the sauce was, Sonia replied, "Love! Love is the special sauce."

Opt for a double with cheese because a single thin patty will not sate your appetite. Available condiments are the standard lettuce, tomato, onion, and pickle. Mayo, ketchup, and mustard are also available, and the menu lists a burger that comes with "special sauce." When I asked Sonia what the sauce was, she replied, without pause, "Love! Love is the special sauce."

The next time you visit Irv's, meet Sonia and Mama and feel proud to be an American. Eat your waxed paper-wrapped burger, take in the vibe of old Route 66, and remember the fight that saved this burger spot from the wrecking ball—each bite will taste that much better.

JIM-DENNY'S

816 12TH STREET
SACRAMENTO, CA 95814
916-443-9655
WWW.LEAVEYOURTEETHATHOME.COM

MON &TUES 6 AM–3 PM
WED–SAT 6 AM–9 PM
CLOSED SUNDAY

For its first 40 years Jim-Denny's was never closed. From 1934 to the late '70s the tiny ten-stool hamburger stand in downtown Sacramento was open 24 hours. Most of those odd late night/early morning hours fed bus drivers from the Trailways depot just across the parking lot and late-night revelers at the long-gone dance hall across the street. The bus depot is no longer active and the restaurant's hours have been reduced, but Jim-Denny's survives thanks to its fourth owner and chef, Patsy Lane.

"We call these the ten hottest seats in town," Patsy said referring to the cramped but cozy seating in the burger stand she bought with her daughter and son-in-law in 2005. Upon taking the helm at Jim-Denny's the first order of business was removing decades of grease and grime that had almost rendered the place unusable. "The ceiling had almost caved in, it was caked with so much grease. If you put your hand on the wall it would just stick there!" Patsy told me as she flipped my burger.

Regardless of the rebuild and deep cleansing that the restaurant went through, Patsy still serves beautifully greasy griddled burgers that are slightly larger than those that Jim Van Nort and subsequent owners served for the first 70 years. And with the exception of new curtains on the windows, everything else is pretty much the same. The wooden candy and cigarette shelves behind the counter labeled with features of the old menu (Fancy Cheeseburgers and a Fancy Cube Steak Sandwich for 25 cents) remain intact. The original red leather swivel stools are still anchored at their spots facing the worn Formica counter. The griddle continues to occupy the same spot just inside the front window.

Jim and a friend Denny started Jim-Denny's just before World War II. After the war, Jim and Denny parted ways and Jim opened a new restaurant with the same name around the corner. That location (also known as #2) is the only one that remains, and thanks to the efforts

of Jim in 1988, this classic American burger stand has been designated a historic landmark by the city of Sacramento.

"We use the same butcher for fresh ground beef that Jim used since the early days," Patsy pointed out. The burgers come in two sizes—a smaller three-ounce patty and a larger six-ounce. Both arrive at Jim-Denny's daily as fresh, preformed patties.

The burger menu is extensive. You can order a Megaburger (two half-pound patties), a Superburger (one half-pound patty), or the Five Cent Burger, the original price for the quarter-pound burger. Each is served on locally made fluffy white rolls with lettuce, tomato, onion, pickle, mayo, and mustard standard.

A tradition that disappeared with Jim along with his "my way or no way" attitude was one of the restaurant's most endearing qualities—if you sat at the last seat at the counter you had to answer the phone and take the orders. The rule was created based on the seat's proximity to the phone. Fortunately for lovers of tradition like myself, I was glad to see that Jim's original note to diners at the seat remains, right next to the nonfunctioning pay phone. "If you sit near the phone you must answer it. Take the order, or ask them to hold." This was followed by sample greetings: "Jim-Denny's may I help you?" or "Jim-Denny's, please hold."

JOE'S CABLE CAR RESTAURANT

4320 MISSION STREET
SAN FRANCISCO, CA 94112
415-334-6699
WWW.JOESCABLECAR.COM
OPEN DAILY 11 AM–11 PM

The meat grinder is in the window—what more can I say? "It's there mostly for dramatic reasons, but it's there so the customer can see what they are getting," says Joe Obegi, owner for over 40 years and the man responsible for some of the freshest burgers on the West Coast. The grinder is only five feet from the huge flattop griddle.

Joe emigrated from Armenia to Brooklyn, NY in the early 1960s and jumped a Greyhound for San Francisco the next day. He found his way to what was at the time a small walk-up diner resembling a cable car. In 1965, after working there for a while, Joe bought the restaurant, added his name to the marquee, and has held court daily since. "I see grandchildren now of customers from way back," Joe told me as I inhaled my burger. Since the early days, Joe has renovated and expanded more than once and continually upgrades the service. Over the decades the restaurant slowly added indoor seating, beer and wine, parking (Joe spends half his day chasing off interlopers), and a larger state-of-the-art kitchen. It's an impressive little empire.

The restaurant décor is an eclectic mix of custom neon, oil paintings of butcher shop scenes, an artist's rendering of retail cuts of beef, and a sea of Polaroids taken of regular customers. The black linoleum floor is polished to an impossible shine and a wall of windows into the kitchen gives you the sense that there's nothing to hide here.

Joe takes his burgers very seriously. Don't look for half-pounders and other fractional designations here. Joe prefers to use what he calls "actual sizes," four,-six,-and eight-ounce "fresh ground beef steaks." The burgers are cooked medium-rare unless specified. The menu explains, "Order your beef steak the way you would like your steak cooked."

About halfway through my "beef steak," Joe made a strange but characteristically brazen move. He grabbed a fork and delicately pried loose a small portion of meat from the center of my burger. "Eat that, just like that with no bun or other stuff." My burger experience had been altered and I had seen the light—Joe's burgers really were ground steaks.

A butcher dressed in all white with a white paper cap starts the burger-making process by trimming a large chuck steak behind glass, for all the patrons to witness. The meat is coarsely ground, measured, and portioned into balls using ice cream scoops, then gently pressed into patties six at a time with a special press of Joe's design. When the patties hit the griddle they contain 6 to 8 percent fat.

Driving down Mission in the Excelsior neighborhood, it's hard to miss Joe's. A huge sign, larger than the one with the actual name of the restaurant, announces with incredible candor, "JOE GRINDS HIS OWN FRESH CHUCK DAILY." He really does and it makes all the difference.

How to Buy Hamburger Meat

OK, I've given you 100 reasons to eat out and you still want to make a burger at home? No problem. All you'll need to do is drop in to your local big-box supermarket and grab a plastic-wrapped wad of ground meat on the Styrofoam tray, right? Wrong. The first step is getting the right meat. Here's a guide to shopping for ground beef:

Go to your local butcher, not the supermarket. Fresh ground beef is the prime ingredient of an excellent burger. Supermarket ground beef is rarely fresh. Also, the origin of the cow (or cows) that is in supermarket beef is usually unknown. If you go to a butcher, chances are the beef comes from one cow and is ground right in front of you.

Depending on your preference, choose a fat-to-lean ratio. The best hamburgers have more fat (surprised?) but lean sirloin is always an option for the health conscious. Most butchers will choose an 80/20 percent ratio of muscle to fat if you don't ask. This is because any more fat will cause the burger to shrink substantially as it cooks. Less than 5 percent fat may cause the burger to stick to the cooking surface.

Ask for chuck shoulder. This is the most common part of the cow used for hamburger meat because of its high fat content. Some butchers will blend fatty chuck with sirloin in the grinder to increase the leanness of the mix.

Ask your butcher to grind the chuck "twice" or ask for a "number two grind." This means he'll put it through the grinder twice to ensure that the fat and muscle fibers are blended well. My local butcher insists the beef needs to be sent through the grinder three times for proper blending.

Use the ground beef **the day you purchase it**. After the first day, refrigeration causes the juices to separate from the meat. These are the juices you need to create the perfect burger. Freeze any leftover beef if you need to keep it longer than a day

Making patties from fresh ground beef at Joe's Cable Car

MARTY'S

10558 WEST PICO BOULEVARD
LOS ANGELES, CA 90064
310-836-6944

OPEN DAILY 7 AM–6 PM

In a town where finding old, established anything is getting harder and harder, look for this tiny burger stand in West LA for a genuine blast from LA's past. What's more, Marty's has been serving up quality fast food made with fresh ingredients and has never succumbed to the temptation to serve processed frozen food. For nearly five decades almost nothing has changed. "Nothing," Vicki Bassman told me. "Never will." Vicki is the daughter-in-law of Marty himself. She told me without pause, "There's nothing like fresh meat."

Marty's is the "Home of the Combo" and this fact is proudly displayed on a sign on the roof of the stand. The combo is so basic you'll wonder why more restaurants have not followed suit. Invented in the 1950s, the combo at

Marty's is a hamburger with a hot dog on top. It's a great-tasting way to be indecisive and order both fast-food icons together.

Both meats for the combo come from high-quality ingredients. The hot dogs are Vienna Beef foot-longs and the burgers are pattied on the premises everyday from fresh ground chuck. Angel, manager of 20 years, told me, "We take a three-and-a-half ounce measured scoop of fresh ground beef and press each patty by hand." They use a single press that produces an almost paper-thin patty, one at a time. On the original, perfectly seasoned griddle, the combo is cooked separately, then wed. The foot-long is halved lengthwise, flattened, and then halved again, resembling a small square red raft. The burger is cooked for less than a minute on each side before the hot dog raft is placed on top. The stack of America's two favorite fast foods piggybacked on the griddle and separated by a square of yellow cheese is a sight both absurd and beautiful, a sight that makes you proud to be an American.

Burgers come standard with mayonnaise, ketchup, lettuce, onion, and a tomato slice (which Angel slices as your burger comes off the griddle). Mustard and pickles need to be requested. One time a guy on line in front of me asked for his combo "my way," which naturally sounded very folksy and personal, but he told me, "That just means extra mustard, extra mayo."

Marty Bassman opened the roadside stand in 1958 and worked the griddle until the late 1960s when operations were handed over to his son Howard. At the time Howard assumed the business, he was only 17 years old. Today, Howard and his wife run the stand, as well as a successful catering business that focuses on supplying local schools with high-quality lunches and private barbecues around Los Angeles.

I never would have discovered Marty's had it not been for my LA cousin Dan Appel. The tiny blue and orange burger stand is a blur to most as they speed down Pico. Wedged between a gas station and a fire department, and down the street from popular Rancho Park, the stand is a daily lunch spot for firefighters. "They have a gym upstairs," Angel told me, "they have nothing to worry about." Angel and his hard-working crew take orders without writing a single thing down. "I can remember up to 25 orders at a time, in my head," Angel said, finger to temple.

A throwback to simpler times, the stand offers walk-up service and a few outdoor stools and narrow counters along the sides of the structure. A patio behind the stand (that I only discovered recently) has enough seating for 50.

Howard told me, "When I was a kid, there were mom-and-pop hamburger stands like Marty's all over Los Angeles. They've all disappeared." Across the street from Marty's stand the ubiquitous golden arches of a popular American burger chain. Its garish presence, though, doesn't seem to affect the brisk business being conducted at Marty's. It seems that the waiting customers are smarter than that. They know where to find a real burger.

PIE 'N BURGER

913 E. CALIFORNIA BOULEVARD
PASADENA, CA 91106
626-795-1123
WWW.PIENBURGER.COM

MON–FRI 6 AM–10 PM

SAT 7 AM–10 PM

SUN 7AM–9PM

"That was the last slice of butterscotch pie. Hope you didn't want one," the waitress said to me on my first visit to this forty-plus-year-old burger counter. The customer I had just been speaking to, who had told me he was visiting from London, said he was not leaving California without a slice of butterscotch pie from Pie 'n Burger. No big deal. I didn't know what I was missing. Then I visited two more times and ran into the same problem (one time I showed up on a day they were not even offering the fabled pie). Finally, on my fourth visit, I got my slice. This pie is not to be missed. Their pie motto (written on the pie safe): "Take home one of our famous homemade pies for that special occasion or just when you want to live it up."

But the obvious reason to visit Pie 'n

Burger is for their incredible hamburgers. Since 1963, the long faux-wood-grain Formica countertop has seen its share of burger perfection. The burger they made in the '60s is the same one that is served today. Even the local retail butcher that supplies the ground chuck has not changed in over 35 years. Longtime employee and owner Michael Osborne told me, "The beef we use is top quality and ground coarse. That's why they taste so good."

Two other important factors that go into the great-tasting burgers are the original, well-seasoned, flattop griddle, and the homemade Thousand Island dressing. "We go through about 100 pounds of dressing a week," Michael told me. The recipe came directly from Kraft in the '30s. Original owners Benny and Florence Foote were in the restaurant business long before opening Pie 'N Burger. According to Michael, Benny contacted Kraft and they gave him the recipe. "We still make it the same exact way, using Kraft mayonnaise."

A burger with Thousand Island dressing may sound familiar. California's own burger phenomenon, In 'N Out, also uses the dressing on their burgers. If you order a double-double at Pie 'N Burger, you basically get the same burger, only much better. Both burgers are made with fresh ground beef that has been griddled, served on toasted white buns with iceberg lettuce and the dressing, wrapped in waxed paper. Pie 'N Burger takes a giant leap forward by doubling the quantity of the beef to a quarter-pound per patty. The burgers at Pie 'N Burger are also somewhat hand formed. Quarter-pound balls of fresh beef are measured with an ice cream scoop then smashed flat with a huge can of tomato juice.

The system for cooking and assembling the burgers is all about efficiency. One person flips the burgers while another preps buns with a wedge of lettuce and dressing. The grillmen are seasoned professionals—one, Francesco, told me enthusiastically, "I've been here for 34 years!"

Michael started working at the restaurant in 1972, flipping burgers and going to UCLA full time. When he graduated, he continued to work at the restaurant, gradually helping out with managerial duties. In the late '70s, Michael bought a piece of the business and in 1992 the Foote family, in search of retirement, sold the remainder of the shares to him.

Pie 'N Burger looks exactly as it did in 1963 (with some obvious wear and tear). The wood-paneled walls and plaid wallpaper look beautifully out of date, as does the hand-painted wall menu. A cup of buttermilk is still offered with the usual diner fare of tuna sandwiches and chicken pot pie.

I asked Michael why he had stuck with the burger counter for so long and he told me, "I took the job because it was fun working here. To me, life is about having fun."

TAYLOR'S AUTOMATIC REFRESHER

933 MAIN STREET
ST HELENA, CA 94574
707-963-3486
WWW.TAYLORSREFRESHER.COM
OPEN DAILY 10:30 AM–8:30 PM

The drive to Taylor's takes you right through the heart of the Napa Valley. You'll pass rows and rows of vineyards and welcoming wineries with products to sample. Take a deep breath and smell the dense, pungent odor of freshly pressed grapes. It seems like the last place you'd find a good hamburger joint. That is, of course, until you pull into Taylor's Automatic Refresher.

Taylor's is in the center of it all. Most of the patrons of this updated classic '40s burger drive-in seem to be the buttoned-down wine-tasting types, but the stand does get its fair share of working-class locals as well. A bit of an anomaly in this part of the Napa Valley, Taylor's has endured the influx of luxury hotels, inns, and spas as well as a number of high-end restaurants.

The burger stand opened in 1949 as Taylor's Refresher. In the late '90s, two brothers with a long family history in winemaking, Duncan and Joel Gott, bought the ailing stand and added the word "Automatic." The structure received a first-class face-lift but they made sure to maintain the integrity of the original stand.

The city of St. Helena allowed the Gott brothers to expand only slightly, as Duncan put it, "for health reasons." He explained, "Before we bought the place, the refrigerators used to be outside, out back." Today's Taylor's is a superclean, contemporary version of the former stand with an upgraded kitchen and menu full of gourmet road food.

The hamburgers at Taylor's are well thought out, tasty, and like so many quality hamburgers of the Pacific Northwest, socially conscious. Duncan explained, "We spent weeks of testing to come up with the right blend for the burgers." The one-third-pound fresh patties come from naturally raised, hormone-free California cattle. They are cooked on an open-flame grill and served on locally made soft, pillowy buns. A "secret sauce" also goes on all of the burgers at Taylor's. It's a creamy, tangy mayo-based sauce, a sort of proprietary version of "Goop," (see page 287) the standard condiment on most burgers of the Northwest. "The spices in the sauce we keep secret," manager Dave told me. All of the burgers are served with lettuce, pickle, and tomato in a red-checkered paper basket.

The burger selection at Taylor's ranges from the traditional with American cheese to gourmet creations topped with guacamole or blue cheese. The extensive menu also includes healthy options like a chicken club, veggie tacos, and a Cobb salad, but no meal at Taylor's would be complete without one of their extraordinary milkshakes. The first time I was there the flavor of the day was mango. The woman in front of me tasted hers and proclaimed, "Oh MAN, that's good!" I had an espresso bean milkshake that I still dream about today.

There's no indoor seating and the carhops on roller skates are long gone, so find a spot at one of the many large red picnic tables in front, or on the spacious back lawn. Save your wine tasting for Taylor's too. There's a separate "bar" here that serves a rotating selection of over 40 local wines and eight small-batch beers like Sierra Nevada and Anchor Steam. I'm not too confident about the pairing of a cheeseburger and a good Cabernet, but I can tell you there's nothing like a great burger and a cold beer.

Add Napa Valley to the equation and you'll be in heaven.

I asked Duncan why the offspring of a wine family (his brother is a fifth-generation winemaker in the region) decided to buy a hamburger stand and he told me, "We have a family love affair with food." They weren't even sure the venture would work. "The day we opened 500 people showed up, and we thought, 'We could do this . . . we *could* be successful!'"

WESTERN STEAKBURGER

2730 UNIVERSITY AVE.
SAN DIEGO, CA 92104
619-296-7058
MON–SAT 10 AM–9 PM

On a trip to San Diego to film a TV show, I made plans to visit one of my favorite burger stands in America, Hodad's in Ocean Beach. But a crew member of mine alerted me to another nearby out-of-the-way burger spot that I had to try.

Western Steakburger sits on the edge of the up-and-coming San Diego neighborhood of North Park. Opened in 1983 by Greek immigrant "Gus" Constantinos Anastasiu and his effervescent wife Maria, the Greek-influenced restaurant kept burgers and gyros separate for the first year. But sometime in 1984, Gus piled a wad of sliced gyro meat on a finished burger and the Western Steakburger was born.

The restaurant is set back from the street, fronted by a large palm tree. If you sit on the small front patio, the soundtrack for your meal is the rustling of palm fronds and the occasional thump-thump of a passing urban party-on-wheels. Members of the San Diego police department make regular stops at this burger restaurant and have been for decades (cops always know where the good burgers are). But before you plan to sit beneath the palm fronds on University Avenue, plan on taking the afternoon off—this burger is a beast.

The menu lists many "steakburgers" and their toppings (e.g., pastrami, bacon, and chili) but there's no mention of the burger that made them famous. The gyro-topped burger is listed simply as the half-pound "Western Steakburger." "Gus never wanted to list the contents of the Western, he always says 'let them ask,'" Maria told me.

The burgers are cooked over an open flame in full view of waiting patrons. Oval-shaped patties of fresh-ground beef are grilled to perfection and placed on toasted white squishy buns. Grillman Ricky then places a one-third-pound pile of the salty gyro meat on the patty and delivers the burger with mustard, ketchup, mayonnaise, lettuce, tomato, pickles, and onion.

After my first bite I was in heaven. The familiar spice of the gyro meat complemented the burger well and somehow the pound of ingredients managed to stay neatly tucked into the soft bun. About 20 minutes after ingesting this glorious grease-bomb, I had to pull over in my rental car because I was having food coma hallucinations. My advice to you—do not operate heavy machinery or a motor vehicle after enjoying this burger.

Maria was working the counter when I visited. "You have to love what you do. Mom-and-pops are a dying breed." Western Steakburger was the first burger available to residents of North Park. Today, the tiny family-owned burger joint feels the heat from a McDonald's, Wendy's, and a Burger King only a few blocks away. But thanks to recent development in the neighborhood (a condo just went up across the street), people are starting to take notice of Western Steakburger and their flair for coupling Greek and American foods. Maria told me, laughing, "How come after 24 years people are just starting to come? Why couldn't they come when we were younger and had more energy!"

BUD'S BAR

5453 MANHART STREET
SEDALIA, CO 80135
303-688-9967
MON–SAT 10 AM–10 PM
SUN 11 AM–7 PM

Bud's Bar is not in Denver. On a map, the town of Sedalia, Colorado, looks like it could be a suburb of the Mile High City, but in person, the tiny town, surrounded by cattle farms, feels as remote as any town on the Kansas Plain.

Bud's is one of only a few businesses in the small downtown of Sedalia. The 60-year-old bar sits between two busy railroad rights-of-way that are only a few hundred feet apart. It's not uncommon to be stuck at either crossing for longer than 20 minutes waiting for a long coal train to pass. "Some guys walk out, see the train,

and say 'Oh well!' and head back inside for another beer," Mike Steerman told me. Mike should know. He owns the place.

Mike is only the third owner of Bud's since Calixte "Bud" Hebert converted an auto shop into a bar in 1948. In the 1960s, Bud became a local judge and decided that judges shouldn't own bars. He sold his tavern to an employee, Thurman Thompson. In the 1980s, current owner Mike started tending bar part-time to relieve stress from his job as a salesman. When Thurman decided to sell the bar, he set his sights on Mike, knowing that he would change little about the place.

The one thing I'll bet most people were afraid he would change was the burger. Rest assured that Mike has kept it the same. With a name like Steerman, it would be stupid to question his Colorado heritage or his affinity for fresh beef. The burger at Bud's is a classic griddled quarter-pounder with American cheese on a white squishy bun. It's absolutely amazing and transcends the standard notion of bar food. The burger bursts with flavor and is one of the juiciest griddled burgers I have ever eaten.

People go to Bud's for two reasons—because they know everyone in the bar and for the burgers. Outside of drinks at the bar, Bud's has served only burgers since the beginning. "It's simple," Mike explained, "we don't offer lettuce, we don't offer tomato, and we only use one kind of cheese." Fries? Nope. Chips will have to do. But trust me, you'll be focusing on this burger and nothing else.

The burgers start as 80/20 chuck hand pressed in a single patty maker. They are cooked on a smallish flattop griddle in a bright, clean kitchen next to the bar. As a burger nears doneness, both halves of a bun are placed on the burger and covered with a lid to steam the bun to softness. Your order is served with a bag of chips and a slice of onion in a plastic mesh basket lined with waxed paper. "That's it," Mike told me, proud of the simplicity of his product. Locals in the know request jalapeno slices that Mike has stashed in a small jar in the kitchen.

Sunday is the busiest at Bud's, a day where the griddle can see up to 500 burgers. "That griddle stays full for six hours on Sunday," Mike told me.

Mike seems to be one of the newer members of the Bud's family, and the only male in an all-female staff. Amiable bartender Nancy has been serving drinks for two decades and I'm told that Judy, the head grill cook, has been at Bud's since Neil Armstrong first set foot on the moon.

People go to Bud's for two reasons—because they know everyone in the bar and for the burgers.

Bud's interior is cozy and simple. One side is lined with vintage stools, there's booths on the other side, and a few tables in the middle. An original jukebox sits just inside the front door and one wall displays a unique item—the branding board.

Of course, being from New York I was very intrigued by the branding board, something that probably seems mundane to a ranching community. The idea is simple—it's a long piece of wood attached to one wall of the bar that displays actual cattle brands of the local ranchers. To me, it was a viable piece of "bar art." One glance at the board and you are reminded of just how close you are to fresh beef.

Despite its roadhouse appearance, Bud's has become a place for family and friends. Since smoking in bars was banned in 2006 Mike has seen an increase in business. "A little while ago we had an entire Little League team in here. That never would have happened a year ago."

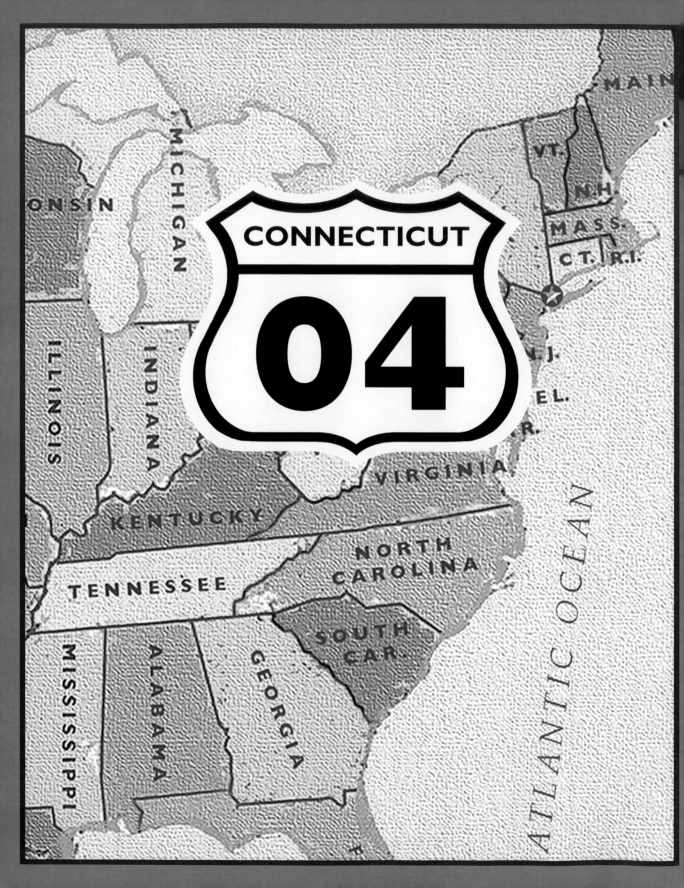

CLAMP'S HAMBURGER STAND

ROUTE 202 (NEAR MARBLEDALE, CT)
NEW MILFORD, CT 06776
NO PHONE
OPEN LATE APRIL TO LABOR DAY
11 AM–2 PM, 5 PM–8 PM DAILY

Way up in the northwest corner of Connecticut is a tiny burger stand that is definitely worth the drive. It has no real address and no phone but doesn't need these things. If you show up on a summer day at lunchtime, you'll find a crowd that somehow found its way there regardless of its off-the-grid status.

I asked owner Tom Mendell why, after all these years, there still was no phone at Clamp's. He told me, smiling, "It's always been that way and I don't see any reason to change it." Tom's great-uncle Edwin Clamp opened the little white-shingled stand in 1939 because he had tired of his job as a door-to-door hardware salesman. "I think he came up with this idea because he didn't like to work," Tom told me. The stand is still open only during the warmer months, which gave Edwin the winter off.

When World War II started, meat rationing caused Clamp's to shut down temporarily. During that time, Edwin used the tiny stand to manufacture a faucet washer that he had patented. After his death, Edwin's wife, Sylvia, ran Clamp's and worked there into her late eighties. "She was a worker," Tom told me.

Tom, who lives in Baltimore in the winter and assumed the business 10 years ago at the young age of 30, has changed very little about Clamp's. He expanded ever so slightly the tiny kitchen, but the structure still remains under 450 square feet. Tom himself mans the griddle at the front of the stand and spends most of his day flipping patties to perfection. And like most great keepers of the lunchtime grill, Tom stays focused and politely refused to answer my questions as he managed the incoming orders.

Clamp's gets a daily delivery of fresh ground beef from a local butcher, delivered as quarter-pound patties. Tom is very serious about the quality of the ingredients that go into his roadside fare. Everything is fresh and he makes his own coleslaw and the chili that goes on the hot dogs and hamburgers.

Somewhat recently, the griddle was replaced. Tom wasn't exactly sure but he thinks it happened around 20 years ago because the original finally gave up. Janine, on staff for 15 years at the stand, told me, "The old griddle had a big slope in the middle from being cleaned so much."

Clamp's is an outdoor place. The stand is basically a kitchen with walk-up order windows. You place an order at one of the windows, find a table (made from those huge industrial wire spools) in the grassy grove on either side of the stand, and wait for your name to be called. Don't expect a loudspeaker to summon you back for pickup. The girls that take your order literally shout your name, sort of like your mom calling you for dinner.

The cheeseburgers are served on white squishy buns with the traditional Yankee white American cheese. Locals know to order theirs topped with a Clamp's specialty—a pile of sweet, slow-cooked, caramelized onions.

I asked why there still was no phone at Clamps. Tom told me, smiling, "It's always been that way and I don't see any reason to change it."

The drive to Clamp's is half the fun. If you are coming up from the quaint, historic town of New Milford, Clamp's is exactly 5.9 miles north on Route 202 from the gazebo on the town's square. Trust me, you'll need this info as you pass farm after farm, nearly hit a deer (as I did), and wonder if you've gone too far. Look for the small white building tucked into the trees with an American flag tacked to its side. The only identification the building offers is a postcard-sized sign just over a side door: a small plaque that reads "Clamp's Est. 1939."

Tom told me, "Most of the time I'm as busy as I can possibly handle." The only break he gets is when it rains, but even then, some like to show up for his famous burgers. "I think we have a cult of people who like to show up during thunderstorms," Tom told me. "It's funny. They sit in their cars, eat burgers, and watch the rain."

LOUIS' LUNCH

261-263 CROWN STREET
NEW HAVEN, CT 06510
203-562-5507
WWW.LOUISLUNCH.COM
TUE & WED 11 AM–4 PM
THU–SAT 12 PM–2:30 AM
CLOSED SUNDAY & MONDAY
CLOSED DURING AUGUST

There are many claims to the origin of the first hamburgers in America. One of them is Louis' Lunch (pronounced LEW-EEZ). Even if the claim here can be disputed, it is without a doubt the oldest continuously operating hamburger restaurant in the country. What's more, one family, the Lassens, has owned and operated the tiny burger haven since 1895—four generations of passionate hamburger making. Operating Louis' today are the third and fourth generations: Ken Lassen, his wife Leona, and their two sons Jeff and Ken Jr. My wife likes to call Louis' "hamburger church"—there is no excessive banter or typical diner orders being barked, just the clanking sound of the upright flame broilers opening and closing and the crinkling of wrapped burgers going into paper bags. People stand at the counter waiting patiently for their order to be handed to them.

The structure that houses Louis' Lunch is a tiny box with 100-year-old Victorian flair. Small as it seems, it's the largest it's ever been. The original Louis' was a tiny-wheeled lunch cart that eventually went terrestrial as a three-sided

cube attached to one side of a large downtown New Haven tannery. When the tannery was torn down in the early 1970s, the three sides were salvaged, dragged four blocks, and an expanded fourth wall was constructed, along with a basement.

A burger at Louis' starts with fresh-ground lean beef, ground daily in the spotless basement. Every morning Ken and his son Ken Jr. roll the meat into small balls. Two balls are pressed together to make a patty, which is placed vertically in a metal grate and then slid into an ancient upright broiler. The grill cooks from both sides and juices drip into a pan below. The burgers are then placed on Pepperidge Farm white toast, simply because when Louis Lassen invented the "hamburger sandwich" in 1900 there were no buns (in fact buns didn't come around for almost another 25 years). In the 1970s, Ken felt the pressure to add cheese to his

Louis Lassen in his lunchwagon

famous sandwich. If you ask for cheese, you'll get a cheese spread that seems Velveetaesque. Due to the unique method for cooking the burgers, cheese slices take a back seat to the spread. Fresh-cut tomatoes and onions are standard, but don't ask for ketchup or you may be shown the door. As Jeff Lassen explains, "We honestly believe you don't need ketchup because it's the best burger there is." And Ken told me, "Ketchup is a strong flavor. If we gave you that, it would destroy everything we are trying to give

you." Jeff also pointed out that students from nearby Yale frequently try to sneak in small packets of ketchup only to be told that the burger they wanted to sit down and eat is now a to-go order.

It's not uncommon to walk into Louis' and find matriarch Leona, or "Lee" Lassen operating the vintage burger broilers at a fever pitch. For over 50 years Lee has grilled burgers to perfection for the lunch crowd. In 2006, she was hospitalized with a heart condition and after only a few months rest she surprised us all by returning to her spot at the grill.

The Lassens are salt-of-the-earth burger royalty and they are quite aware of their status in American food history. Regardless of the provenance that surrounds Louis', the prices are fair and the burgers always fresh and tasty.

SHADY GLEN

840 EAST MIDDLE TURNPIKE
MANCHESTER, CT 06040
860-649-4245

MON–THURS 7 AM–10 PM
FRI & SAT 7 AM–11 PM
SUN 11AM–10PM

The inside of the Shady Glen looks like a cheeseburger. The yellow-striped wallpaper, warm lighting, and low brown Formica countertops mimic the colors of their famous cheeseburger concoction. Ice cream may be the number-one seller at this Manchester, Connecticut institution, but the cheeseburger is what has made them famous. In 1949, Bernice Rieg invented the "Bernice Original" which became an immediate success and still accounts for 80 percent of their sandwich sales today. The four-ounce cheeseburger comes with four slices of cheese. The cheese is not just stacked atop the burger; it is symmetrically placed, centered on the burger as it cooks on the hot griddle. An understandably large portion of this cheese makes direct contact with the griddle. When the cheese cooks through it is curled skyward by the deft grillman until it resembles a cheese crown. Amazingly, I watched burger after burger leave the grill with the same dramatic cheese. The same burger, over and over, since 1949.

"It's a special cheese, but that's all I can tell you," Michael the manager smiled. Michael started working at the Shady Glen over two decades ago as a dishwasher. "At 22 years, I'm still the new kid on the block." Shady Glen is a very busy place. There are more than 15 employees in constant motion, waitresses in little ruffled aprons and grillmen in paper caps and black bow-ties. This is the real deal, not a mock-up like Johnny Rockets.

There are no menus at the Shady Glen, just wall menus, and they are basic. You can order a "cheeseburger" or a "big cheeseburger;" the latter comes with the four slices of cheese. The smaller "cheeseburger" comes with only three slices. It's served on a white squishy bun and delivered to your spot at the counter with your own personal condiment tray of relish, raw onion, mustard, and ketchup. The Shady Glen

can sell up to 4,000 "Bernice Originals" on a busy week. That's a lot of cheese sculpture.

I stood by the grill and watched closely—the cheese, which looked like a house-sliced mild cheddar, really does not stick. One of the grill men offered some shaky science. "The carbon, uh, buildup on the griddle over the years acts sort of like Teflon." I think he's right. I had a hard time trying to figure out what do with my cheese wings once I had my burger in front of me. Two guys sitting near me at the counter had opposing views. One told me, "Fold the crisps onto the burger and eat it that way." "Not me," said the other, "I like to break them off and eat them separately." A girl sitting on the other side of me was chewing on some cheese crown crisps with no burger in sight. "This is an order of Crispy Cheese," she told me. This guilty pleasure is served on a bed of lettuce and is not on the menu.

At first I was concerned about the large mural that spans the entire west end of the restaurant. It depicts strange elves having a picnic of burgers, hot dogs, and ice cream. As I left the restaurant I looked again at the mural and fully understood its significance—the Shady Glen is a necessary fantasy. I hope it never goes away.

The " Bernice Original"

TED'S RESTAURANT

1044 BROAD STREET
MERIDEN, CT 06450
203-237-6660
WWW.STEAMEDCHEESEBURGER.COM
MON–SAT 11 AM–10 PM
SUN 11 AM–7 PM

If you are looking for a truly unique hamburger experience, go to Ted's. If you are looking for a potentially healthy burger, go to Ted's. If you are looking for a char-grilled cheeseburger, don't go to Ted's. Ted's Restaurant is the epicenter of the steamed cheeseburger world—a burger that only exists in central Connecticut. The current owner of Ted's Restaurant, Ted's son, Paul Duberek, told me, "Within 25 miles of here there are about seven steamed cheeseburger places, but we're the only ones that make ten hot dogs a week and 800 steamed cheeseburgs."

The steamed "cheeseburg," as it's referred

to at Ted's, is just what you'd think it would be—a steamed patty of ground beef on a bun. What you wouldn't expect is that the cheese is steamed too, steamed to a molten goo. The process starts with a steaming cabinet that holds 20 small stainless steel trays. Specially ground fresh chuck is pressed into the trays and these are placed in the cabinet. The meat cooks through but stays amazingly moist and unfortunately, looks like gray matter. The result is a burger that loses most of its fat content (it gets poured off) and retains a truly beefy flavor. A "secret" cheese (Paul told us it's an aged Vermont cheddar, but that's as far as he'd go) is also placed in the small trays in the steamer. Once gooey, the cheese is poured onto the burger, served with tomato, ketchup or mustard (or both), lettuce, and a slice of onion, and placed on a hand-sliced soft kaiser roll.

The origins of the steamed cheeseburger are a bit murky, but it's believed to have originated at Jack's Lunch in Middletown sometime in the '30s. Ted Duberek opened his restaurant in 1959 to feed the immense local factory worker population. For over 100 years, that area of Connecticut was home to some of the largest silverware manufacturers and they had shifts around the clock. Ted's used to stay open until 4 a.m., but started closing earlier as the factories moved their business overseas.

There are other spots in the Meriden/Wallingford area to experience the tradition of steaming beef in metal cabinets, but none are as focused or competitive as Ted's. Paul Duberek is a guarded but extremely proud burger-man and he makes sure that every burger that goes out is perfect. Try doing that to 200 burgers a day.

YANKEE DOODLE COFFEE & SANDWICH SHOP

258 ELM STREET
NEW HAVEN, CT 06511
203-865-1074
WWW.THEDOODLE.COM
DECEMBER 1ST–JUNE 1ST
MON–FRI 6 AM–7:30 PM
SAT 6 AM–4:30 PM
CLOSED SUNDAYS
JUNE–AUGUST
MON–SAT 6 AM–2 PM
CLOSED SUNDAYS

In the bosom of Yale University sits one of the most famous hamburger stands in America, the Yankee Doodle, affectionately known as "the Doodle" to regulars. Lew Beckwith named his burger counter after the song of the same name, a song his father sang to him as a child. I'm going to go out on a limb here and assume that just about every Yale student has had at least one Doodle burger. That's a lot of meat, since the Doodle has been cranking out burgers for almost six decades. You can wait for up to half an hour for one of the covet-

ed 12 stools when Yale is in session, but it is well worth the wait.

The cheeseburger is a thin two-ounce patty cooked on a cast-iron griddle, served on a toasted white bun with cheese, butter, and some sort of hot jelly. They go down quick, which usually results in placing a second order—or better yet, get the Dandy, which is a double cheeseburger with tomato, lettuce, bacon, butter, and onion on a kaiser roll. Pattied fresh ground beef gets slapped on the hot, well-seasoned griddle and sprinkled with a few onions. By the time the patties have been pressed by the spatula it's time to flip them. Burgers barely spend two minutes on the griddle and the average dining experience at the Doodle is only five minutes long. "My job was simplified many years ago by my father and grandfather" said Rick Beckwith, third-generation owner of the small burger counter. Rick is standing in the front window of the Doodle at the impossibly small griddle. It looks like it might be from opening day in 1950, but Rick tells me the original was replaced in the early '70s when it cracked. "My dad had a habit of pushing grease off the griddle, then tapping hard right here," and he demonstrated gently on the top center of the cooking surface.

The Yankee Doodle is only a few blocks away from the world-famous Louis' Lunch (which holds a claim to the invention of the hamburger), but Rick explains, "It's a lot easier for a first-time customer to walk into this place than Louis.' You ask for ketchup over there and you're finished." He told me there are still some customers who patronize only one of the burger havens and would never think of setting foot in the other. "Sometimes we'll get some of their regulars when they close for August."

Not surprisingly, based on its proximity to an institution of higher learning and the proposition of free burgers, the Doodle has its own eating competition and an honor; roll of past eating heroes. The rules are simple: break the record and the burgers are free. Only problem is, the record is currently at 34, which were consumed in less than two and a half hours (another important rule). There is no date for the competition, one needs only to give Rick a day's notice to try and set a new record. "They get as many burgers as they want, and a bucket." Bucket? "Just in case."

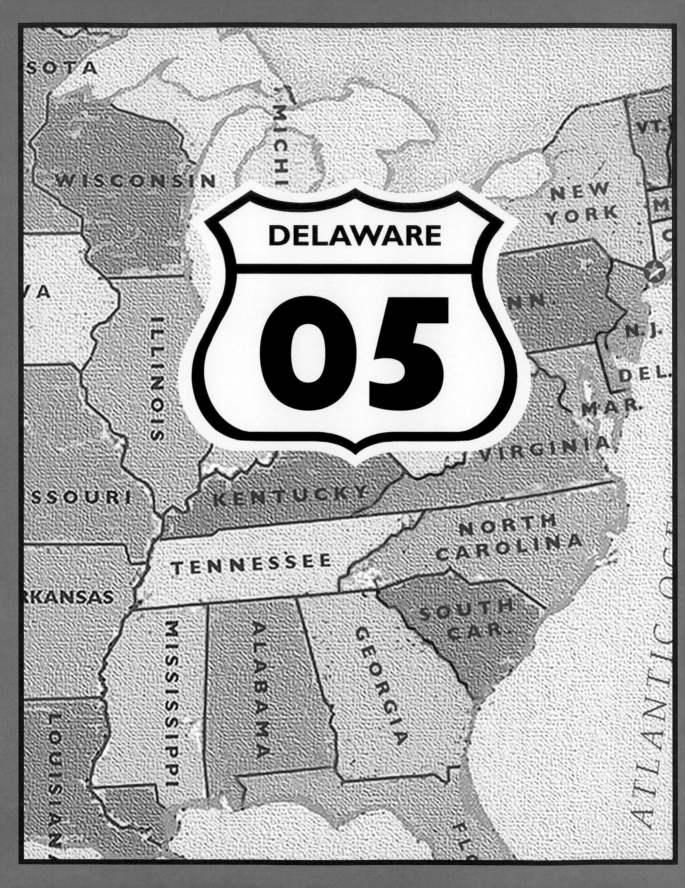

CHARCOAL PIT

2600 CONCORD PIKE
N. WILMINGTON, DE 19803
302-478-2165
(3 OTHER LOCATIONS
AROUND WILMINGTON)
WWW.CHARCOALPIT.NET
MON–THU 11 AM–MIDNIGHT
FRI & SAT 11 AM–1 AM
SUN 11 AM–12 AM

When Charcoal Pit opened in 1956 it was way out on the Concord Pike surrounded by fields and very few other businesses. "It was all farmland and nothing but a two-lane road," manager of 38 years Frank Kucharski said, looking out the window of this time-warp diner. "Hard to imagine now." Yes, it is. Concord Pike today is a densely packed commercial strip. It's a wonder this burger gem is still standing.

From the outside, Charcoal Pit looks virtually unchanged since the 1950s. The restaurant's boomerang-inspired marquee with its pudgy pink neon lettering is authentically retro. The interior has seen a few upgrades and design changes over the years and blends styles from the past five decades. If you're lucky, you'll be seated at a booth with a tabletop jukebox. These are not props. They actually work. Holly Moore, Philadelphia area food writer and a man who knows where to find the best greasy food anywhere, told me, "Think Richie, Potsie, and Ralph Malph in a corner booth and Al flipping burgers behind the counter." There's something unmistakably genuine about eating at Charcoal Pit that needs to be experienced.

The burgers are cooked over an open flame, as the restaurant's name implies. The large gas grill, in full view of the dining room, is outfitted with a bed of lava rocks that help to evenly distribute the heat. Grillman of 16 years, Lupe spends hours inches from the flames, flipping hundreds of burgers a day.

For some reason, for the first time in all of my burger exploits I did not order the burger suggested by my host. A burger at Charcoal Pit comes in two sizes, a thick half-pounder and a thinner quarter-pounder. He said to get the big one; I opted for the smaller. The thing about flame-grilling burgers is this—thicker burgers taste much better when cooked on an open flame because all of the moisture stays inside the burger. Thin patties have a hard time retaining that moisture. It's much easier to cook a thin burger on a flattop griddle because the burger stays moist and tasty no matter what you do. I found myself eyeing a neighboring booth's half-pound burger dripping with juices, cooked to temperature, and realized I should have listened to Frank.

The half-pound burger is served on a kaiser roll and the quarter pounder comes on a seeded, toasted white bun. Seems as though someone was paying attention to burger physics when bun decisions were being made. The fresh Angus patties are delivered daily to Charcoal Pit from a local supplier. "We probably go through over a thousand pounds of meat a week," Frank told me, "and it's always fresh."

Not only are the burgers fresh, other items on the menu are house made, like their crab cakes, soups, and coleslaw. The first time I visited Charcoal Pit I found Frank and another employee in the kitchen straining what looked to be about 10 gallons of homemade vegetable beef soup. "We're hands-on here," Frank said as he hoisted the steaming vat of soup.

Outside of burgers, Charcoal Pit is ice cream nirvana. A sign out front proclaims simply, "Ice Cream Creations" and they are not kidding. The menu is heavy on ice cream and there is a sundae named after each of the nine local high schools. The thick, hand-dipped milkshakes are enormous and not to be missed.

Every year as the local high schools are letting out for the summer, Charcoal Pit can count on one thing—the prom. "It's total chaos in here," manager Joseph Grabowski told me, "They're really into the Kitchen Sink." For a minute I imagined a burger with enough embellishment to fill a sink, but Joe explained, "It's 20 scoops of ice cream, whipped cream, nuts, etc., and two bananas." Whoa.

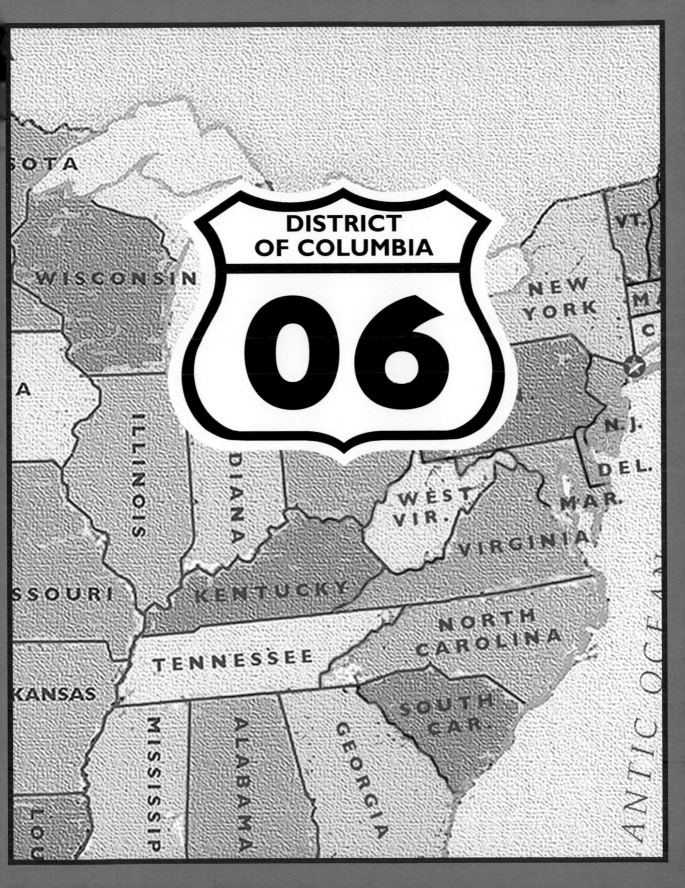

BEN'S CHILI BOWL

1213 U STREET NW
WASHINGTON, DC 20009
202-667-0909
WWW.BENSCHILIBOWL.COM
MON–THU 6 AM–2 AM
FRI 6 AM–4 AM
SAT 7 AM–4 AM
SUN 11AM–8PM

"Most people don't want to eat with a lot of loud music. It's just part of our culture," a regular for four decades named Marshall Brown told me as we sat at the counter of this 50-year-old Washington, D.C., landmark chili restaurant. Marshall was referring to the sounds of Bob Marley and Luther Vandross that were oozing out of the jukebox, not necessarily loud, but definitely present. One time when I was enjoying a breakfast chili cheeseburger, the guy next to me at the counter was eating his eggs, so consumed by the music that he started dancing in his seat. I'm positive that moving to the music made the food taste that much better.

Ben's was opened in 1958 by Ben and Virginia Ali in a former silent movie theater known as the Minnehaha. Ben, who had emigrated from Trinidad, met his wife at the bank just down the street. "She was a bank teller," the couple's son Nizam told me. Ben and Virginia have retired, but two of their sons, Nizam and Kamal, run the restaurant today.

Ben's is known for its tasty chili that glori-ously adorns hot dogs, half smokes, and hamburgers. The bright, airy, neighborhood restaurant, with its incredibly colorful façade, also serves a memorable breakfast, but many return from all corners of the country for their chili dogs and burgers. Over the years it also became known for the role it has played in Black American history. Ben's fed many celebrities performing at the clubs along the U Street corridor in the '50s and '60s, including Ella Fitzgerald, Miles Davis, and Cab Calloway.

The 1968 riots sparked by the assassination of Martin Luther King started just a block away when someone threw a brick through a drugstore window. The riots devastated the neighborhood, a curfew was imposed, and the city shut down while attempting to restore order. But Ben's remained open by special police permission to feed firefighters, police, and members of the Student Nonviolent Coordinating Committee located just across the street. When they did close for the night, Ben stayed behind to protect the business from looters. "He kissed my mom goodnight, sent her home, and sat inside with a gun all night," Nizam told me. To identify the restaurant as a black business Ben painted the words "Soul Brother" across the front window.

Ben's survived the riots, the crack hell of the '70s and '80s, then the construction of a Metro extension that cut off traffic on U Street for almost five years. "We had two employees and were making only about $200 a day during

that time," Nizam told me. "The construction was more devastating than the drugs." Massive publicity from Bill Cosby and other black luminaries kept the business alive during the bad times. Cosby and his wife had many dates there while he was stationed in the Navy nearby.

Today Ben's thrives. Even the Clintons are fans. Nizam told me, "We sent a lot of takeout over to the White House when they were in office." The U Street corridor is in the midst of a revival and the new Metro stop is directly across the street. There must be twelve people behind the counter and the atmosphere is lively and fun, with all of the employees joking and flirting with each other. The large front room with its long counter and booths gives way to two more rooms that are somewhat hidden from view. The enormous dining room in the back has a projector and screen and the walls are lined with adoring photos of a virtual who's-who in Black America. One great photo shows Cosby and Al Green smiling, the front window of Ben's as their background.

The burgers are quarter-pound patties and arrive fresh daily from a supplier in Baltimore. The chili that goes onto the burger is a simple family recipe that contains only finely ground meat in a dark red, tangy sauce. The burger comes on a toasted bun in a plastic basket with a side of potato chips. If you need more, go for a chili dog, or better yet, the sublime chili cheese fries.

Ben's is a successful family business that has endured incredibly hard times. "We've gotten the most ridiculous amount of press, more than we could ever dream of," Nizam pointed out. Then, remembering the importance of having a fan like Bill Cosby, he said "this place is a big part of his history." I'm sure Ben's is also a big part of the collective histories of all of the diners who have passed through its doors, and the future stories that have yet to be written there.

TUNE INN

331 ½ PENNSYLVANIA AVENUE
WASHINGTON, DC 20003
202-543-2725
SUN–THU 8 AM–2 AM
FRI & SAT 8 AM–3 AM

Johnny Cash on the jukebox, cheap beer on tap, and copious amounts of taxidermy on the walls . . . sounds like a recipe for your favorite country crossroads bar. But the bar is the Tune Inn and it's only steps from the Library of Congress and the Capitol Building in our nation's capital. It'd be easy to assume the country bar trappings are an urban design choice, but all of the stuffed game was bagged by the three generations of the Nardellis, owners of the Capitol Hill watering hole since 1955. This place is the real deal—a comfortable neighborhood dive bar with an excellent burger on the menu.

"I shot that one. That's my first doe," Lisa

Nardelli told me, pointing to a stuffed deer head directly over the bar. Lisa is young and pretty and doesn't strike you as the hunting type. Her grandfather, Joe Nardelli, hunted most of the stuffed game, ranging from deer to squirrels to pheasant. "They would get drunk and shoot at anything," Lisa said of her father Tony and grandfather hunting together. Mounted over the bathroom doors in the rear of the narrow tavern are the other ends of deer. "That's my grandfather's sense of humor—deer asses over the bathrooms." The collection is so vast that the local Shakespeare theatre borrowed a bunch of the Nardelli's stuffed birds for a production of *King Lear*.

Lots of well-known politicos and other Capitol Hill heavies have been drinking and eating at the Tune Inn for the last five decades. One of the most famous couples in American politics, James Carville and Mary Matalin, had their first date here (they left abruptly because it was too crowded). Janet Reno was a regular (for the burgers) and JFK the senator had his favorite booth (second one on the left). The bar also hosts regulars who have been coming in for decades. "It's like a big family, which is unusual in a big city, so close to the Capitol," Lisa pointed out. It's also home to countless numbers of students looking for cheap beer and good burgers, yours truly being one of them a few decades back.

"Many people find their own true love at the Tune Inn," Susan told me.

The menu is mostly modest comfort food. The burger takes center stage and starts as a six-ounce ball of 80/20 ground chuck. Chef Mike Tate told me, "We use a measured scoop, then form a patty." The meat is delivered fresh every morning from a local butcher that also supplies the well-known upscale Old Ebbitt Grill, a Washington landmark near the White House. "It's the same exact meat," Lisa told me.

The patty is cooked to perfection on a flat-top griddle and served on a buttered, toasted bun. The result is a loose, moist burger that melts in your mouth. It really is the perfect bar burger—not so big that you can't finish your beer and not so small that you go hungry.

The Tune Inn was the fifth bar in the District to receive its liquor license after Prohibition was repealed, and today is the oldest drinking establishment on Capitol Hill. During Prohibition the bar served as a speakeasy and regulars have told stories about that time for decades. One day recently, Lisa was wondering about a certain out-of-place wall in the basement. She tapped on it, found it hollow, and proceeded to smash the wall with a sledgehammer. What she uncovered was an indelible piece of American history. "There was a trap door that led to right here," and she pointed to a spot behind the bar. "Apparently they used to pass the booze through here to the bartender."

You can visit the Tune Inn for a burger, for a few drinks, or as long time bartender Susan Mathers believes, for love. "You think I'm kidding. Many people find their own true love at the Tune Inn," Susan told me with a straight face. "I have observed many people meet and fall in love here." She looked over at the third-generation Nardelli. "Lisa met her husband here."

Notable Burger Chains

In the corporate burger world, all burgers are created equal by design. Most are frozen, then shipped for miles to their intended fast-food outlet. There are, however, a few hamburger chains that buck the system and offer burgers made with fresh ground beef: places like Red Robin, Cheeburger! Cheeburger!, and the Northwest's own Burgerville. Below is a list of my personal favorites, from West to East.

In-N-Out Burger

LOCATIONS THROUGHOUT CALIFORNIA AND THE SOUTHWEST
WWW.IN-N-OUT.COM

It may look like a Big Mac, but the In-N-Out double-double is anything but. Made from the freshest ingredients, the burgers at this Southern California burger stand celebrate the marriage of fast-food and car culture like no other. Since 1948, family-owned In-N-Out has expanded to over 150 locations and has never lost sight of its commitment to freshness. They have a processing facility that grinds 100 percent pure chuck shoulder, makes the patties, and ships them by refrigerated truck to the restaurants. In-N-Out can proudly boast that none of their locations have freezers because nothing is ever frozen (except of course the ice cream for the milkshakes).

Steak 'n Shake

LOCATIONS THROUGHOUT THE MIDWEST AND THE SOUTH
WWW.STEAKNSHAKE.COM

This classic drive-in burger stand opened its first location in Normal, Illinois in 1934. Since then, Steak 'n Shake has expanded to over 450 locations and still serves burgers made from fresh-ground strip steak, sirloin, and T-bone. A seat at the counter offers excellent views of the white paper-capped grill man preparing your "Steakburger." A wad of beef is smashed thin and seared on a super-hot flattop griddle. Within just a few minutes, a moist yet crispy patty is placed on a toasted white bun and delivered to you on real china. Get a double with bacon for an unforgettable meal.

Oh, and the shakes are pretty good too.

Five Guys

LOCATIONS THROUGHOUT THE EAST COAST
WWW.FIVEGUYS.COM

I'm guessing this relative newcomer to the burger scene is making quite a dent in the business corporate fast food is doing up and down the East Coast, especially since the Five Guys business plan calls for up to 1,000 new locations in the next few years. One college student I spoke to told me he'd *never* visit a Mickey D's if there was a Five Guys nearby. What's all the fuss about? Great burgers made in large portions from fresh ground beef. Corporate burger biggies are in trouble when even drunken students can tell the difference between fresh and frozen burgers.

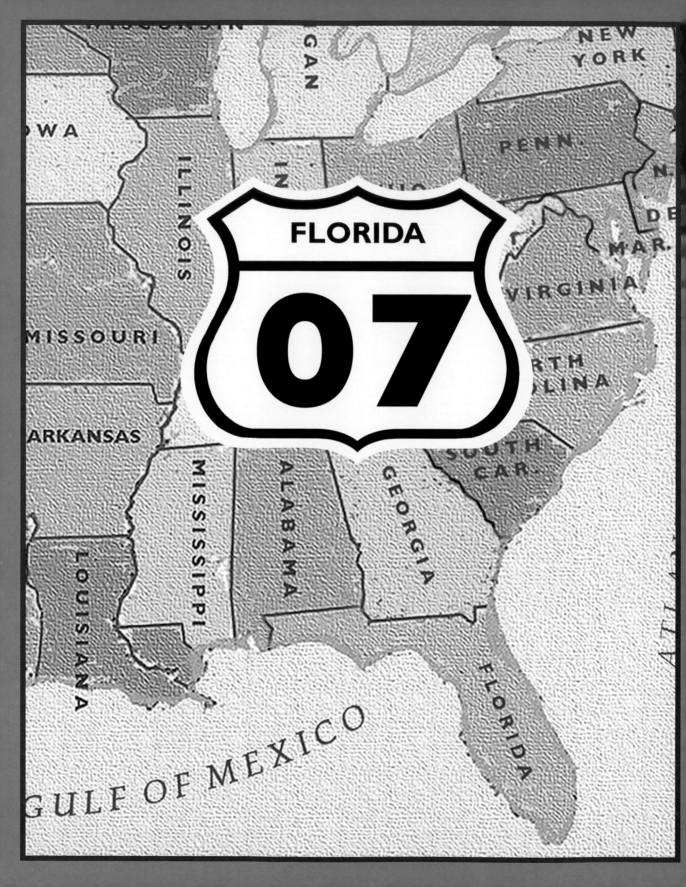

LE TUB

1100 NORTH OCEAN DRIVE
HOLLYWOOD, FL 33019
954-921-9425
OPEN DAILY NOON–4 AM

Le Tub had quite a year in 2005. After it was chosen by *GQ* magazine for having the #1 burger in America, the Oprah show did its own report backing up the claim. The only problem is, the most crowded no-frills burger shack in Florida just got more crowded.

Located on a stretch of A1A just a half hour north of Miami, Le Tub is a former gas station converted into a strange pile of flotsam collected over three decades. Most of Le Tub's seating is outside on a meandering multilevel porch surrounded by lush foliage, worn wood, chirping birds, and hot breezes. Its proximity to the Intracoastal Waterway offers a constant boat show. We sat at a table on the water and watched an entire bachelorette party in bikinis float by, the bride opening gifts of lingerie and giggling.

The restaurant got its name from owner Russell Kohuth's collection of discarded commodes, tubs, and sinks, which basically hold the place together. In addition to the porcelain collection are parts of boats, buoys, and other planks that actually make up the basic structure of the restaurant. Russell started collecting stuff on early morning jogs along Hollywood beach and opened the restaurant in 1975. "This place wouldn't hold up in a hurricane," the guy at the next table told his wife.

The burger at Le Tub is a beast—eight or more ounces of fresh-ground, hand-pattied, char-grilled sirloin served on a soft kaiser roll. When I prodded the waitress for the actual size of the burger, she told me, "They are big and messy!"

The grill cook works at a small three-foot-square grill on a level just below the bar in basically an enclosed un-air conditioned space. There is smoke everywhere and the smell of searing sirloin permeates your clothes if you spend any time at the bar. Why the grillman does not pass out from the heat three times a day is beyond me.

The crowd at Le Tub is a mixed bag—confused tourists, beachgoers, and boaters fill the tables. A dock on the patio allows you to arrive by water if so inclined.

Order your burgers THE MINUTE YOU WALK IN THE DOOR. I'm not kidding when I say that mine took one hour and twenty minutes to arrive. When I asked our waitress upon ordering if their famous burgers really took that long, she warned, with a straight face, "Could take up to an hour and a half." I placed an order for myself and a friend who had just landed at Miami International Airport. By the time she got off the plane, got her luggage, rented her car, and drove to Le Tub, she still had to wait 45 more minutes for her burger.

The good news is that the burger is worth the wait. Also, don't forget, you are in a bar, on the water, in Florida—the beers will go down easy, especially because you'll be sitting there for a while.

Is there really a "Cheeseburger in Paradise"?

Imagine that you are sitting in a beachside bar somewhere in the Caribbean or south Florida eating what you consider to be, at that moment, the best-tasting burger you have ever had. You tell the waitress or bartender, and they say, "Well it should be the best. This is the burger Jimmy Buffett wrote the song about!" This hypothetical conversation plays out every day somewhere in the warm climes of vacationland, in claims that stretch from the Bahamas to New Orleans and back to the Florida Keys. Places like the Cabbage Key Inn on Captiva Island, Florida, where the wait for the fabled burger can be up to two hours because up to 500 people a day are there just for the burger "Jimmy sang about." Or Le Select, a comfortable beach dive on St. Barths where the claim has some merit because Buffett has been known to swoop in on his Cessna seaplane, go straight to the bar, and put on an impromptu concert.

One claim that seems to make the least sense but is worthy of inspection comes from Rotier's in Nashville, Tennessee. The burger at Rotier's has been on the top of every poll in Music City for decades. It's a worn-in, dark, friendly place that has served excellent burgers since 1945. Pointing at the bar, Margaret Crouse, the giggly owner and second-generation Rotier,

told me, "He used to sit right here and write songs," referring of course to Buffett, who lived and tried to make a go of his music career in Nashville in the late '60s. It's easy to see how over the years a connection could be made between the best cheeseburger in town and a starving artist-cum-star's early low-income diet. Alas, there is no connection.

Where is the famed cheeseburger then? Turns out Buffett came clean a few years back and told the truth. The "cheeseburger in paradise" stemmed from a hallucination. As the story goes, he was sailing near Puerto Rico in the mid-'70s and ran into weather and equipment trouble. He and his crew floated at sea for over five days eating nothing but canned food and peanut butter, and naturally fantasized about juicy cheeseburgers. Eventually the ship limped in to the Village Cay Marina on Tortola, BVI, and the hungry sailors headed for the dock bar. There they feasted on what he recalls as overcooked American-style burgers on burnt buns that tasted "like manna from heaven." The song that followed was not about that burger, but about the fantasy. Buffett made his dream burger a reality in 2002 when he opened the first of his 44 Cheeseburger In Paradise restaurants.

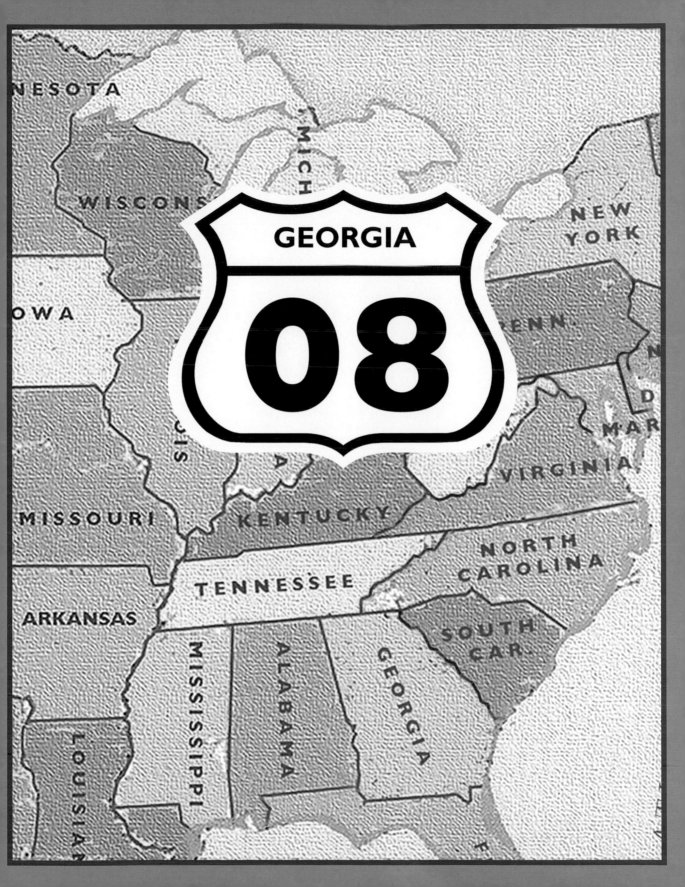

ANN'S
SNACK BAR

1615 MEMORIAL DRIVE SE
ATLANTA, GA 30317
404-687-9207
MON–SAT 11 AM–9 PM
CLOSED SUNDAY

A visit to Ann's Snack Bar is not for the faint of heart. I warn you now, the list of rules posted on the wall covers only a fraction of how you should behave in Miss

Ann's small outpost on the southeast side of Atlanta. I'll do my best here to prepare you for the onslaught that will lead to one of the best hamburgers in America.

"When I die, I want them to say, 'She was a mean bitch but she made a great hamburger!'" While she works alone in the burger and hot dog shack she has owned and tended to since 1972, she keeps the waiting patrons amused with a running comedy routine that covers everything from new condos going up down the street to her retirement and Social Security woes. The guy sitting next to me explained, "It's like a barbershop in here." The routine is real, though, no acting here. I found out the hard way when she threw me out of the restaurant for wanting to interview her. "I threw *Southern Living* out just last week! I don't give a damn . . . Get out!" I stuck it out and was rewarded with the only thing that seems to get ordered from her short menu—the Ghetto Burger.

In 1994 a Checkers drive-in hamburger stand opened up just two doors down from Ann's. Realizing that she had to offer something different to maintain her business, Miss Ann (as she is affectionately called by regulars) ditched the frozen patties she was serving for fresh ground beef, and lots of it. The gimmick worked. "If I had known that's all it took to be world famous I would have done this years ago," she told the crowd at the eight-stool counter. But fresh beef was only the beginning. The Ghetto is an enormous burger, a glorious heap of sin, a pile of just about every ingredient in the restaurant. Two hand-formed patties that are unmeasured but look close to a half pound each are slow cooked on a flattop griddle and sprinkled often with seasoned salt as they cook. The construction of the Ghetto Burger includes the two patties, toasted bun, onion, ketchup, mustard, chili, lettuce, tomato, cheese, and bacon. If that were not enough, the bacon is deep-fried. The finished product resembles a food accident and tastes as it should—amazing.

Says Miss Ann: "When I die, I want them to say, 'She was a mean bitch but she made a great hamburger!'"

"One lady came in here and watched everything I did and said 'Miss Ann, how come I can't make a burger at home like yours?' and I told her 'because you ain't Ann, and you ain't BLACK!'" She punctuates her delivery by repeatedly slapping the counter hard. The mostly black crowd laughs at all of it and waits patiently for their burgers, which can take up to 45 minutes.

Ann wants to retire, though she keeps pushing the date back. "I want to be retired by the end of 2008." Preventing her retirement has been the search to find the right buyer. "I don't want some developer coming in here and tearing the place down," but she smiles, "though the money would be nice."

HUDSON'S HAMBURGERS

207 EAST SHERMAN AVENUE
COEUR D'ALENE, ID 83814
208-664-5444
MON–FRI 9:30 AM–6 PM
SAT 9:30 AM–5:30 PM
CLOSED SUNDAY

If you had found yourself in Coeur d'Alene at the turn of the century, chances are you would have paid a visit to Harley Hudson's tiny canvas burger tent for some greasy nourishment. The great news is that over a hundred years later you can still visit this landmark burger counter for the same greasy nourishment. The tent may have gone brick-and-mortar and has moved four times (only a few blocks each move), but the burgers are still made with pride by the fourth generation of the Hudson family.

This classic burger counter is just what you'd expect to find in picturesque downtown Coeur d'Alene, Idaho. From the front window of the restaurant you can see a piece of the enormous Lake Coeur d'Alene and imagine the hydroplane speedboat races that took place there in the 1950s and 1960s. Find a spot at the long counter and order a burger, the only thing on the menu.

"We also have drinks and pie," grillman Eli told me, "but that's it. No fries, no chips, no nothing." By design, the menu focuses on the hamburger, as it should, because this one was worth the drive.

The choices are single or double, cheese or no cheese. Condiment options are pickle and a slice of raw onion. If you request pickle, watch closely what happens. You'll witness something you'd be hard-pressed to find anywhere else in America. The grillman takes a whole dill pickle and hand slices five or six pieces and neatly arrays them on a waiting steamed bun. The same happens for a slice of onion, sliced in a worn groove on the butcher block in front of the griddle. Nothing is presliced.

> ## "We also have drinks, and pie," said Eli, "but that's it. No fries, no chips, no nothing."

A pan of high-quality, fresh ground round sits to the left of the small flattop griddle. The grillman takes a guesstimated quarter-pound wad of the fresh beef and swiftly forms it into a patty, and it hits the griddle with an audible splat. The griddle only holds 18 burgers at a time, so expect to wait for a stool during peak times. Eli told me that during the summer, the line can go out the door and down the street. "When it's busy, we are behind all the time."

Hudson's serves what could be considered a nearly perfect burger. Relish the moment and plot your return because you'll be forever changed. The simplicity of the elements and the burger's ideal proportions will win your heart (and stomach).

One unique feature of the burger experi-

ence at Hudson's is a proprietary "spicy ketchup" that locals and regulars put on their burgers. Fair warning: this stuff is HOT and looks like regular ketchup in its traditional squirt bottle. Todd explained that the ketchup was invented not for culinary reasons but for economic ones. "During the Depression, some people would come in and load up their burgers with ketchup to stretch the meal." Todd's grandfather added fiery spice to discourage the practice. Over 70 years later, Hudson's still does not offer the classic red stuff.

Today, brothers Todd and Steve Hudson run the historic burger counter. They each take a three-day shift and do their share of burger flipping. Burgers have not been the sole passion of the Hudson family, though. Their proximity to the lake has led to a lifetime on the water. Great-grandfather Harley flipped burgers in the early part of the century, but also owned a steamboat that he rented for excursions on the lake. During the decade that speedboat racing was allowed on the lake, it was the Hudson

family's unofficial job to set up the racecourse markers. When you have finished your burger at Hudson's, wander into the back of the restaurant, where you'll find one of the most impressive collections of hydroplane racing ephemera and memorabilia anywhere.

A few years ago, a McDonald's Express opened four doors down from Hudson's and it lasted only two years. Seems as though the fast-food empire was no match for a 100-year-old burger institution. Todd told me that people would ask if they could go buy McDonald's fries and eat them with their burger at Hudson's. He repeatedly told them, "Sure, as long as you bring enough for everybody."

"The secret is our longevity," Todd explained as he smiled and shrugged. In 2007, that longevity was recognized when the state of Idaho issued a proclamation to honor the Hudson family for a hundred years of business. 100 years of great burger making is definitely cause for celebration.

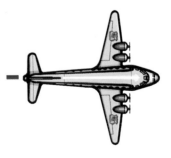

BILLY GOAT
TAVERN & GRILL

430 N. MICHIGAN (LOWER LEVEL)
CHICAGO, IL 60611
312-222-1525
WWW.BILLYGOATTAVERN.COM
OPEN DAILY 6 AM–2 AM

The Billy Goat is responsible for one of the most famous lines in hamburger history, delivered by John Belushi on *Saturday Night Live* on January 28, 1978. But the Goat is more than just "Cheezborger! cheezborger! No Pepsi, Coke! No fries, cheeps." The Goat is steeped in history, so much that it makes you wish you were a Chicagoan, and probably makes many Chicagoans proud. All this from a tavern opened in 1934 by Greek immigrant William "Billy Goat" Sianis.

No one is really sure if the Billy Goat got its name from the far-fetched story of how a goat wandered into the bar one day and became a mascot/pet, or if the name came from the grey

The history of the Goat, carried on today by Sam Sianis and his son Bill (Billy Goat Jr.), along with the 8x10 glossies of past newspapermen who drank and debated there and the bizarre subterranean location, actually add a different type of flavor to the burger. The Goat has what I like to call the "whole burger experience"—it's not just about the burger. It includes the place you are eating it, and who you are eating with.

The "cheezborgers" at the Billy Goat start as fresh beef that is machine pattied into quarter pound slivers. "Triple much better!!" is the call you are likely to hear as the countermen take your order. Just try and order a single cheeseburger. A "Sosa" is four patties, named after the home run king of the Cubs. There really are no fries so don't even ask. You remember the call "No fries, cheeps, no Coke, Pepsi!" They actually do have Coke, no Pepsi; Belushi flipped that in the skit. You dress your own burger with onions and specially made pickle slices, then take a seat at the bar, one of the longest I've ever

goatee Sianis sported, but the nature of its origins is part and parcel of all stories emanating from the Goat. The famous "Curse of the Billy Goat" was also dreamed up by Sianis, a curse that has endured and still exists today: a curse that has spiritually kept the beloved Chicago Cubs out of the World Series for over 60 years despite Sianis' nephew Sam's attempts to "remove" it. And it's all because the media-friendly tavern owner and his smelly goat were denied entry to the 1945 World Series.

photo courtesy of The Billy Goat Tavern

Above: The goat at the bar with friends

Opposite: "Billy Goat" Sianis and his young nephew Sam buy the goat a drink.

seen. There are so many things to look at that it would take days to read all of the clippings and photo captions. Not a problem here, since the Goat is open every day, 20 hours a day.

Probably every old hamburger joint has its share of stories and lore, but none wears it on its sleeve like the Billy Goat. There are so many stories to hear that you'll have to go there and ask Sam or Bill yourself. I'm sure they'd be glad to tell a few—ask about the butter on the ceiling, or the goat that ate the $20 bill.

MOONSHINE STORE

6017 EAST 300TH ROAD
MOONSHINE (MARTINSVILLE), IL 62442
618-569-9200

MON–SAT 6 AM–1 PM, GRILL CLOSES AT 12:30
CLOSED SUNDAY & MAJOR HOLIDAYS

The Moonshine Store is one of those places you hope no one finds out about. I never would have known about the Moonburger if I had not seen a clip on *CBS Sunday Morning* calling it the "Best Burger in America." A claim like that makes me a skeptic from the start but naturally my interest was piqued. I had all but written the place off when I just happened to be in the neighborhood. Believe me, this is not an easy thing to do. Thanks to Ryan Claypool, a resident of nearby Marshall, Illinois, I was coaxed into giving the Moonburger a shot.

The Moonshine Store is at a crossroads in east central Illinois surrounded by cornfields. The drive to Moonshine (population two) is a blur of cornstalks and soybean fields for hours on two-lane roads and the nearest *city* is Terre Haute, Indiana. There's a reason the lines are not out the door with city people—it's too damn far away. But it's true; the Moonshine does make one of the best burgers in America.

Helen mused with a serious gaze, "We do no advertising. I believe the Lord has a hand in this business."

The large country-store-turned-burger-spot does a brisk business regardless of its remote locale. There are no tables inside, just recycled church pews and chairs that line the counters and cases. You place an order at the back of the store and when your burger is ready, you take it to the bountiful condiment table in the center of the room. If you can't find a spot on a pew, there is ample seating out back at the picnic tables.

The staff is a sight to behold—a bevy of chatty country women all taking turns at the grill and register. "I don't work here, I'm just helping today," laughed one behind the counter. Helen Tuttle, owner and grillmaster, explained, "Friends and family all come down for the lunch hour to help out. When we're busy we'll even ask someone in the store to do dishes—we're not bashful."

The Moonburger is a beauty: pure and simple, 80/20-ground chuck cooked on a hot gas griddle until moist inside with a delicately crunchy exterior. I asked what the size of the burger was and Helen told me, "All sizes. Depends on what my hand grabs." They look to be around a third of a pound and served on an untoasted white squishy bun. Cheese is treated like a condiment and tossed on cold. Trust

me—this burger needs no cheese.

The new gas griddle can hold up to 50 burgers, which is an improvement over the previous electric griddle that only held 15. "We can sell 50 to 600 burgers a day depending, and at least 400 on a Saturday," Helen told me. Over 25 separate motorcycle tours made the

Moonshine a destination for food last year, and one visit resulted in a record. "We made 712 that day." Helen then mused with a serious gaze, "We do no advertising. I believe the Lord has a hand in this business." Believe it. These burgers are touched by something.

TOP NOTCH BEEFBURGER SHOP

2116 WEST 95TH STREET
CHICAGO, IL
773-445-7218
WWW.TOPNOTCHBEVERLY.COM
MON–FRI 8 AM–8 PM
SAT 7:30 AM–8:30 PM
CLOSED SUNDAY

I was tipped off to Top Notch by a friend in Chicago who is a key grip in the film business, the same friend, incidentally, who told me about Mr. Beef on North Orleans (for which I am eternally grateful). This is definitely the kind of spot you need to be tipped off to because it is very far from downtown Chicago. In fact it's about 25 minutes by car south of the Loop in a neighborhood called Beverly. The journey to Top Notch is worth it because it makes, without a doubt, one of the best burgers in Chicago.

Top Notch has the standard-issue brown Naugahyde booths, fluorescent lighting, and wood paneling from the '40s but takes it a step further to include Bob Ross–inspired oil paintings of soothing waterfalls and mountain scenes. The staff is extremely friendly and the menu lists true diner fare. The shakes, fries, and tuna sandwiches are all good, but the reason to visit Top Notch is of course for the "beefburgers." They come in three sizes—the quarter pounder, the half pound "King Size", and the three quarter pound "Super King Size." A deal breaker for me is the absence of fresh ground beef in a burger restaurant, so I always ask the question "fresh or frozen?" I was directed to the manager of 16 years, Sam Gomez, who, without asking for credentials, dragged me into the kitchen and into their small meat locker. There I was surrounded by the real thing—about five sides of beef and various cuts waiting for their turn in the grinder. Sam told me "our burgers are very fresh." I had a hard time doubting him.

The burgers are cooked on a large vintage cast-iron griddle in plain view of the counter patrons. They are griddled wide and flat, allowing more of the beef to have contact with the griddle surface. A favorite condiment is the grilled onions, so much so that burgers requested without onions still gather an onion essence. The bun is my favorite kind—white and squishy with sesame seeds, probably six inches across, toasted in the same upright conveyor toaster that Louis' Lunch in New Haven uses. Sam describes the fries as "pre-WWII," which I took to mean from a time before fries were frozen. Sure enough, there in the kitchen one employee had the task of gathering up fresh-cut fries that soak in cold water and bringing them to the fryer. The fries are excellent.

I want to have a party there someday—the place is huge and can hold over a hundred hungry burger lovers. Bring your appetite and order at least the half pounder with cheese.

HEINNIES

1743 WEST LUSHER AVENUE
ELKHART, IN 46517
574-522-9101
WWW.HEINNIESRESTAURANT.COM
MON–THU 10 AM–10 PM
FRI & SAT 10 AM–11 PM
CLOSED SUNDAY

Friend and food columnist Marshall King led me to this hamburger. He told me about a decades-old bar down by the train tracks in an industrial part of town that had been serving burgers forever—I was sold.

When I first visited Heinnies, Bill DeShone, third-generation owner, was doing what his grandfather and father did for decades before him—he was walking around the dining room, greeting people, and checking on their food. "There's always a family member here," Bill told me, "whether it's me or my brother." It's that kind of pride of place that keeps people loyal. That, and of course, a world-class hamburger.

In the early 1950s, Henry "Heinnie" DeShone chose a spot for his tavern that was a bit remote for the residents of Elkhart. His new venture would be located across the street from one of the busiest railroad hubs in North America. "There was nothing else out here," Bill explained, and told me that most of the clientele were railroad men. "It has always been a place where the working man could come get a burg-er, though back then it was a *beer* and a burger." True to its roots, the area is still very industrial, though today the local industry is focused on motor home repair and manufacturing.

When Heinnies opened in 1951, the low-ceiled bar had a sign on the door prohibiting women (but by 1956 the sign was removed). A small dining room was added to the bar in 1983, and in 1996 a full renovation was completed. Bill's younger brother Troy did the decorating and his obsession with NASCAR is apparent—the walls are lined with an impressive collection of American racing memorabilia.

The menu is loaded with burgers, but the ones to focus on are the classic Heinniecheeseburger and the Claybaugh. The latter is a larger version of the classic that includes two one-third-pound patties and a wild pile of ingredients including, but not limited to, bacon, mushrooms, and four types of cheese. This one should be reserved for the truly starved. The burger is named after a local policeman and regular named Scott Claybaugh who, Bill explained, just like the burger, "is big and full of shit." But it's the Heinniecheeseburger that they come back for, a moderately priced, well-seasoned, great-tasting burger.

Made from fresh-ground prime beef, the Heinniecheeseburger in its simplest form (no condiments, on a bun) is a taste explosion.

The Heinniecheeseburger

That's because of a not-so-secret ingredient included in the DeShone family burger recipe—chopped onions mixed into the beef. "We used to mix in bread crumbs and egg too," Bill told me, "It was sort of like a meat loaf." But because the meat turned bad quickly, the DeShone family decided to stick with the basics—chopped onion, salt, and pepper.

The meat for the Heinniecheeseburger comes from a local butcher, the same butcher Heinnies has been using forever. The butcher uses scraps from sirloin, filet, and strip steaks and grinds them for the restaurant.

After the ground prime arrives, it is blended with chopped onion and pattied on an ancient family heirloom. The tool is a unique patty maker that presses the burgers one at a time to the proper thickness without forming the traditional cylindrically "squared" sides. The result is a patty with craggy edges that looks hand formed.

Bill is slightly befuddled by a newfound group of fans who have discovered the decades-old tavern—the Amish. On Friday nights the back room is full of people from the nearby Amish communities of Nappanee and Shipshewana. Bill assumes that they are drawn to the restaurant by the huge, horse stable–themed dining room that was added in 1985 to the back of the restaurant called "Heinnies Back Barn." Knotty pine frames each booth like a horse stall and vintage farm equipment lines the walls. "They come in by the vanload," Bill told me. "Strawberry daiquiris and steak for two!"

HAMBURG INN NO. 2

214 NORTH LINN STREET
IOWA CITY, IA 52245
319-337-5512
WWW.HAMBURGINN.COM
OPEN DAILY 6 AM–11 PM

Chances are that if you've been to Iowa City you've been to the Hamburg Inn. Since 1948 this hamburger destination has been serving fresh-ground burgers to University of Iowa students and professors and faithful regulars, and more recently has become a sort of base camp for politicos rambling through town on the campaign trail. Everyone from local politicians to presidential hopefuls has made press stops at the Hamburg Inn. They are there to talk to the people and, naturally, be photographed enjoying America's favorite food. But the burger at Hamburg is not just a photo-op prop, it's the real deal and, thanks to second-generation owner Dave Panther, a high-quality one at that.

Dave inherited the Hamburg Inn No. 2 from his father, Fritz Panther. Fritz' older brother Joe opened Hamburg Inn No. 1 in the mid-1930s, a small, classic ten-stool hamburger stand featuring burgers for a nickel. In 1948, Fritz and another brother, Adrian, bought a defunct restaurant (the current location) and called it Hamburg Inn No. 2. At one point there was a No. 3 in Cedar Rapids but today both No.1 and No. 3 are long gone. Only No. 2 remains.

Dave, who moonlights as a professional clown, started working for his parents at the restaurant at age thirteen, peeling potatoes. After a stint in the U.S. Air Force, Dave started working full time at the Hamburg Inn and in 1979 assumed ownership.

Since the beginning, chuck steaks have been ground daily on premises. A six-ounce ice cream scoop is used to measure the balls of ground beef. The balls of meat are pressed on the griddle and assume a somewhat uneven beauty. Dave's father, Fritz, bought a patty maker back in the 1950s but returned it after three days, fully dissatisfied with the results. "He said the patty maker changed the complexion and nature of the whole product," Dave remembered. Five decades later not a single pre-formed patty has ever graced the griddle at the Hamburg Inn.

I ask Dave where Bill Clinton sat on his visit. "Just to the left of Reagan's table."

The burgers are served on large, toasted, cornmeal-dusted kaiser rolls. Five different types of cheese are available, as are an abundance of toppings ranging from the standard tomato and lettuce to the slightly bizarre pineapple. Honestly, don't be blinded by the options—this burger, made from choice beef, is so fresh it'd be a shame to cover it with anything other than a bun.

The menu at the Hamburg Inn is enormous, offering every type of comfort food imaginable. Dave gradually expanded the menu over the decades and was responsible for adding a favorite breakfast item, the omelet. The burger takes center stage for lunch and dinner but it's the omelet, served in unlimited combinations, that captivates the morning crowd. "We have a guy that comes in and orders a cream cheese, black olive, and raisin omelet," Dave told me. "That's about the weirdest combination we've made." One of the restaurant's most popular omelets contains, not surprisingly, a healthy dose of the Hamburg Inn's ground beef. It's called the "Zadar" and is named after a local movie that was filmed at the restaurant. With ground beef and American cheese, it's basically a hamburger omelet. A great idea and probably the only one of its kind in America.

The walls of the Hamburg Inn are covered with vintage photos and one wall is dedicated to American politics. There's even a plaque over table #6 that trumpets a visit by former president Ronald Reagan. President Clinton visited as well, but has not been honored with a plaque (yet). I asked Dave where Clinton sat on his visit to the Hamburg Inn and he told me, "Just to the left of Reagan's table." The political humor was not lost on me.

TAYLOR'S MAID-RITE

106 SOUTH 3RD AVENUE
MARSHALLTOWN, IA 50158
641-753-9684
WWW.TAYLORSMAIDRITE.COM
MON–SAT 8 AM–10 PM
SUN 10 AM–10 PM

Taylor's does not serve hamburgers. Taylor's serves the only "loosemeats sandwich" in this book. For those not familiar with the popular Iowa hamburger-influenced sandwich, a loosemeats, or Maid-Rite (and sometimes referred to as a "tavern"), is basically a deconstructed hamburger, or a sloppy joe without the slop. The recipe is simple: fresh ground-on-premises beef is steamed and crumbled in a cast-iron cooker. Nothing is added but salt. Upon getting an order, a member of the extended Taylor family or longtime employee grabs a bun that has been "doped" with pickle and mustard, and with the other hand scoops up an impossible amount of the pebbly, moist meat. That's it, and there's nothing else on the menu but shakes, ice cream, pie, and soft drinks, and they have been doing it this way since 1928. The order is wrapped up even if you are eating at the counter. "Wrapping makes the bun soft," Zac told me. Zac is a fifth-generation Taylor helping out for the summer and proving that Taylor's is clearly a family-run business.

Cliff Taylor purchased the franchise for the

third Maid-Rite in Iowa for $300 and called it Taylor's. His son Don Taylor took over the business in 1944. In 1958, Taylor's moved across the street into a new *modern* building, its current location. Cliff Taylor's granddaughter Sandy remembers the move well. "We moved the entire contents of the restaurant overnight making trips back and forth across the street. I remember helping to carry the plates." One element of the move that didn't work out so well was the new steam cooker. "My dad thought the meat just didn't taste right so he brought the cooker over from the old place," Sandy told me.

"This could be the same cooker from 1928," Sandy said, pointing to the strange stainless cabinet with the deep, cast-iron trough.

Taylor's is a bright, clean, friendly place with floor-to-ceiling windows in the front of the restaurant. A large horseshoe counter surrounds a short-order kitchen that offers amazing views of your food being prepared. One wall of the restaurant is covered with enormous world and U.S. maps with the phrase above, "Go 'round the world, but come back again."

Unlike other Maid-Rites in the well-known Midwestern franchise, Taylor's has kept things simple. The other Maid-Rites offer everything from roasted chicken and corn dogs to tacos. At Taylor's, a loosemeats sandwich has always been the solitary sandwich on the short menu.

The loosemeats sandwich may be some of the fastest food you'll ever come across because the meat is already cooked and warm. An order can arrive at your spot at the counter in under a minute. Unwrap and sink your teeth into one of the softest, tastiest sandwiches around and you'll start wondering why the rest of the country has not caught on yet.

The last time I visited the Central Iowa eatery there was a debate going on about the proposed introduction of ketchup, not to the sandwich, but *to the counter*. The sign out front announced "STOP IN VOTE YES OR NO FOR KETCHUP." The votes were tallied, and in August 2006 ketchup was introduced to the counter, 77 years after opening day.

Sandy retired from a job as a schoolteacher in North Dakota only to return home and find herself drawn to Taylor's. Her son Don Taylor Short was looking to move on after 20 years managing the popular loosemeats institution and Sandy agreed to jump in. "This is my retirement!" she told me laughing. She's there every day and makes a point to warn customers about the pitfalls of the metal cup that holds your "extra" milkshake. "You need to stir it before you pour it," she reminds me. "Someone dumps their shake on the counter everyday."

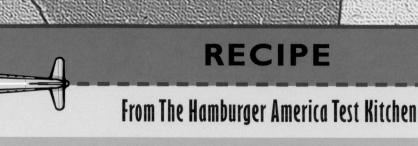

THE BEER MAID-RITE SANDWICH

This is an interpretation of the Iowa classic loosemeats sandwich. At Taylor's Maid-Rite in Marshalltown, there are no secrets and their recipe is simple. They grind meat at the restaurant, add salt, and use a cast-iron steam cooker that has been in use for almost 80 years.

MAKES 5-6 SANDWICHES
1 pound fresh ground 80/20 chuck
5 pinches salt (to taste)
1 cup beer
3 squirts (teaspoons) yellow mustard
6 white squishy buns
Pickle slices
Chopped onion
More yellow mustard

Place a heavy cast-iron skillet over medium heat to warm for five minutes. Turn heat to medium high and crumble the beef into the Skillet. Add salt. Using the blade end of the spatula, chop the beef as it cooks until it is pebbly. When the beef loses most of its pink, add the beer and turn the heat up to high. Add the mustard as the beer begins to bubble and stir to mix contents. Cook over high heat, stirring constantly, until most of the liquid has evaporated. Scoop onto buns that have been "doped" with onion, pickle, and more mustard. Enjoy with the remaining beer.

BOBO'S DRIVE IN

2300 SW 10TH AVENUE
TOPEKA, KS 66604
785-234-4511
MON–SAT 11 AM–8:30 PM
CLOSED SUNDAY

Bobo's is one of only a handful of original drive-ins in America still using carhops. That's right, the ones who come to your car, take your order, then come back with food and clip a tray onto your car door. Sonic may have capitalized on the modern version of the drive-in, but there's still nothing like an original one-of-a-kind like Bobo's.

At one point there were two Bobo's Drive Ins in Topeka the one remaining opened in 1953. The first location was opened just a few blocks away in 1948 by Orville and Louise Bobo. "Mrs. Bobo still comes in and buys pies two to three times a week," Kim, a carhop of ten years told me. Bobo's is now owned by Bob Humes—only the second owner in the restaurant's more than five decades in operation. Bob bought Bobo's and all of the secret recipes in 1988 and kept everything pretty much the same.

Bobo's plays the part of the mid century American road icon with a neon tower shooting out of its roof and a large arrow pointing the way. There are 12 stalls for cars and two carhops during the day running orders and food back and forth from the kitchen to waiting drivers. You can see why so many fast-food restaurants moved to the economical drive-thru; the drive-in is without question a lot more work.

"What's on the Spanish burger?" I asked. "Spanish sauce," Jonette told me bluntly.

The burgers at Bobo's are excellent. They start as fresh ground 85 percent lean one-eighth-ounce patties and are cooked on a superhot flat-top griddle, pressed flat. "You don't always get a perfect circle," grill cook Robert admitted. The thin patty is sprinkled with salt and pepper, then griddled until crunchy on the outside but perfectly moist inside.

A strange burger creation proprietary to Bobo's competes equally with their flavorful double cheeseburger—the Spanish Burger. What's on the Spanish? "Spanish sauce," Jonette told me bluntly. Turns out, the Spanish sauce is a tangy, sweet tomato sauce. Just then, someone sat down and ordered one. "You see? We sell as many of them as cheeseburgers."

Not to be missed are the onion rings. I mean it when I say that these were probably the best I've ever eaten. I still think about that inviting pile of not-too-greasy gnarled, deep-fried onions. I couldn't stop eating them. Homemade root beer is also a draw.

In 1998 Bob and his son decided to celebrate Bobo's fiftieth anniversary by purchasing a champion cow at the Shawnee County 4-H Fair. They walked away with the "grand champion" for $1,000. Bob told me, "It was a little more than we expected to pay!" They sent the cow to slaughter and the party went on for days at Bobo's.

Carhops Kim and Jonette know just about everyone who drives up or walks in the door. "For a lot of people who pull in here," Jonette said, "we can have their order on the grill before they even tell us." Now there's a perk that could lure you to Topeka.

COZY INN HAMBURGERS
108 NORTH 7TH STREET
SALINA, KS 67401
785-825-2699
WWW.COZYBURGER.COM
SUN–THU 11 AM–8 PM
FRI & SAT 10 AM–9 PM

The Cozy Inn is a classic well-preserved hamburger stand built in 1922 in Salina, Kansas. Not surprisingly, the Cozy, with its six white-painted steel stools and short counter, was modeled after the successful White Castle hamburger chain. In 1921, only one year earlier in nearby Wichita, a man named Walt Anderson had opened the first White Castle: it was to become the first hamburger chain in America. In the next few years the White Castle model, a clean, small stand serving wholesome burgers, would be copied by entrepreneurs all over the country. The secret ingredient to White Castle's success was chopped onions that, when cooked with the burger, created an intoxicating smell that drew customers from near and far. Bob Kinkel, an amateur baseball player from Salina, liked what he saw (and smelled) and immediately opened the Cozy Inn.

On one of my visits to Cozy a woman sitting at the counter named Phyllis told me, "My father built this place for Bob—$500 turnkey." This would have been a bargain even by 1922 standards, with the possible exception that the place is incredibly small. It takes only a few people to fill up the low-ceilinged burger joint, so understandably, a line builds quickly outside at lunchtime.

To sit and watch the grillman at work is a treat. He stands in front of a smallish recessed griddle that has room for 60 of the *aromatic sliders* for which the Cozy has become famous. A steam cloud envelops his head as he flips row after row of the small onion-covered burgers. The cloud fills the tiny restaurant with an aroma so thick your eyes will tear and make your clothing smell for days. It's an oniony goodness that once saturated thousands of burger stands just like the Cozy Inn from the 1920s to the 1950s. Today Cozy is one of only a handful of its kind still in operation.

So now you're thinking. Can I get a slider without onions? No. For over 80 years the same sliders have been sold at Cozy. If you don't like onions, you won't like their burgers. But if you do, you'll be in heaven. A burger "all the way" comes with ketchup, mustard, pickle, and a pile of steam-cooked onions. Today you can choose any combination of these condiments, but in the old days you had no choice—a burger at the Cozy came "all the way" and that was that. And for all of these decades, cheese has never graced a burger at Cozy, so don't even ask. No fries either. Grab a bag of chips at the counter.

The burgers are small, so order a bunch. A familiar call from a customer might be, "A sack and a pop, please," which is local vernacular for, "six sliders and a soda to go."

"We roll our own meat here," Nancy said, referring to the one-ounce wads of fresh bull beef that make up a Cozy slider. The tiny stand will go through 500 pounds of onions and an incredible 1,000 pounds of meat a week. "On our 80th anniversary we sold 8,800 burgers in three days," Nancy boasted. The buns, soft and pillowy, are made especially for the Cozy Inn and come all the way from Missouri.

On my first visit to the Cozy Inn I was walking out, reeking of onions, and an older woman on her way in stopped me and excitedly asked, "Was it as good as you remembered?" Now that's the kind of sentiment the Cozy deserves.

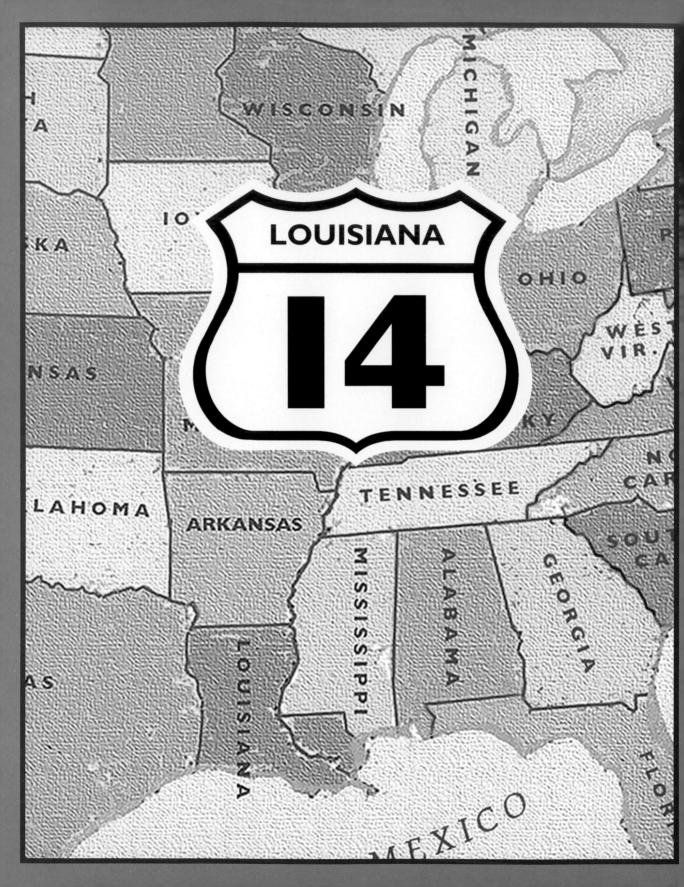

BOZO'S

3117 21ST STREET
METAIRIE, LA 70002
504-831-8666
TUES–THU 11 AM–3 PM, 5 PM–10 PM
FRI–SAT 11 AM–3 PM, 5 PM–11 PM
CLOSED SUNDAY & MONDAY

Bozo's is not the kind of place you'd expect to find a great burger. The restaurant is a destination for fresh oysters and excellent fried seafood and the burger is listed at the bottom of the menu. Southern food writer and friend, John T. Edge, led me to Bozo's, calling their burger a "sleeper." Nevertheless, Bozo's has sold the same amazing hamburger po'boy (Louisiana vernacular for submarine or hero sandwich) for almost 80 years.

Bozo's sits in a fairly nondescript industrial neighborhood in Metairie, a half block from the Lake Pontchartrain Causeway. The low wooden building is set back from the street with a large parking lot in front. If you didn't know what you were looking for you'd drive right past. No ostentatious signage or loud neon here—just a small stained-glass window with the name Bozo's subtly printed on it. The dining room is pure function, clean and well lit with wood-grain Formica tables and sturdy industrial seating. The only real decoration is a floor-to-ceiling mural of two fishing boats near a dock. "Those were two of my dad's boats," second-generation owner and septuagenarian chef Chris Vodanovich pointed out to me.

Yugoslavian immigrant Chris "Bozo" Vodanovich Sr. opened Bozo's Oyster House on St. Ann Street in New Orleans in 1928. At one point Bozo had a fleet of eight boats to service the needs of his restaurant. Fresh oysters, shrimp, and catfish were the reasons most locals patronized the tiny restaurant, but from the beginning, Bozo offered a hamburger po'boy as an alternative to seafood.

The burger at Bozo's is a combination of almost 80 years of experience, a proprietary mixture of meat and onions, and a twist on a regional specialty—the po'boy sandwich. Among those for whom the perfect po'boy is a passion, it is understood that the bread used is as important as what goes on it. Because of this Chris uses only the best—French bread from Leidenheimer Bakery, an institution in New Orleans for over 100 years.

I asked Chris how big the burger was and he didn't know. "We just make them to fit the bread," he told me, smiling. The bread is not small, making this hamburger po'boy a filling meal. The fresh ground beef has onions and "other spices" mixed in before being hand patted and cooked on a flattop griddle. The combination of the perfectly cooked burger and the pillowy bread makes for a great regional hamburger experience.

Chris inherited Bozo's and moved his father's business out of downtown New Orleans to Metairie in 1979 because, as he put it, "the neighborhood was gettin' rough." The Metairie location was expanded to accommodate 120 diners in two dining rooms separated by a large bar.

While I talked to Chris, every patron said "Thanks, Mr. Chris" as they paid their tabs and left. He speaks with a gentle Louisiana twang and has piercing blue eyes and wavy grey hair. I asked him "Why Bozo?" "In the old country, Bozo was the word for Christ," he told me, "and my name is Chris."

PORT OF CALL

838 ESPLANADE AVENUE
NEW ORLEANS, LA 70116
504-523-0120
WWW.PORTOFCALLNEWORLEANS.COM
SUN–THU 11 AM–MIDNIGHT
FRI & SAT 11 AM–1 AM

Port of Call is a bar and restaurant that sits on the far northeast end of the French Quarter in New Orleans. I say this because when people tell you this place is in the Quarter your thoughts first go to drunken tourists with their souvenir hurricane glasses, lame strip clubs, and big-ass beers. Not so here.

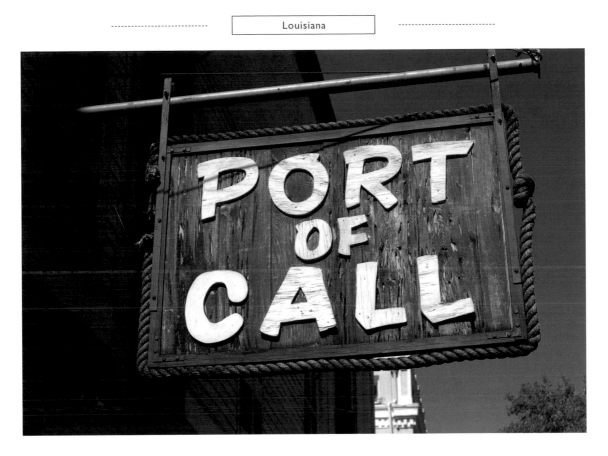

Port of Call is on the other end of the quarter, in a quiet, beautiful neighborhood.

The building Port of Call calls home dates back to the turn of the century, where it started as a sailor bar. Over the years it went from grocery store to tavern and then opened as a steakhouse in 1962. Burger sales one day eclipsed the steak, and today Port of Call is the most popular (and best) burger destination in New Orleans.

The decor is comfortably nautical and has dark wood floors, wood walls, wood tables, and a wood bar. The entire ceiling is a web of sisal rope and the whole place feels like it might start rocking with the tide.

There are four burger choices–Hamburger, Cheeseburger, Mushroom Burger, and Mushroom Cheeseburger. It's the Mushroom cheeseburger that keeps them coming back.

Port of Call grinds its own sirloin and forms burgers into eight-ounce patties. The burgers are char-grilled and served on a bun that seems too small for the amount of meat provided. In order to make the patty fit, the burger is a tall, inch-and-a-half-thick, perfectly cooked fist of meat. The cheese is shredded cheddar and the mushrooms are sautéed in wine, butter, and garlic and melt in your mouth. It looks like a mess when it arrives at your spot at the bar (or at one of the many tables in two dining rooms) but is actually easy to handle once you get going.

Port of Call was spared major damage during the devastating Hurricane Katrina in 2005. "The flooding stopped two blocks that way," general manager of over thirty years Mike Mollere told me, pointing north. "We were extremely fortunate and had little damage. After the neighborhood opened back up I just turned the key and we were open for business." Mike followed his post-hurricane opening by serving first responders and the press.

I arrived at Port of Call just before open- ing, hoping to beat the crowds. No such luck. By the time the ancient, windowless wood doors were unlatched there were over 20 people wait- ing on the sidewalk to get their mushroom burger fix. "It's like that every morning," Mike said, shaking his head. I took a spot at the bar and watched as the restaurant filled almost to capacity with an additional 50 hungry tourists, locals, and construction workers. Within *ten minutes* the Port of Call was transformed from an empty, dark bar into a bustling, lively hot spot. Mike pointed out that they have the best jukebox in town. "Hey, where else can you hear Zappa on a jukebox?"

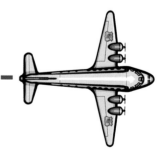

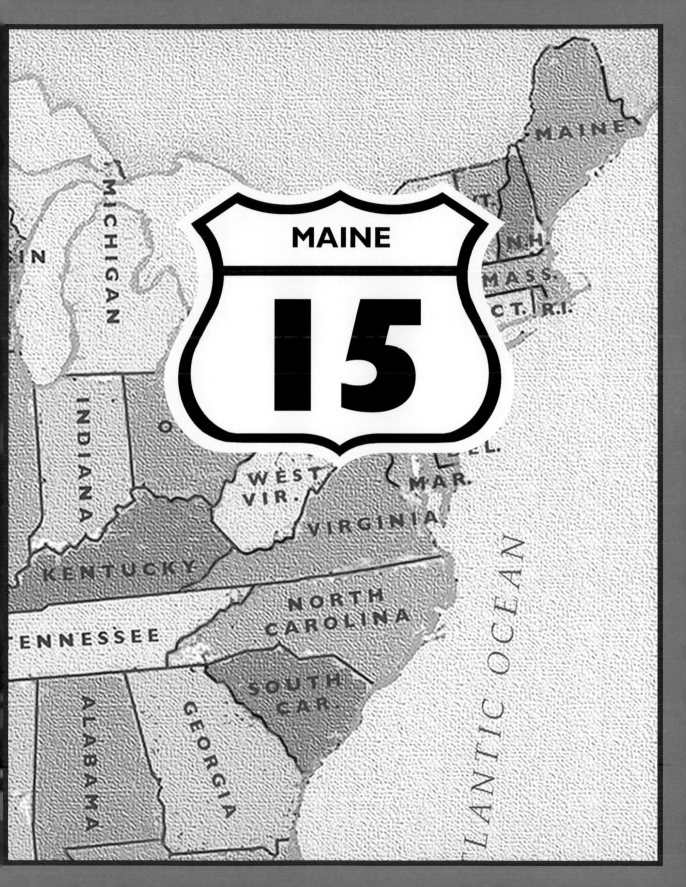

HARMON'S LUNCH

144 GRAY ROAD
FALMOUTH, ME 04105
207-797-9857
MON–FRI 10:30 AM–3 PM
SAT 11 AM–7 PM
CLOSED SUNDAY

My first question for owner Pete Wormell was a dumb one—I asked, "Why Harmon's *Lunch*?" Through a thick monotone Maine accent he told me, "We're only open for lunch." Even though this tiny burger spot in Maine is open for only four and a half hours a day, they still manage to sell over 80,000 burgers a year.

Amazingly, Pete knows exactly how many burgers he sells every year because he jots down the day's total on a calendar. When I asked him why, he said, "I'm weird, I guess." You can ask him how many he sold on any day in the last decade and he'll be able to tell you. "Look," he said, pointing to the calendar, "We only sold 144 that day because of snow."

Pete and friend Cliff bought Harmon's in 1995 from Marvin Harmon, who was looking for the right people to buy the place. "I blame him," Pete said, pointing at Cliff, who was working the grill. Cliff had seen an ad in the paper that the restaurant was for sale. He has since sold his portion to Pete, who joked, "We're still friends part-time."

Marvin built the small wood-frame burger joint in 1960. Today, not much has changed, but Pete started an impressive collection of vintage Maine dairy bottles that line the walls. It's a collection that is rooted in his family's dairy past.

Both Pete and Cliff share time at the busy seasoned griddle cranking out excellent burgers. The menu is limited to burgers, hot dogs, and grilled cheese, but fresh-cut fries are also available. If you ask for milk, specify either "white" or "chocolate" or be pegged a tourist.

The burger at Harmon's is small but tasty. Pete buys fresh ground beef and uses a patty former at the restaurant to make two-ounce patties. "We made them by hand for the first six months," Cliff told me. "That was enough."

A fully loaded burger comes with mustard, fried onions, and a signature sweet red relish.

"Most people think it's going to be hot because of its color," Pete told me. A local bakery provides preservative-free buns that are steamed to limp. The bun creates an impossibly soft, warm pillow that cradles the perfectly cooked thin patty.

The wait at Harmon's, especially on a Saturday, can be up to 45 minutes. "We get backed up," Pete said, "but to have the quality you can't do more."

If you ask for milk, specify either "white" or "chocolate" or be pegged a tourist.

When Pete and Cliff first took the helm at Harmon's, they decided to slightly alter the menu and offer a traditional Maine favorite — the lobster roll. The attempt backfired and the roll was pulled from the menu after only a few weeks. "This is a hamburger place," Pete explained, and attributed the failure to the old adage "If it ain't broke, don't fix it."

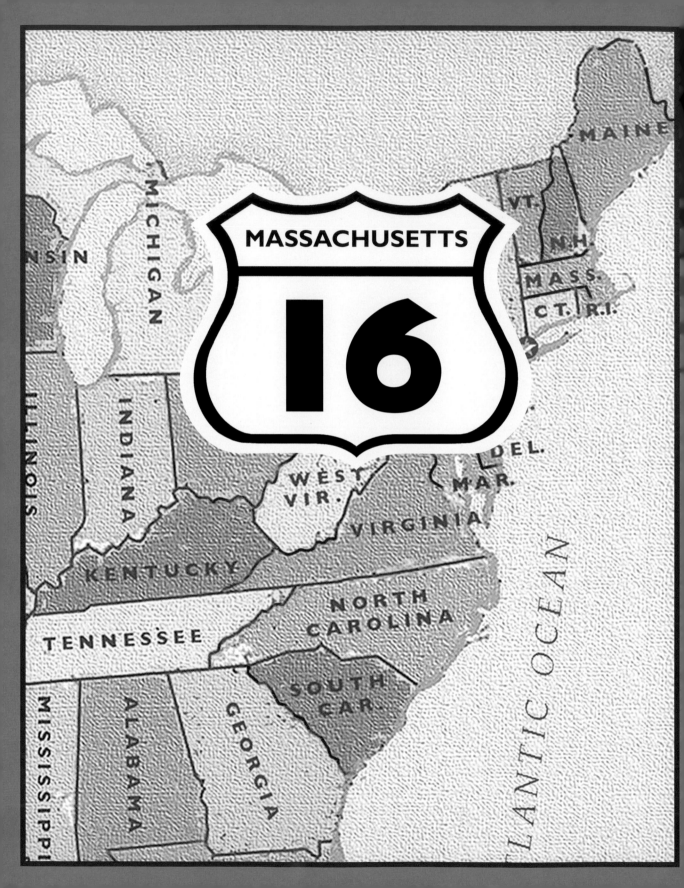

MR. BARTLEY'S BURGER COTTAGE

1246 MASS AVENUE
CAMBRIDGE, MA 02138
617-354-6559
WWW.MRBARTLEY.COM
MON–SAT 11 AM–9 PM
CLOSED SUNDAY

Bill Bartley is an original. He stands at the griddle at his family's Harvard Square eatery shouting things at me like "We're the BEST!" and "This is the greatest burger ANYWHERE!" He's smiling and extremely energetic and has the kind of cocksure confidence and running dialogue usually reserved for someone like Muhammed Ali in his prime. Fortunately, all of it is true—the burgers at Mr. Bartley's are unbelievable.

"I've probably made over five million burgers in the last 30 years," Bill told me as he shifted some burgers on the 600-degree griddle, "All good ones too, all cooked to temp." If you ask for medium-rare, that's what you'll get. Every burger goes out exactly the way Bill wants them to, which means perfect. If you ask for cheese it's cooked *separately* from the burger. Where most chefs melt the cheese atop the burger as it nears completion, Bill cooks the perfect burger, tosses a thick slice of cheese directly on the griddle for a minute, then gently transfers it to the burger as it is dispatched to a table. As Bill eloquently explained, "The cheese is ambivalent to the temperature of the burger."

Mr. Bartley's is a busy place. Just across the street is Harvard University, so you can imagine the crowd. The restaurant feels like a big broken-in bar, yet no booze is served and the walls are covered with Red Sox stuff, political ephemera, and the types of posters a student might have in their dorm room. Many tables, including a long communal one, and green plastic chairs complete the scene.

The first time I visited, there was a line out the door at 2:30 p.m. on a Thursday. The man who started it all, Joe Bartley, was taking names outside, his wife Joan was managing the tables inside, and their son Bill was at the grill cranking out perfect burgers. "You don't have a line outside because you're slow," Bill explained, "you have a line because you're GOOD." The turnover is quick and the service lightning fast.

> **"You don't have a line outside because you're slow," Bill explained, "you have a line because you're GOOD."**

The burger selection is enormous. With the same seven-ounce patty, Bill and his team can add any one of the over forty dressing concoctions on the menu. Everything you can imagine on a burger is available here, from feta cheese to baked beans, but the big seller is the Viagra Burger. The Viagra is topped with blue cheese and bacon, and the menu asks you to "rise to the occasion." The reality is that these

The Viagra Burger

to almost a burn to seal in the juices.

Even though the burger selection is daunting, your toughest choice will be deciding what to drink. Mr. Bartley's serves up some of the city's greatest frappes (milkshakes) and an amazing raspberry lime rickey. My advice? Get both.

Joe Bartley ran a lunch counter seven days a week in the back of a pharmacy in Garden City, New York in the 1950s. "I was going to be a cop on Long Island, can you believe that?" He decided to move back to his native Boston one day and opened a grocery store in 1960 in Harvard Square. By 1962 he was making burgers because, as he told me, "When I started there wasn't a good burger around."

As I stood and watched Bill's genius at work I tried to figure out what made these burgers so special. Without missing a beat Bill offered this insight: "The person who has this skill level thinks they should be doing something better. Not me. I make the best burgers anywhere."

burgers need no condiments. They are that good and don't even need a bun. Of course Bill put it best when he explained, "The bun is just the envelope for the good news that's coming."

Mr. Bartley's burger starts as fresh-ground chuck that come from a local butcher daily. A special patty former in the restaurant is designed not to compress the meat too much as it creates the fist-sized burgers. "We use an Acu-Pat," Bill told me. "It's made of stainless steel so it doesn't use heat during patty forming like most. Heat is the worst thing for an uncooked burger." On the intensely hot griddle the burgers are seared

WHITE HUT

280 MEMORIAL AVENUE
WEST SPRINGFIELD, MA 01089
413-736-9390
WWW.WHITEHUT.COM
MON–WED 6:30 AM–6:30 PM
THU–FRI 6:30 AM–8:30 PM
SAT & SUN 8 AM–6 PM

White Hut is one of the few remaining "White" restaurants in America. During the 1920s and 1930s America was blanketed with ten-stool hamburger joints with names like: White Tower, White Diamond, White Clock, and the one that started it all—White Castle. Placing the word *white* in your name conveyed a sense of cleanliness, an important tenet in a time when hamburgers were considered dirty food for wage earners. By the 1930s in America, thanks to the tremendous success of White Castle, the word white also became synonymous with quality fast food.

And then along came White Hut. In the late 1930s, Hy Roberts opened a small three-stool hot dog shack on a busy corner in West Springfield, Massachusetts. A year after opening, Edward Barkett was asked by Roberts to run the stand for a few weeks. Barkett liked what he saw and negotiated the purchase of the business for $300. He bought a plot of land across the street soon after and built a tiny 600-square-foot burger counter. That same burger counter, over 60 years later, serves a thousand burgers a day and is still run by the third generation of the Barkett family.

The interior of White Hut is a classic burger counter with 12 vintage stools facing a large flattop griddle, bare white walls, and a long counter supported by a wall of glass block. The floors are sprinkled with a generous amount of sawdust, giving the place an old-time meat market feel. "That's so people don't slip—this floor can get slippery," manager Kathy told me. The place was built during the Depression, at a time when most building materials were scarce. "The White Hut was built with black-market lumber," current owner and grandson EJ Barkett pointed out. "Nothing else was available during the war." His grandfather was also forced to use the only flooring available, a slick beige terrazzo. Booths lined the back wall of the restaurant for the first few months, but were removed when Barkett noticed that people tended to hang around in them too long. "My grandfather needed the turnover and replaced the booths with a large table to stand around."

Don't look for a menu—there is none. White Hut offers only three things: hamburgers, cheeseburgers, and hot dogs. And, as of only a few years ago, fries. If you love onions, you'll love the burgers at White Hut. Every morning a large pile of chopped Spanish onions is placed on the griddle. The onions cook slowly until they are translucent and limp, then hearty amounts are spooned onto the burgers. "We go through about 250 pounds of onions a day," counterperson Roberta told me. Roberta is actually owner EJ Barkett's mother and a fount of White Hut lore. White Hut receives an order of fresh, thin, two-ounce patties every morning made of a special blend they have been using for years. "There's less fat so there is less shrinkage," Roberta pointed out.

The daily lunch crowd is large and the method for ordering a burger at peak times requires well-tuned survival instincts. Order your burgers when a counterperson *makes eye contact with you*. Roberta told me, "People will stand four and five deep at the counter at lunchtime." Nothing is written down and somehow everyone's order is produced perfectly. Regardless of the hungry mob and apparent lack of order, the average dining experience at White Hut lasts only 15 minutes. A unique rule, imposed at the counter, may help. "No newspapers between 12 and 2," Kathy told me, "because they are not paying attention."

White Hut is a family place, run by family and visited by families. A regular named Michael, in a suit, standing and eating a quick lunch told me, "I bring my kids here just like my dad brought me here years ago." "We've had four generations sitting at the counter at the same time," EJ told me, "I love to see that." For many in this part of Western Massachusetts, White Hut is an enduring tradition that shows no sign of fading any time soon.

KRAZY JIM'S BLIMPY BURGER

551 SOUTH DIVISION STREET
ANN ARBOR, MI 48104
734-663-4590
MON–SAT 11 AM–10 PM
SUN NOON–8 PM

A visit to Blimpy Burger can be a daunting but rewarding experience. Theatrically, the cooks behind the counter engage in a sort of Soup Nazi berating of customers who do not follow the cafeteria-style rules of ordering. "Just answer the questions I'm asking you," grill cook Brian told a group of newcomers the first time I visited. In reality, the rules are there to help you, not scare you. They are there to allow the cooks to get your food to you fast, which is a good thing because you'll need this burger in your mouth as soon as possible.

Blimpy Burger is on the edge of the University of Michigan campus, surrounded by student rental houses with mud lawns. For students, the positioning of this decades-old greasy spoon could not be better. The interior of Blimpy Burger is wholly utilitarian and the opposite of a comfy dive. A low drop ceiling and greenish fluorescent lighting give the place a construction trailer feel. A collection of vintage cast-iron swivel stools bolted to the floor serve most tables. The original owner, Krazy Jim Shafer, purchased the stools from a department store that had gone out of business in the 1950s for $1.75 apiece.

In 1953 Jim Shafer turned a corner grocery into a burger stand to sell cheap burgers to University of Michigan students. At his previous burger venture, shoehorned into an alley in downtown Ann Arbor, a friend at a neighboring business called Jim "crazy" for selling food for so cheap. The moniker stuck, as did the famous phrase that greets customers at Blimpy Burger: "Cheaper Than Food." Current owner Richard Manger told me, "Back then it was cheaper to buy a 20-cent burger than to eat at home."

Richard bought the restaurant in 1992 from Krazy Jim, who was already in retirement. Jim and Rich had a past together at that point—Rich had worked as a cook flipping burgers in the late 60s for Jim at Blimpy, had met his wife Chris there (also a student), and had designed the Blimpy logo that is still used today. It's a drawing of a seated, chubby bear smiling and hoisting a burger. "Jim wanted me to draw a cow. I told him 'I don't draw cows. I draw bears.'"

Richard's menu design is an elaborate piece of R. Crumb-inspired line art that is suitable for framing. It lists a dizzying assortment of comfort foods and toppings for the burgers. Rich told me, "When Jim opened he only had burgers, American cheese, pie, and coffee." Not so today. The selection of toppings and burger sizing is so vast it prompted a math student to deduce that there are more than 2,147,483,648 possible burger combinations.

The fresh chuck that is used for Blimpy

shaped, flat patty. The burgers are pressed and pressed until they can get no thinner, flipped, pressed some more, then tossed on a bun. You'd think these guys had pressed the life out of your burger, but relax; you are in good hands. The result is a glorious grease bomb—a pile of loose, griddled meat that is crunchy in parts and soft in others. The meat is so loose it's practically pebbly. Mohawked grill cook Brian told me, "These things are held together by hope."

Jim was considered "crazy" for selling food for cheap. The moniker stuck.

The choice of roll for your burger, toasted on the griddle, includes pumpernickel, onion, or kaiser, the latter offered with *or* without sesame seeds because, as Rich explained matter-of-factly, "Some people have diverticulitis." The onion roll is hands-down one of the best I have ever eaten, soft and tasty and able to soak up the copious amounts of grease a Blimpy burger produces. "Onion rolls most places suck," Rich told me bluntly. "These really are great rolls."

Following the rules for ordering is impor-

burgers is ground daily in the back. When you ask for a burger, you tell the grill cook how many you'd like (up to five, a "quint") and he'll grab that number of 1 ½-ounce-balls of beef. The balls are tossed onto the hot griddle and smashed together, creating a sloppy, mis-

tant. Start by grabbing a tray and getting in line. Everyone gets a tray because, as Rich pointed out, "It keeps the tables clean when we're busy." Then grab a drink and order your fried food of choice first. French fries and onion rings are offered, but skip the usual for excellent deep-fried vegetables like mushrooms and cauliflower. My vegetarian wife, Casey, was in heaven. Next, order your burger, but hold your cheese selection until the end of the process. Follow the rules and be rewarded with one of the best burgers in America.

A group of healthy-looking 60-somethings were enjoying their burgers the last time I visited and told me, "This is where we celebrate our birthdays. We've been coming here for over 50 years." When one of the grill guys, Skinny, heard that, he blurted out, "And they STILL don't know how to order their burgers."

MILLER'S BAR

23700 MICHIGAN AVENUE
DEARBORN, MI 48124
313-565-2577
WWW.MILLERSBAR.COM
MON-SAT 11 AM-12:30 AM
CLOSED SUNDAY

The first time I visited Miller's it was in the middle of a torrential springtime downpour. It was 11:15 am on a Wednesday, the bar was packed and everyone was eating hamburgers. Doesn't that pretty much say it all?

Miller's is on a commercial stretch, six lanes wide, in Dearborn, Michigan. Across the street from a large Ford dealership, the windowless bar is painted with a fresh coat of red paint and emblazoned with enormous white letters spelling out the name of this nearly 70-year-old institution. Despite the cool functionality of the exterior, the interior, with its original 1940s Brunswick bar of undulating high-gloss wood and booths made of supple deep-red leather, feels more like a long-lost private men's club than the bunker that the outside evokes. The immaculate well-preserved dining room is dark and cozy and, according to part-owner Mark Miller, has not needed renovation since 1964.

There is no menu at Miller's but the options are simple—burgers, fries, and onion rings are available, as are tuna, ham, and corned beef sandwiches and of course drinks from the bar. The clientele is mostly local devotees and regulars from the nearby world headquarters of the Ford Motor Company. They come for the burgers and have been since 1941, when Mark's uncle, George Miller, opened the bar. Today, thanks to topping many "Best-of" lists in America, Miller's Bar sells over 1,200 burgers a day. Every one of those burgers is cooked on a griddle next to the bar that is no more than three feet square.

"Our butcher starts grinding beef for us at 4 am everyday," Mark told me. Mark owns the bar with his brother Dennis, and the two are

second generation owners. The Miller's father Russell bought the bar from his brother George in 1947.

The sprightly grill cook Kim, who has been flipping burgers at Miller's for over 20 years, is responsible for griddling the hundreds of perfect, award-winning burgers during the lunch rush. I overheard her take an order for a few burgers "well-done." Well-done? "Oh gosh yes," she sighed, "People don't know how to order their burgers here." Mark told me he won't eat anything over a medium, and rightly so, because Miller's meat is some of the freshest I've ever tasted.

The Millers have been using the same butcher for over 40 years. The bar used to get a

400-pound delivery daily of fresh ground beef that would have to be hand pattied by the kitchen staff. "It got to be too much," Kim told me, so the butcher offered to start delivering preformed patties. Knowing that the Millers wouldn't accept just any patty, he employs a special patty maker that injects a blast of air back into the beef. "It makes the patty looser," Mark explained, "and it has an almost hand-pattied feel."

The seven-ounce burger is served on a steamed white bun and delivered to you on a square of wax paper. Lettuce and tomato are not offered. Swiss or Velveeta are available, as are the standard condiments like ketchup, mustard, pickle, and sliced onion. But this burger needs no embellishment—so forgo the condiments. The meat is so good you could eat it plain. I asked what it was that made the burger taste so great and Mark told me, "It's the meat. The meat is great. There are no seasonings and we have no secrets."

The secret may be in longevity. The staff is great and many have been with Miller's forever. The day-shift bartender Jeff has been pouring drinks for almost 30 years and a waitress named Linda has been delivering burgers at Miller's since Nixon was in office. The secret may also be in the Miller brothers commitment to the family business. Every Sunday, when the bar is closed, Mark and Dennis take apart the entire kitchen and grill area for a thorough cleansing. Mark told me, "We completely disassemble the griddle, dishwasher . . . everything." What did *you* do last Sunday?

★ ★ ★ ★ ★

REDAMAK'S

616 EAST BUFFALO STREET
NEW BUFFALO, MI 49117
269-469-4522
WWW.REDAMAKS.COM
MON-SAT NOON–10:30 PM
SUN NOON–10 PM
CLOSED IN WINTER

Redamak's is a burger destination. Vacationers come from miles around for a weekend at Lake Michigan and most visit Redamak's for nourishment. George and Gladys Redamak opened a tiny mom-and-pop burger restaurant in the late 1940s. In 1975 the Maroney family bought the restaurant from Gladys, with the stipulation that they keep it the same. It didn't really turn out that way, though—they actually made it better.

Redamak's is enormous. Years of expansion and updating to the structure have created a profoundly successful restaurant that can comfortably seat 400. Crowd control is aided by two sets of double doors at the front—one marked ENTER, the other EXIT. If you have kids, you won't be alone here—kids and families populate the place. There are two separate video arcades and a sizable kids, menu. If you need a drink, there's a bar right in the center of it all. And of course, if you need a burger, Redamak's makes one of the best in the country.

The menu is round, the size of a large pizza, and has more text on it than the front page of the *Chicago Tribune*. You won't believe the options you'll have. Everything from corn dogs to clam strips is offered, along with seven different types of French fries. There's even lake perch on Fridays. The endless selection of lakefront comfort food can't disguise the fact that the burgers are the star attraction here. The menu proudly proclaims the Redamak's burger is "The Burger That Made New Buffalo Famous."

Fresh Iowa beef chuck steaks are ground in the kitchen for the five and one-third-ounce burgers at Redamak's. Manager Matt told me, "They are grinding all of the time back there." They *have* to keep grinding because the kitchen cranks out over 2,500 fresh patties a day. "We broke our record last year," Charles Maroney pointed out. In 2006 Redamak's ground over 110,000 pounds of chuck steaks for burgers, which is amazing for a restaurant that's only open eight months of the year. What's even more baffling is the method by which this astounding number of burgers is cooked every day—*each one is cooked in a pan by itself.* This sounds impossible, but I saw it with my own eyes. There must have been ten stovetops lined up. On each burner, a single skillet. In each pan, a single burger. "We do it that way to keep the juices with the burger," Charles told me, "On a griddle, those juices dissipate." Charles also pointed out that, along with their use of Velveeta cheese, the Maroney family is commit-

ted to doing things the way the Redamaks did for so many successful years.

Tomato and lettuce are not offered with a Redamak's burger. "Redamak's started as a tavern and there was no place for lettuce and tomato in bar food," Charles told me. Again, a tradition the restaurant holds dear. A burger with everything comes with ketchup, mustard, pickles, a slice of raw onion, and melted Velveeta. Don't panic. The oldest and most venerable burger destination in America, Louis' Lunch of New Haven, also indulges in the yellow stuff. Besides, it tastes good.

Bring the family, bring your friends, bring everyone you know—Redamak's can handle the crowds with ease. You'll probably have to wait, so go to the video arcade or browse the merchandise at the front. It might be the only place in America where you can buy a souvenir yo-yo in the shape of a hamburger.

MATT'S BAR

3500 CEDAR AVE SOUTH
MINNEAPOLIS, MN 55407
612-722-7072
WWW.MATTSBAR.COM
MON–WED 11 AM–MIDNIGHT
THU–SAT 11AM–1 AM
SUN NOON–MIDNIGHT

"**W**e had a bad Sunday," waitress Devon told me on my first visit. Before I realized what she was talking about, I assumed that things were slow at this South Minneapolis bar. Devon pointed out that the bad Sunday was attributed to the large number of Jucy Lucys that had exploded on the griddle that day. If one explodes, the grill cook starts over. There's no way to mend a broken Lucy.

If you have no connection to or have never visited the Twin Cities then there's a good chance you have never met the beloved Jucy Lucy. The famed burger concoction can be found all over Minneapolis, but the epicenter of the Jucy Lucy legacy is a small, friendly,

stuck-in-a-time-warp bar on the south side of town. In 1954, then owner Matt cooked up the first Jucy Lucy for a customer sitting at the bar who asked for "something special." The result was two fresh quarter-pound patties crimped together with a folded slice of American cheese hiding inside. What happened next was pure science.

Over 50 years have passed and the burger recipe remains unchanged. The burger is griddled and closely monitored (much like a science project), delicately flipped, then pin-pricked to prevent it from exploding. As it nears doneness, it resembles a large clam wobbling on the griddle.

The delivery of the burger to your table always comes with a warning. Bartender of 14 years Margaret Lidstone said to me sternly, "You will burn your mouth off if you bite into it too soon. Let it sit." The phrase "Fear The Cheese" printed on the waitstaff's shirts was warning enough. I tried to wait, but became a victim instantly. The molten goo was HOT, really hot, and kept the burger moist all the way through. Everyone who ordered the Jucy Lucy got the same stern speech. "I know," a regular responded, "not my first time." A woman sitting at the next table had no problem saying to me, "You're doing it all wrong. Just nibble at it, take small bites while it cools down."

The Jucy Lucy comes on waxed paper—no plate, no utensils. Onions, fried or raw, are optional and pickles are standard. No tomato, no lettuce. Coke? Sure, no ice. Diet Coke? No lemon. Matt's is bare-bones dining at its very best.

The griddle is positioned behind the bar in full view. Grill cook Nancy told me, "We can sell up to 500 on a good day." Nancy and the owner's wife, and whoever is available, spend hours a day pinching and stuffing Jucy Lucys. "It's endless." said Margaret, and opened a low bar fridge to reveal hundreds of prebuilt Jucys ready for their turn on the grill that day.

The only menu is the one on the wall behind the bar and it has not changed in over five decades (with the exception of the prices, of course). It's on this menu that the "Jucy Lucy" is misspelled. "I think it was a mistake that just stuck," Margaret told me.

Matt Bristol worked at the bar, then named Mr. Nibb's, before purchasing the quiet corner tavern in 1954 and changing the name to his own. Scott Nelson bought the bar from Matt's daughter in 1998 and changed nothing. Even the crazy '50s wallpaper (which can be viewed on the tavern's website) remains. "It's quite tacky, actually," Scott explained, "but people don't want change." In a time when so many restaurants, and even bars, all look the same from city to city because of franchising, Scott believes that there is a place for Matt's. "Everything looks like a chain. We don't."

Matt's commitment to hamburgers starts with a concept that has its roots in the 1950s, and the simple menu is a testament to the fact that great burgers are immune to fads. Scott said it best when he pointed out, "Burgers and fries don't go out of style, and neither do we."

THE 5-8 CLUB

5800 CEDAR AVENUE SOUTH
MINNEAPOLIS, MN 55417
612-823-5858
WWW.5-8CLUB.COM
SUN–WED 11AM–10:30 PM
THU–SAT 11 AM–11:30 PM

"5-8" was the address for this former speakeasy in south Minneapolis on the corner of 58th and Cedar Avenue. In 1928 when it opened illegally, it was a small stucco house out in the country where the owners had constructed a secret underground garage to make smuggling booze easier.

Today the 5-8 is a crossroads restaurant that is no longer rural. The dirt road that ran beside the building is now a highway, and the end of the runway for the Twin Cities airport is only half a mile away. It is not uncommon to get a close-up view of the belly of a Northwest jumbo jet as you walk from your car to the restaurant.

The 5-8 is home to the "Juicy Lucy," the same cheese-stuffed burger concoction made famous by Matt's just up Cedar Avenue, though Matt's spells theirs "Jucy Lucy." Regulars and waitstaff were reluctant to talk about the origins of South Minneapolis' favorite burger. "Oh, I don't know," said one regular, "they both make pretty good Lucys." The only person willing to talk was the kitchen manager, coincidentally named Matt. He was still pretty vague saying, "It's always been a thing between here and Matt's on who invented it."

Guaranteed: "Free refills 'till you float." I don't think this applies to the beer, though.

Regardless, the 5-8 makes a great "upscale" Juicy Lucy, because there's a twist to the recipe—you can order one stuffed with classic American cheese, Swiss, pepper Jack, or blue cheese. Matt told me, "People love them—we sell tons." As a burger hits the grill, it is marked with a colored fuzzy-tipped sandwich toothpick to identify its corresponding molten cheese core. Yellow for Swiss, blue for blue cheese . . . you get the idea. Has Matt ever gotten them mixed up? "Never." That's pretty impressive for cranking out over 300 Juicy Lucys a day for the large sit-down lunch and dinner crowd. All of the Juicy Lucys are made from fresh-ground Angus chuck. Two large patties are pinched together and stuffed in-house daily. The buns seem too large to fit in your mouth but are superlight, locally made, and fresh.

It's recommended that you wait to eat your burger after it shows up in the basket at your table. The hot cheese interior will burn your mouth if you are impatient. I made the mistake of cutting mine in half to let it cool; I was left with a cheese-goo mess.

Don't do what I did and enter the 5-8 through the welcoming front door, complete with a lawn, low hedges, and a flag. True to its speakeasy heritage, the back door is the way to enter. And don't be put off by its clinical looking rear entrance—behind the door is a com-fortable dining room with a large outdoor patio.

The 5-8 may be known for its burgers but don't miss out on its long list of comfort food like jojo potatoes, pork tenderloin sandwiches, and the Midwest's own fried cheese curds. And if you order a drink with that, the 5-8 guarantees "free refills 'till you float." I don't think this applies to beer, though.

BILL'S HAMBURGERS

310 NORTH MAIN STREET
AMORY, MS 38821
662-256-2085

SUN–FRI 7:30 AM–5:30 PM
SAT 7 AM–5 PM
BAR OPEN TILL MIDNIGHT

The drive to Amory is quintessential back-country Deep South—miles of two-lane roads lined with cotton fields, cotton gins, and, when I visited, lots of loose cotton all over the road. Amory is a small town and Bill's is a small restaurant at a spot where Main Street bends. Locals affectionately refer to this spot as "Vinegar Bend."

Bill's has 23 stools and about two tables, so chances are you'll probably be sitting at the counter. Nothing fancy here—in keeping with tradition, burgers are still served at your spot at the counter on waxed paper.

Before it was Bill's it was Bob's. In 1929 Bob Hill borrowed $48 from a local baker named James Toney to open a hamburger restaurant. A stipulation of the deal was that Bob had to buy all of his hamburger buns from Toney's bakery.

One year after opening, Bob hired Bill Tubb to help slice and prep buns with the only two condiments available in the '20s at Bob's—mustard and onion. World War II meat rationing forced Bob's to close, but after the war Bob reopened and later sold the business to Bill in 1955. Naturally, Bill changed the name to his own, then turned around and sold it in 1957 to another Bill, who then rehired Bill to work there. After a string of Bill's relatives owned and operated the small burger stand, Bill's was sold to the current owners, Reid and Janice Wilkerson.

"I grew up eating here. It was such a big part of my childhood. When it came up for sale I had to buy it," Reid told me as he emerged from the back room of the restaurant. He grinds fresh beef there every day for the burgers as it has been done since 1929. Another tradition Reid and Janice adhere to—mustard and onion only—also dates back to the beginning. "Not much has changed here, except that the burgers got bigger," grill girl Amy told me. Toney's bakery closed in 1970, which led Bill's to start using standard four-inch buns. The new burger size was determined by the size of the buns.

The burgers start as quarter-pound balls of beef that are pressed onto a well-seasoned flat-top griddle. The burgers at Bill's are unbelievably tasty, beefy, and rich with grease flavor. The mustard, onion, beef, and bun combination is heaven. Cheese is unnecessary, though available, but tomato and lettuce are nowhere to be found. If you really need ketchup or mayo, Amy hides packets behind the counter. "They're really only for takeout orders."

Ever had a burger for breakfast? Bill's opens at 7:30 most mornings and does not serve eggs or bacon. "We serve burgers all day. People do come in here first thing and order burgers, especially the third shift at the local factories," Amy told me as I polished off my double.

On the front of the restaurant is a large painted portrait of the beloved former employee Junior Manasco, a gently disabled fixture at Bill's for over 20 years starting in 1977. On a wall opposite the counter is a framed resolution from the State of Mississippi presented to Junior "for his service to his community." Reid recalled, "He knew and greeted everyone that came in the door."

As I was leaving an old-timer at the counter told me, "The first time I came here the burgers were 25 cents." When I pressed for just how long ago that was he said, "A long time ago."

PHILLIPS GROCERY

541 EAST VAN DORN AVE.
HOLLY SPRINGS, MS 38634
662-252-4671
MON–THU 10 AM–4 PM
FRI–SAT 10 AM–8 PM
CLOSED SUNDAY

Downtown Holly Springs, Mississippi, looks like it may have looked 70 years ago. American flags and freshly painted turn-of-the-century storefronts line the streets. Phillip's Grocery is not here though. Phillip's is down the road by the train tracks across from a semi-restored 150-year-old ornate train depot. There's a '60s era Ford Galaxie with four flat tires out front, and the area looks a lot like William Eggleston's photography of the South—gritty and real. I got lost trying to find this burger destination, and you will too.

Phillips serves one of the best burgers in America. Not just because I said so; their burg-

ers have been the subject of many journalistic accolades, including being awarded, "Best Burger In America" twice by *USA Today*.

The restaurant was first established as Phillips Grocery in 1948 when the Phillips family bought an existing grocery that sold hamburgers. Current owner Larry Davis told me, "The burger's been made here since the '30s." Mrs. Phillips had planned to do away with the burger when they bought the store, but changed her tune when she saw how many they were selling. "She put her kids through college with burger money."

Their success is no accident. The secret lies in the mixture of ground beef and other "secret" ingredients. Adding breading to ground beef was popular in the South during the Depression, and I suspect the burger at Phillips may be a vestige of this lost art. I arrived at Phillips before it opened and interrupted Larry's morning ritual of making the ground beef mixture for the day's burgers. He actually disappeared behind a closed door and reappeared a few minutes later with rubber gloves and large stainless mixing bowls filled with ground beef. "It's the same recipe since the '30s," Larry said of the secret recipe he purchased with the store in 1989. "I do this every day, sometimes 40 to 50 pounds on Saturdays."

A burger at Phillips can be ordered as a single one-third pound patty, a double with two quarter-pound patties, or a deluxe half-pound patty. That sounds confusing, but not to the kitchen staff who electronically weigh and portion each ball of ground beef. The balls are pressed on a well-seasoned flattop griddle and served on white buns with only mustard, pickle, and onion. Mayo, ketchup, cheese, and bacon are offered (but unnecessary). The burger is so tasty as is you could eat it with only a bun and emerge contented.

Phillips no longer sells groceries. The business shifted in the '50s when supermarkets killed the corner store. The décor is pure country store kitsch today—Coke advertising from every decade is represented as well as old grocer's scales, saws, and a vintage John Deere bicycle dangling from the ceiling.

You can sit at one of the random tables offered or find an old school desk to enjoy your burger and one of Larry's homemade fried pies. Look out the window of this 120-year-old building toward the train crossing and savor the sounds of locomotive whistles and the clanking of the active Mississippi Central Railroad rumbling by.

TOWN TOPIC

2021 BROADWAY STREET
KANSAS CITY, MO 64108
816-842-2610
OPEN DAILY, 24/7

Most people might drive by Town Topic and see a cute old hamburger stand, an icon of the past, or a relic in a rundown neighborhood. Not me. The people who know better see a vibrant keeper of the flame, a lesson to learn from, and a restaurant that knows its place in history. I couldn't drive by anyhow. Every time I try, I need to stop for a burger.

There are three Town Topics left in Kansas City where there once were seven. Today, only the Broadway location, also known as #3, is open 24 hours. At one point all of the Town Topics were open 24/7, as were many other ten-stool mid century hamburger joints across America.

When I approached the Town Topic for an interview for this book I had already been there a few times. The night I chose to visit I hit the jackpot—Bonnie Gooch was at the grill. Bonnie should be defined as a hard-boiled sweetheart. She's just what you'd want from a short-order lifer—a woman who takes no crap but takes care of the regulars. "See that guy down there?" she said to me, pointing down the counter to an older man. "He's been like a daddy to me. I've known him since the day I started so I try to take care of him." With that she slid an unordered slice of lettuce onto his burger and sent it off.

Bonnie started working at the little burger counter in 1965 when she was 13. For the next 23 years she worked the night shift alongside her husband Richard. When he passed away, she switched to the early evening shift. To date she has put in over 30 years at the Town Topic. Needless to say, she knows how to make a great hamburger.

The burger at Town Topic is a classic thin patty. Small one-eighth-pound wads of fresh ground 80/20 beef are delivered to the restaurant daily. Bonnie presses the meat thin on the hot, well-seasoned griddle and drops a small handful of shredded onions on the patty. Not unlike the fried onion burgers of El Reno,

Oklahoma, these onions are then pressed into the patty as it sizzles on the grill. The result is a tasty combination of griddled beef and caramelized onions.

"Ninety-nine percent order their burgers with onions," Bonnie told me as she built my double cheeseburger, the most popular burger on the menu. It comes with pickles on a white squishy bun and resembles a burger *Popeye's* Wimpy might have eaten—a classic American burger. Bonnie imparts to each burger a sort of nonchalant perfection that is reserved for those who have made short order burgers for decades.

Fortunately, those of us who understand the significance of a counter like Town Topic need not worry about its future. "The city tried to turn this place into a parking lot," Bonnie's counter partner Keisha told me, but a grandfather clause spared the restaurant based on its age. "Some people have been coming in here since they were kids," Bonnie reflected during a lull at the grill. "They just love the place."

WINSTEAD'S

101 EMANUEL CLEAVER II BOULEVARD
KANSAS CITY, MO 64112
816-753-2244
WWW.WINSTEADSKC.COM
MON–SAT 11 AM–8:30 PM
CLOSED SUNDAY

In the hearts of many Kansas City natives Winstead's is the only place in the world that serves great hamburgers. Even Kansas City's own Calvin Trillin, food writer and journalist, once said jokingly about Winstead's, "Anyone who doesn't think his hometown has the best hamburger place in the world is a sissy." More than three decades have passed since Trillin made that statement and almost nothing has changed—Winstead's still serves one of the best burgers in America.

Gone are the carhops, replaced by a drive-thru in 1989. On my first visit to the vintage time-warp diner I was led to longtime employee Judy Eddingfield. Judy started working at Winstead's when she was only 16 years old, over 40 years ago. "When I was just a kid my father would take me here for a strawberry shake and a single burger," she told me. Over the decades her mother, brothers, sisters, and aunts would all work at Winstead's in some capacity.

I asked Judy how she was on skates as a

carhop and she quickly pointed out, "No, no. There were no skates back then. Winstead's opened in 1940, which predates skates." True, carhops on skates were a fad and gimmick for some drive-ins of the 1950s. Winstead's maintained carhops for 50 years until the popular drive-thru was installed.

Today there are ten Winstead's restaurants in the Kansas City area but the mini-chain was actually started in Springfield, Illinois by sisters Katherine and Nellie Winstead. Their first location in Kansas City, located adjacent to the Midwest shopping mecca Country Club Plaza, remains the flagship restaurant in the chain.

The physical structure of Winstead's is a stunning, well-preserved example of midcentury restaurant architecture. The entire building is sheathed in pastel pink, and yellow, glazed enamel brick. The dining room is large and seats 280 comfortably. The wide, clean, open space is a sea of well-laid-out booths sitting beneath enormous hot pink neon-rimmed ceiling light fixtures. On one of my visits, an entire elementary school (close to 75 kids) had comfortably taken over the restaurant for an early lunch and there was still plenty of room for regulars.

The menu at Winstead's is split—one half lists food items, the other shakes, malts, and drinks, reminding one and all that ice cream is just as important as burgers to drive-in clientele. Winstead's has built its reputation on the "Steakburger," which served with "everything" includes a toasted white bun, a fresh-ground two-ounce patty, pickles, a very large slice of onion, and a "secret sauce" that is really just a mixture of mustard and ketchup. Make it a double and add cheese and you have a meal.

Bobby Chumley spends his entire morning at a patty maker in the restaurant's basement making hundreds of the day's burger patties. I met him as he emerged at noon one day to be greeted with a high five from the manager. The burgers are smashed thin and cooked on a flat-top griddle. The result is a moist, loose burger with a salty, crunchy exterior. Order a limeade and fries with your Steakburger to round out the perfect diner eating experience.

Winstead's today does a brisk business and employs over eighty people at the Country Club Plaza location. Judy told me as I took a sip from my ice-cold Mr. Pibb, "There are still a handful of us that have been working here for over 30 years." Now that's commitment to making and serving great burgers.

THE PEANUT BUTTER "GUBERBURGER"

In 2007 America almost lost one of its greatest assets—the Wheel Inn Drive Inn of Sedalia, MO. Highway expansion forced the decades-old small town burger counter to close its doors, and America bid farewell to one of the strangest burger creations ever—the peanut butter slathered 'guberburger'. But at the last moment a woman named Judy Clark, an employee since she was 13, saved the American icon by moving the business around the corner to a defunct video store. Thanks to Judy this burger lives on. It can also be re-created in your kitchen. The concept is surprisingly simple. Fresh ground balls of meat pressed thin, griddled, then dressed with melted peanut butter. To the uninitiated, the concept sounds bizarre. But to those in the know, the combination of ingredients is elementary.

MAKES 4 QUARTER-POUND BURGERS
(minus the peanut butter, this recipe is the "Motz Burger" (see page 176)
1 cup smooth peanut butter
1 pound fresh ground 80 percent lean chuck
Salt
4 white squishy buns
Butter

In a small saucepan, heat peanut butter over a very low flame. Divide the meat into quarters and form into loose balls. Place a heavy cast-iron skillet over medium heat to warm for one minute. Turn heat to high, wait a minute, then place balls of beef into pan. Sprinkle some salt on the meat and with a strong spatula press ONCE into the shape of a patty Cover the pan. Once the pink in the meat is almost gone from the surface (about two minutes), flip the burgers and cook for another two minutes. Remove from heat and place on toasted white buns (to best toast buns, butter and place in pan over medium heat). Spoon some hot peanut butter onto the patty and enjoy.

I prefer my Guberburger with peanut butter alone, but the Wheel Inn makes a practice of including lettuce, tomato, and mayonnaise. Give it a shot if you've got the stomach.

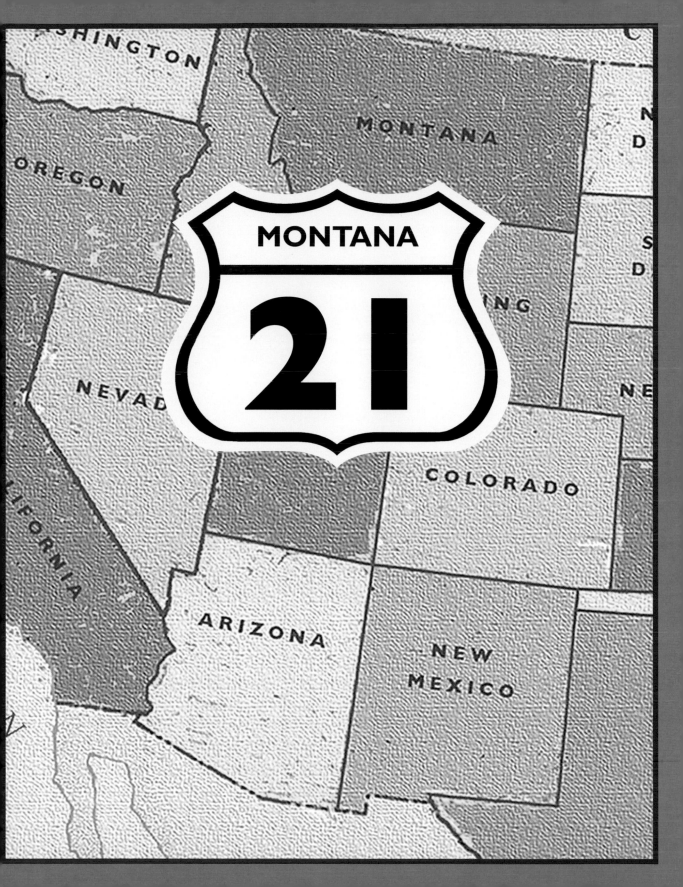

MATT'S PLACE
DRIVE-IN

2339 PLACER ST.
BUTTE, MT 59701
406-782-8049
TUE–SAT
11:30AM–6:50PM

Matt's Place is a drive-in on the edge of the boom-bust Old West mining town of Butte, Montana. As you approach the hillside town on I-90, you'll notice first the abandoned copper mining equipment and the brick buildings of a somewhat underpopulated downtown. The streets of Butte are lined with vintage neon signage that reflects its colorful past—Irish pubs and Chinese restaurants among many others that existed to entertain and feed the large number of immigrant mine workers.

Matt's Place opened in 1930 during the peak of copper mining in Butte. Through it all, Matt's has survived, so much so that it can proudly boast that it has a spot on the National Register of Historic Places. Recognized as historically important for its contribution to early American road culture, Matt's also serves amazing, fresh-beef burgers and milk shakes made from homemade ice cream. I visited Matt's for all of these reasons, but mostly to sample their fabled "Nutburger."

Of the thousands of burgers I have eaten across America, few piqued my interest like the Nutburger. Maybe it was the remote, beautiful, Western locale, or the fact that Matt's has been in existence for over 70 years, but it was the description of the Nutburger that had me planning a trip almost immediately.

In 1930, after a visit to Southern California, Matt Korn returned home and opened a small drive-up burger stand only a few feet from a busy railroad right-of-way. After a few years of hanging trays on car doors, Matt built a structure 25 feet away that would serve as a drive-in, a counter with 16 stools, and living quarters upstairs for him and his new wife Betty. That structure still stands today, a vestige of car culture stuck in time that was placed on the National Register in 2002.

Today, nonagenarian Mabel Laurence, only the second owner in the burger counter's long history, owns Matt's. Mabel started at Matt's in 1936 as a carhop, and in 1943 she and her husband bought the restaurant. Many people from "Mae's" family have worked at the vintage burger counter. For the last 25 years Matt's has been run by Laurence family members Brad Cockhill and Paula Parini. Brad and Paula are intensely proud of their family's heritage and committed

to quality burgers.

Matt's is split in two; one half is a horse-shoe counter, the other an efficient short-order kitchen. Paula works the counter while Brad flips patties at the freestanding griddle in the kitchen. "This is the original cast iron griddle from the 1930s," Brad told me. "There's nothing like cast iron." He's right. Very few burger restaurants in America cook on vintage cast-iron because they are impossible to find.

Brad and Paula use an ice cream scoop to make balls out of the fresh, lean ground round. When I asked Brad about the size of the burgers, he shrugged and showed me the scoop. "They're this big. We should probably have better portion control, but we don't." Brad believes the burgers are around a quarter pound each.

The most popular burger at Matt's is the double cheeseburger deluxe, which comes with mustard, pickle, onion, lettuce, and tomato. But do yourself a favor and indulge in a Nutburger.

"We don't really sell many Nutburgers anymore," Paula told me. " Maybe six a day?" Just then the phone rang and in came an order for two Nutburgers.

Paula spoons chopped salted peanuts from the sundae bar into a coffee mug and adds Miracle Whip. It's that simple. The texture of the nuts and the creamy sweetness of the Miracle Whip synthesize perfectly with the salty, greasy meatiness of the burger. Standard condiments are available to dress up the Nutburger, but why mess with the simplicity? I understand if you are a little squeamish at the concept, but after your first bite you'll be a convert.

The interior of Matt's is worth the price of admission alone. Grab a seat at the small horse-shoe counter and take in the décor. You'll be hard pressed to find a single fixture not dating back to the 1950s. Everything, from the knotty pine walls to the Coke dispenser, is original. Even the cash register dates back to simpler times. Paula told me, "The register only goes up to $5, so you have to ring up big orders $5 at a time."

A carhop at Matt's will still take your order from your car if you drive up and toot your horn. "We'll still go out and hang a tray on a window," Brad told me as he dumped out a basket of fresh-cut fries. Imagine that. A functioning drive-in where you can pull up and order a fresh-beef Nutburger with a side of nostalgia. Can it get any better than that?

The Nutburger

THE MISSOULA CLUB

139 WEST MAIN STREET
MISSOULA, MT 59802
406-728-3740
OPEN DAILY 8 AM–2 AM

The Missoula Club is not the only bar in town. In fact, there are more great bars and vintage neon signage in this western Montana town than I've ever seen in such close proximity to one another. Having 10,000 students at nearby University of Montana probably helps, but the Missoula Club is a local institution that has been serving beer and burgers to students and regulars, some believe, since 1903.

If you were expecting a cozy, dark pub you'll be shocked by the Missoula Club's first impression. During the day, the "Mo Club" (as it's affectionately known) looks like any well-worn watering hole, but at night the daylight seems to linger. Thanks to super-bright bluish overhead fluorescent lighting, the place is lit up like an operating room in the midst of triple bypass surgery. There's no hiding at the Mo Club, and the lighting allows one to observe every detail of the bar. The lighting also seems to make patrons overly sociable, so expect to be involved in a random conversation with a stranger almost immediately. The first time I visited the famous burger and beer destination, I walked in with my friend Greg Ennis and we were greeted by a group of rugby players and a boisterous "Hello, LADIES!" It's a rowdy, drinker's bar that serves great burgers. You have been warned.

The burger at the Mo Club is legendary. "The hamburger is the best thing on the menu!" employee Jim Kelly told me. Of course the joke is that the hamburger is the only thing on the menu, aside from chips and milkshakes.

Tell the bartender what kind of burger you want. The choices are single, double, or the absurd triple known as the "Griz" (named after the University of Montana's sports teams, the Grizzlies). American, Swiss, "white," horseradish, and hot pepper cheeses are available and the burger is served with a slice of raw onion and a pickle. The preferred burger at the Mo Club is the double with hot pepper cheese, a tasty pepper jack that doesn't really melt, but softens on the burger. Add some of the Mo Club's signature hot mustard and you'll be in burger heaven. As my friend Greg, a Montana native, squirted copious amounts of the fiery mustard onto his double cheeseburger, grillman Tyler warned, "Whoa, have you had this mustard before?" Greg just laughed and said, "Oh yeah, the hotter the better!"

Soft, white buns are toasted on the tiny electric bar griddle alongside the burgers. I asked Tyler if the buns were buttered and he told me, "No, but the burger grease might work its way over there."

The burgers at the Mo Club are hand patted from unmeasured scoops of ground beef. The beef comes in fresh daily from the same butcher they have been using forever. One time

while I was at the Mo Club, a man rushed in and dropped two enormous white paper-wrapped wads of fresh meat on the bar right next to me. They had run low and needed to augment the meat supply before the night crowd showed up hungry.

"Our burgers are over a third of a pound each," owner Mark Laslovich said of the large, juicy patties. Mark also revealed that the amazing tasting burger has chopped onions mixed into the raw meat before they are pattied. Mark has owned the century-old bar since 2000, but has worked there at some capacity for over 40 years. One of the recent changes Mark made at the Mo Club was installing a larger griddle. Well, not too much larger. "This one's a burger wider than the old one," Mark said of the tiny two-foot-wide griddle.

Expect to find all types enjoying burgers and beer at the Mo Club. "We get lawyers, doctors, bums, whatever," Mark pointed out. There is an old-school sports bar feel to the place, but not the kind that hangs gaudy memorabilia on every usable inch of wall space. The Mo Club's walls are blanketed with decades of UM team photos up to the high ceiling, as well as signed sports portraits of Missoula natives who went on to professional fame elsewhere in America.

As bars go, the Mo Club is a clean one. "It wasn't always this clean," Mark told me. "When I took over, this place was a mess." I asked Mark why the lighting was more conducive to a well-lit truck stop than a cozy Irish pub and he explained, "People come in here and look for themselves in these team photos." He and the other bartenders also believe it keeps people honest and the fights to a minimum. Mark told me that a group of women who frequent the bar once asked him to install a dimmer because they were getting older. His advice: "Have another beer."

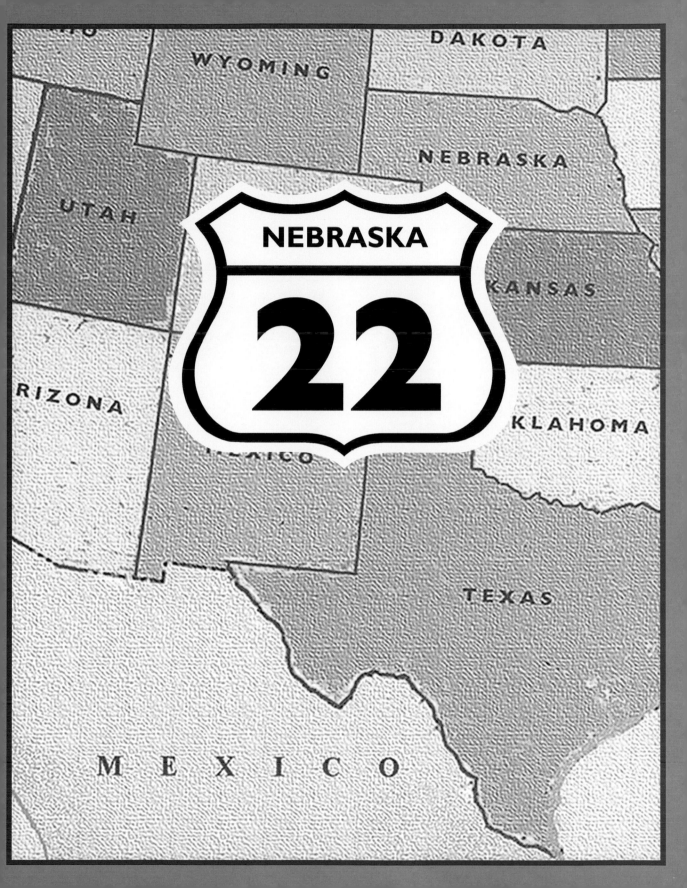

STELLA'S HAMBURGERS

106 GALVIN ROAD SOUTH
BELLEVUE, NE 68005
402-291-6088
TUE–SAT 11 AM–8 PM
SUN 11–4ISH
CLOSED MONDAY

There's no fancy sign out front letting you know you've arrived at Stella's, no pictures of burgers in the window, and no bright colors. Just look for the small, plain-look-ing house on a hill surrounded by a hard dirt parking lot. Smallish vinyl lettering on the front window unevenly spells out the name of the restaurant. And if you arrive at lunchtime, that dirt parking lot will be full of cars.

Stella's is not a fancy place. If you are looking for tablecloths and silverware—go elsewhere. If you are in search of a burger fix and don't mind eating off a napkin, you've come to the right place. The wood-paneled walls are covered with crayon art by local kids and you dine on aged orange Formica tabletops. Look for the framed drawing of a smiling Stella with the inscription "OUR FOUNDER." Expect your clothing to maintain a bouquet of grease long after you leave Stella's.

Tiny Stella Francois Sullivan Tobler opened the sunroom at the front of her home to burger lovers in 1936. Within a few years, her home had morphed into a restaurant with a gas station and a general store. She purchased the bar next door and in 1949 purchased a plot of land a mile away and moved both the house and bar. The bar became the restaurant, and the house and sunroom went back to being a home, and since then nothing has changed.

If you don't mind eating off a napkin, you've come to the right place.

"I added bacon to the menu, that's it," Lisa Metz told me. Lisa is Stella's granddaughter and a third-generation family member working at this burger haven south of Omaha. When she added bacon, she was even afraid to adjust the vintage plastic, light-up menu board, so she just taped the addition to the bottom. "I guarantee that if I change anything she'll come down and haunt me!" The only major alteration to the restaurant occurred after a grease fire destroyed the kitchen in 1976. Lisa told me, "Louise the cook ran out the back door with the cash register while Stella tried to put out the fire."

Local Nebraska beef for the burgers comes from a purveyor that Stella's has been using for years. "We age our ground beef, out of the cooler, for a week," Lisa told me. Both 81 percent and 75 percent lean ground beef are blended at the restaurant to make the perfect fat-to-lean ratio. 5.2-ounce hand-formed balls are pressed and cooked on a cast-iron griddle that has been in use since the 1950s. Every evening after closing time, the griddle is salted to maintain its decades-old seasoning.

The burger at Stella's is an explosion of grease and flavor. Lisa put it best when she told me, "You don't come to Stella's because you are watching what you are eating." It's served on an impossibly soft white pillow of a bun with lettuce, tomato, pickles, and a choice of either grilled or raw onion. Both top and bottom halves of the bun receive a generous layer of mayonnaise, and the burger is delivered no-nonsense on a paper napkin. Stella believed that good food didn't need to be fancy.

Stella's son Al took over the restaurant in 1974 and Stella continued to come in daily. "She worked up to three days prior to her death," Lisa told me. Al still comes into the restaurant just like Stella did in her retirement. Lisa's four children all help out in the restaurant just as she did as a child. Kelly, Lisa's oldest daughter, started peeling potatoes when she was six and as a teenager today preps the buns for the burgers. It seems as though the future of Stella's is secure.

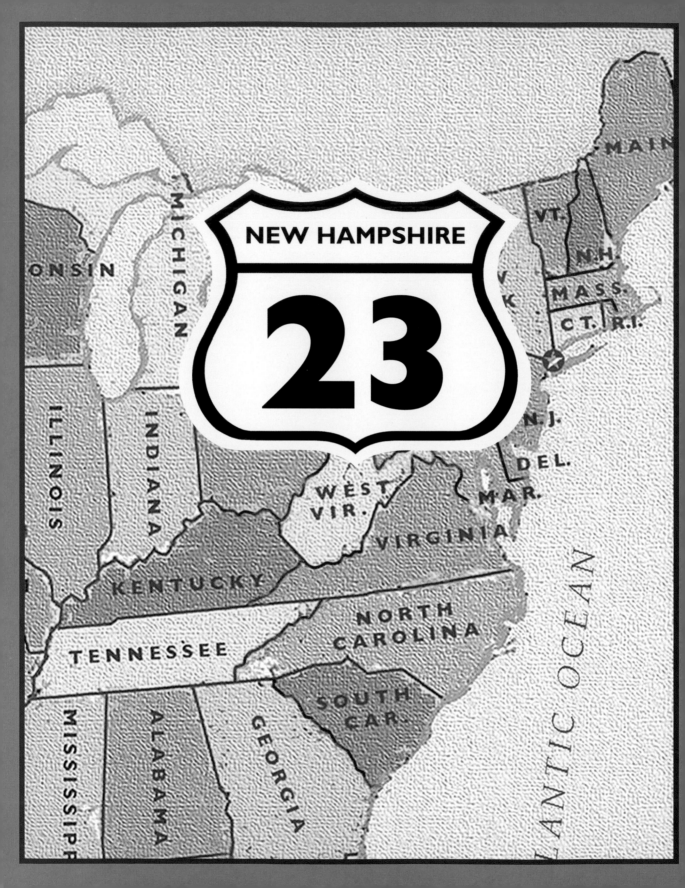

GILLEY'S PM LUNCH

175 FLEET STREET
PORTSMOUTH, NH 03801
603-431-6343
WWW.GILLEYSPMLUNCH.COM
TUE–SUN 11:30 AM–2:30 AM
MONDAY 11:30 AM–6 PM

"**Y**ou can always tell that it's someone's first time here when they pull the door like that," short-order chef Bambi told me. I had trouble getting in the front door of this six-decade-old diner because the door is not normal. It slides open like a pocket door, revealing one of the most beautiful hidden gems in all of New England.

Gilley's PM Lunch is an old Worcester diner. In the first half of the twentieth century the Worcester Lunch Car Company of Worcester, MA, was the premier supplier of mobile lunch carts and prefabricated diners. Their distinct design set the precedent for all diners that followed in America.

Gilley's is now permanently situated on a lot donated by the City of Portsmouth, but prior to 1973 the cart was towed out to the center of town and served food to late-night work-

153

Gilley's is one of the last Worcester diners in America

ers and other hungry people until the wee hours of the morning. There was a time in America, especially in New England, when carts like this were everywhere at night. Many of them were Worcester diners and very few exist today. Gilley's is one of the last.

Though slightly modified, Gilley's retains its barrel-shaped roof and enamel steel paneled interior, and its kitchen still occupies one narrow end of the car. It's a true step back in time with its tiny griddle and eight stools lining the wood-framed windows. New owner (as of 1993) Stephen Kennedy told me, "I had to take two stools out because it gets pretty crowded in here from 11 p.m. to 2 a.m." He says sometimes over 40 people are crammed into the tiny diner waiting for their hamburgers and hot dogs. During the late shift Gilley's can move over 500 burgers.

"Isn't that beautiful?" a customer said as he tilted his plate showing off his double cheeseburger. Both hamburgers and hot dogs are served at Gilley's; the hot dogs preceded the burgers by more than sixty years. Starting in 1912, the first owners had a horse-drawn cart with wooden wheels that sold mostly hot dogs. Hamburgers were introduced in the 1970's, and share equal popularity today.

The burger to order at Gilley's is a bacon double cheeseburger. Gilley's uses only fresh-ground pattied chuck loin that is 85 to 88 percent lean. The patties are small, thin, and just under 3 ounces. Stephen pointed out that it was done that way traditionally for speed, adding, "A smaller burger cooks faster." The white squishy bun is toasted and no lettuce or tomato is offered. The tiny fridge next to the minuscule two-foot-square griddle is really only big enough for the day's hot dogs, hamburgers, and cheese.

In 1996 Stephen attached a construction trailer to the original lunch car to expand the kitchen. This allowed him to add a deep fryer and more refrigeration. Adding a barrel roof to one end of the trailer mimicked the original structure and preserved the integrity of the restaurant. The last truck to pull the mobile diner is still attached to one end of Gilley's, as are the diner's wheels, now covered by wood paneling.

"Portsmouth is the kind of place where things don't change much," cook Bambi mused as I ate my burger. That's a good thing, especially when it involves a historically significant slice of Americana like Gilley's. Thanks to people like Stephen Kennedy this tiny lunch cart may be around forever.

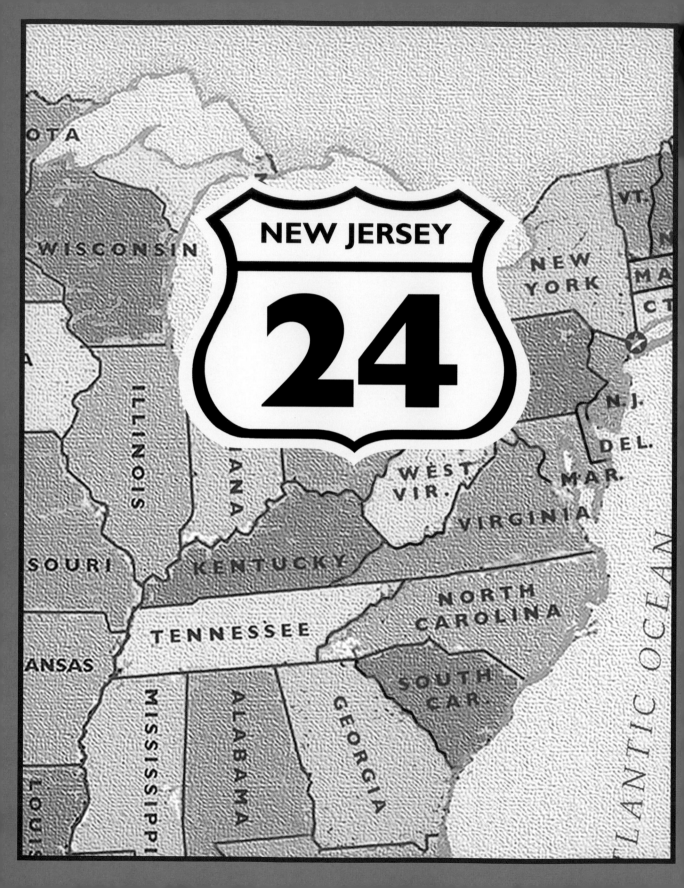

ROSSI'S BAR & GRILL

501 MORRIS AVE.
TRENTON, NJ 08611
609-394-9089
WWW.ROSSIBURGER.COM
MON–SAT 11 AM–2:30 PM, 5 PM–10 PM
CLOSED SUNDAY

" **N**ow we'll see if he knows how to eat a Rossiburger!" Sharon Jemison, part owner and Rossi family member, was heckling me and warned, "If you cut it in half, you're a wuss." As I stared at the enormous, inch-thick burger, I did the smart thing—I put the knife down.

Most great burger joints have their share of multi generational family pride, but few are as proud as Rossi's. Throw in an Italian-American pedigree and you have a recipe for a burger born of unrelenting pride.

In the early 1930s, Michael Alfred Rossi bought a corner soda fountain in the Italian neighborhood of Chambersburg in Trenton, NJ, and lived upstairs. When prohibition was repealed in 1933, Rossi promptly turned the fountain into a bar. "Back then," Sharon told me, "they just had a meatball sandwich [on the menu]." Rossi eventually expanded the menu to include other Italian fare and made a dining room out of the family's living space. But it was Michael's son, Alfred Michael Rossi, who would bring their now-famous burger to the menu in the early 1960s.

Al Rossi had a promising career in professional baseball and played for the Washington Senators farm team for 11 years. Just as he was offered a spot on the Philadelphia Athletics roster, his brother shipped off to fight in World War II. Al's dad told him to leave baseball, come home, and help run the restaurant. In this family, that's just what you did.

Maybe if Al Rossi had continued on his path to be a major league ballplayer there would be no Rossiburger, a thought most would probably not like to entertain.

There's only one burger to order at Rossi's and it is very large and only comes in one size. "That's the million-dollar question, 'Can we get a smaller burger?'" Sharon told me, "Nope."

Don't be put off by the enormous mound of meat in front of you though. Despite its size, the burger at Rossi's is moist and loosely packed, its center almost pebbly. It's actually a breeze to eat, especially if you are hungry.

Rossi's gets a delivery of fresh-ground 87/13 chuck daily and can go through 250 pounds over the weekend. The burgers are unmeasured but are around a half pound. They are loosely hand pattied by Rossi family member and head chef Ted and cooked by indirect heat in a steak broiler. Nothing is added, no salt, no pepper, and it's served on a freshly baked kaiser roll with nothing but a slice of raw onion.

Just about everyone involved at Rossi's is family. Sharon explained, "When we run out of family, we pull in other people." Today, Rossi's is run by Al's children Sharon and Michael. They have both been at Rossi's for over 35 years. The Chambersburg neighborhood is also like one big family. At one point during my interview with her in front of the restaurant, Sharon stopped a passing car for some fact-checking on the history of Rossi's.

Thanks to his involvement with professional baseball, Al Rossi had an impressive roster of buddies. Joe DiMaggio was a frequent visitor, as were Mickey Mantle and Ted Williams. Joe D didn't go to Rossi's for the burger though he went to see his good friend Al and have a bowl of his lentil soup. The restaurant is filled with authentic baseball memorabilia and the bar evokes a time when baseball greats might have mingled freely with their fans. For years, a pair of Mickey Mantle's cleats that were given to Al hung in a corner of the dining room.

Al worked at Rossi's right up until the day before he died in 2007. "He loved it," Sharon recalled of her father, "People came here just to talk to him." Al was involved with the business his entire life and, according to Sharon, "He'd see a pasta dish go out that wasn't right and he'd send it back."

★ ★ ★ ★ ★

WHITE MANNA HAMBURGERS

358 RIVER ROAD
HACKENSACK, NJ 07601
201-342-0914
MON–SAT 8:30AM–9 PM
SUNDAY 10 AM–6 PM

White Manna is, beyond a doubt, one of the most historically important burger joints in America. As the burger business began widespread franchising in the 1960s, most of the tiny burger counters across America were wiped out. Amazingly, White Manna survives and thrives, even with a McDonalds directly across the street.

There was a time in America when the burgers you ate were small and came from a tiny stainless steel or white porcelain paneled diner. Thanks to the success of White Castle in America, most burger counters used the word *white* in their names to convey cleanliness. In the case of this diner, the biblical word "manna" is used, as in *bread from heaven*.

White Manna is a vintage Paramount diner that still proudly serves the early-century American classic "slider" burger. The diner is the descendant of the 1939 Worlds Fair "Diner of the Future" that was built to represent the future of fast food. The original White Manna was purchased by Louis Bridges and brought to Jersey City, where it remains today. Louis built four other White Mannas around Northern New Jersey, but only the Hackensack and Jersey City locations survive. Inside and out, the tiny diner remains true to its original design. The structure is sheathed in stainless steel, has vertical white porcelain panels beneath the windows, and includes Paramount Diner Company's signature use of glass block throughout.

Strip down to the least amount of clothing—otherwise, your clothes will be infused with the unmistakable fragrance of grease and onions.

The interior cannot be more than 30-square feet. Behind a small horseshoe counter surrounded by stools, a short-order cook takes one order after the next, never putting pen to paper. You sit patiently, taking in the thick oniony aroma, until the cook makes eye contact with you. When you place your order, the cook reaches into a pan below the counter, grabs golf ball–sized balls of meat, presses them onto the tiny griddle, and places a wad of thinly sliced onion on top. If you ask for a double, two of the

The White Manna in a rare moment—empty

small balls of beef get pressed together. The cook uses a right-to-left system on the griddle to keep track and miraculously keeps all of the orders straight. Similar to the original White Castle system, buns are placed atop the cooking burgers to soften and soak up the onion essence.

The sliders are served on soft potato rolls on a paper plate with a pile of pickle chips. If you order cheese, expect not a picture-perfect burger, but a glorious pile of tangled beef, onions, and cheese that is barely contained by its bun. The burgers at White Manna may not look pretty, but they sure are delicious. You'll need more than a few sliders to fill you up. Order doubles to accomplish a better beef-to-bun ratio. Esteemed food writer and blogger Jason Perlow prefers to make a meal out of four doubles.

Ronny and Ofer Cohen bought White Manna in 1986 as a business venture, but were also seduced by its charm. "You just fall in love with this place," Ronny told me. They have changed very little about the White Manna, but admitted an attempt to add potato salad and coleslaw to the menu early on in their ownership. "People walk into White Manna to buy burgers." Ronny feels the crush of commercial fast food all around him in Hackensack, NJ. "The only way I can survive is to do things the old-fashioned way."

My good friend and expert burger taster, Ports Bishop, always reminds me, before we walk in, to strip down to the least amount of clothing. Not because it's hot in there, but because after you leave, your clothes will be infused with the unmistakable fragrance of grease and onions. There'll be no hiding the fact that you just dined at the famous White Manna.

BOBCAT BITE

420 OLD LAS VEGAS HIGHWAY
SANTA FE, NM 87505
505-983-5319
WWW.BOBCATBITE.COM
TUE–SAT 11 AM–7:50 PM
CLOSED SUNDAY AND MONDAY

A visit to the Bobcat Bite for a green chile cheeseburger results in what I like to call the "Whole Burger Experience." The restaurant, the people who work there, the relaxed environment, and a stellar burger all coalesce into a perfect hamburger moment.

I was tipped off to the Bobcat by my father-in-law, Don Benjamin, a man whose only red meat intake is at this burger spot. He had a perfect burger moment there, sitting on the porch watching the sunset. It was a perfect moment that turned into a decision to move to Santa Fe.

The Bobcat Bite is way out of town, southeast on the long, lonely Old Las Vegas Highway. The low adobe structure sits on a rocky washboard incline at the foot of what once was a

John and Bonnie Eckre of the Bobcat Bite

large quarterhorse ranch. The interior is cozy New Mexican with a low viga ceiling and a large picture window that looks out toward the old ranch and a hummingbird feeder. Seating is limited—there are only eight stools at the counter, five tables, and just recently added, three tables on the front porch (weather permitting). The restaurant got its name from the bobcats that used to come down from the surrounding mountains to eat scraps that had been tossed out the back door. Co-owner Bonnie Eckre told me, "People used to come down and watch the bobcats eat."

In 1953, Rene Clayton, owner of the Bobcat Ranch, turned a gun shop into a restaurant. Today, Bonnie and her husband John keep tradition alive by serving a green chile cheeseburger that has been on the menu since the place opened. Fresh chuck steaks are ground and pattied by Bonnie's brother nearby. In 2006, John decided to switch over to naturally raised antibiotic- and hormone-free beef. He made one of the best burgers in America even better.

A green chile cheeseburger at the Bobcat is a beauty. Steamed and diced Hatch, New Mexico, green chiles are held in place atop a nine-ounce patty by a slice of melted white cheddar. The well-seasoned cast-iron griddle creates a crunchy exterior and leaves the interior perfectly moist. John is also a master of cooking temperatures, so if you ask for your burger medium-rare it'll be medium-rare. He employs a complex system of bacon weights to manage the different temperatures of the burgers.

I beg of you, please do not pollute this burger with ketchup and mustard. The simplicity of the green chile cheeseburger should not be tampered with. The chiles, hot and flavorful, enhance the beefiness, creating one of the greatest marriages of flavors and textures in the burger world.

The decades-old-cast-iron griddle is one of the secrets to the Bobcat's success. John Eckre once told me, "I've tried to find another like it, but it's impossible." John stands at the grill making perfect burgers while Bonnie takes orders, makes change, and delivers food to the tables. Bonnie knows just about everyone who walks into the restaurant and greets them by name with a smile.

The Bobcat has strange hours so check before you go. They are open 5 days a week, but only until 7:50 p.m. Why 7:50? "Apparently there was a curfew in Santa Fe years ago." Bonnie told me. "You had to be home by 8."

BOBCAT BITE COLESLAW

Turns out I was not the only one who has asked John and Bonnie Eckre for their amazing coleslaw recipe. Unlike most proprietary secrets restaurants possess, this recipe was adapted from a Depression-era recipe by a previous owner of the Bobcat, Shelba Surls. During America's economic dark days, the U.S. government issued recipes like this one that could be made with inexpensive ingredients (in this case, no cream).

MAKES A LOT OF COLESLAW
(THIS IS A DAY'S WORTH FOR THE BOBCAT)
2-3 heads cabbage, shredded
1 green bell pepper chopped
1-1 ½ cups sugar
2 cups distilled white vinegar
½ cup canola oil
½ teaspoon salt
1 teaspoon ground black pepper
1 teaspoon celery seed
2 tablespoons prepared mustard

Place the cabbage in a large bowl. Place the green pepper on top of the cabbage. Pour the sugar over both (for 2 heads, use 1 cup sugar, for 3 heads use 1 ½ cups).

In a large saucepan bring to a boil the vinegar, canola oil, salt, pepper, celery seed, and mustard. According to Bonnie, the smell of the boiling vinegar concoction will drive you out of the kitchen. Boil until the mustard is dissolved (about 5 minutes). Pour the hot brew over the bowl of cabbage and peppers and let sit. When the bowl has cooled, mix the contents and refrigerate. Bonnie told me that the slaw tastes best when it has had time to marinate. Bobcat makes its coleslaw the day before serving.

OWL BAR & CAFE

US 380
SAN ANTONIO, NM 87832
505-835-9946
MON–FRI 8 AM–9:30 PM
CLOSED SATURDAY AND SUNDAY

The Owl Bar & Cafe seems an unlikely candidate for producing a world-famous burger. The bar sits at a crossroads deep in the dry desert of central New Mexico. Its adobe structure has barely a window and is one of only a handful on the main drag in the tiny town of San Antonio. Even though you have to wait until your eyes adjust after entering, and there is a large supply of booze behind the bar, the Owl is a friendly place, a family saloon with an excellent burger on the menu.

The Owl Burger is what many call the "other great green chile cheeseburger in New Mexico." I drove 280 miles to eat this burger so my expectations were high. I sat at the bar at 11 a.m. and watched as burger after burger was dispatched to the booths opposite the bar. Thankfully, mine showed up in only four minutes—the smell of green chile wafting through the air was making me very hungry.

All of the burgers are served on plastic plates with a napkin between the burger and the plate. Their famous green chile cheeseburger starts as a patty of fresh ground beef that has been pressed flat on a flattop griddle (the Owl grinds its own beef daily). Cheese, onion, tomato, mayo, and pickles are standard, and the green chiles pack a punch. They come from Hatch, New Mexico, and are lovingly prepared by Pinto, the kitchen prep cook. Pinto has been preparing the green chile for the Owl for over 40 years.

The clientele is a mix of silver-haired motor-home enthusiasts and servicemen in fatigues. The bar's entrance celebrates its proximity to the infamous Trinity Site, the spot where scientists tested the first atomic bomb only 25 miles away. Large photos of the mushroom cloud and other missile-site ephemera are proudly displayed. Frank Chavez opened the Owl Bar in 1945, just in time to accommodate the entertainment-starved scientists who were frequenting the area. At the request of these scientists, a griddle was installed and the Owl

Burger was born.

The shelves of the bar are covered with hundreds of donated servicemen's uniform patches from all over the country. Current owner Rowena Baca, Frank Chavez' daughter, started the collection years ago. Bartender of 28 years, Cathy Baca, explained, "Rowena told a cop she liked the patch on his uniform so he ripped it off and gave it to her. Since then, we get patches from everywhere."

Another item tacked to the walls is money. Tourists are encouraged to sign and donate a bill of their choice and pick a spot on the wall. Once a year the money is taken down, counted, and given to charity. "We've collected over $15,000 in the last six years," said Cathy. The walls account for up to $2,500 a year, with the exception of a recent late-night robbery. "They stole $600," Cathy told me. "I don't know how they got it off the walls so fast— it takes us forever."

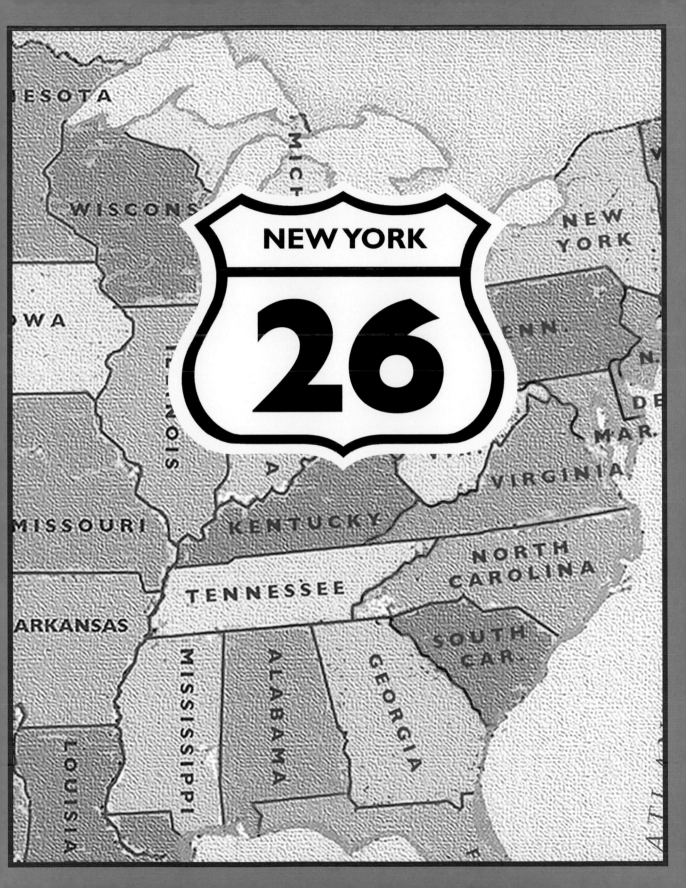

CORNER BISTRO

331 WEST 4TH STREET
NEW YORK, NY 10014
212-242-9502
MON–SAT 11:30 AM–4 AM
SUN NOON–4 AM

For two decades the Corner Bistro in Greenwich Village, New York City, served my "hometown" burger. It's the burger that became the standard by which all others would be measured. I've eaten over a thousand burgers at the Bistro in different states of intoxication or sober, for lunch and dinner, and a few times I even ate them with friends at 3 a.m. on a Tuesday. For five of those years I lived a block away and secretly wondered if my motive for moving had been burger proximity. I knew the right times to visit to avoid the crowds, and their phone number was in the speed dial of my cell phone. I placed phone orders and used the quiet side door to sneak in, grab my waiting hot paper bag, and make a swift exit. My burger quest started here and ends here as well. I went forth into Hamburger America, ate well, returned, and was confident that the Bistro Burger really is one of the best in the nation.

Inside and out, the Corner Bistro defies its name and looks the part of the Irish pub.

Carved-up wooden tables, well-worn wide plank floorboards, and a long bar with a noticeable dip in the center create your lasting first impression. "The building is still settling," Bill O'Donnell said in defense of the sloping bar. Bill has been the owner of the Bistro for over 40 years and its famous burger has been on the menu just as long.

The building housing the Corner Bistro dates back to 1827 and before it was a bar it was an inn. The existing décor surrounding the bar (stained-glass cabinetry and mirrors) as well as the brass-foot-railed bar itself is said to date back to 1880. After Prohibition was repealed the bar became Barney McNichols and attracted mostly the longshoremen who populated the neighborhood. After its short stint as a gay bar, in 1961 a Spanish woman bought it and attempted to put a European spin on the old tavern by calling it the Corner Bistro. It didn't last and went back to being what it has been for well over a century—a cozy dive with a great jukebox.

In 1977, Mimi Sheraton, the well-known food critic from the *New York Times*, wrote a favorable piece on the Bistro Burger that kick-started the surge of popularity that has not slowed since. "I came in the next day and the place was packed," Bill told me. "I was shocked." Bill himself admits that there's nothing special about the burger and nothing has changed in 40 years. "We still use the same butcher around the corner. It's good meat,

mostly chuck and sirloin but I think he puts some porterhouse in there too." Two hundred and fifty pounds of the fresh ground beef gets walked over by hand cart from 14th Street to the Bistro everyday. This was the way all restaurants received their meat in the first half of the twentieth century, delivered by hand from a local butcher.

The Bistro Burger doesn't try to be anything but a great hamburger. It's a thick, 8-ounce burger whose only flourish is three crispy strips of bacon that have been flash-fried in the deep fryer (ever wonder why those fries taste so damn good?). It's served on a toasted white squishy bun with lettuce, tomato, and a thick onion slice hidden beneath the burger. It's cooked in a tiny, postage-stamp-sized kitchen staffed by two. They cook the burgers to your preferred temperature in a salamander broiler, a small, specialized oven that cooks the burgers slowly by indirect, overhead heat. Bartender of 40 years, Harold, explained, "It keeps the burgers soft and juicy."

Hard-working Louis has been the head chef and chief of burger operations at the Bistro for over 25 years. He is a man of few words but will always get your order right. Louis is in charge of the line that builds most nights for people waiting for a table and will take your order. The infamous line starts at the phone booth and can go all the way to the front door, so grab a beer at the bar first.

Many people try to bad-mouth this burger

because they are embarrassed by its simplicity. In a city with no tangible burger identity (you really can find any type of burger in New York City, from the bloated wallet busters to tasty sliders), the Bistro Burger stands out as an unflappable success grounded in modesty. The success has spread to other bars in the neighborhood that claim to "know the secret of the Bistro Burger" and have even hired cast-off Bistro kitchen staff to boost business. "There are no secrets," Bill told me laughing, "The recipe is 'good meat,' you idiots."

★ ★ ★ ★ ★
DONOVAN'S PUB

5724 ROOSEVELT AVENUE
FLUSHING, NY 11377
718-429-9339
OPEN DAILY 11 AM–11 PM

Regulars, God bless 'em, show up at this Woodside, Queens, Irish pub at 11 a.m. daily to slowly drink their Guinness stout and just talk. They are cared for by Robert Kansella, bartender of 40 years who was at the pub before there was even a restaurant. The bar he tends to is an impressive one—long, dark, solid and with the type of patina that only comes with age. It's a great bar to sit at, drink a Guinness, and just talk, but even better to enjoy a burger, one of the best I've ever eaten.

I asked Robert how big the burgers were and his only response was, "They are pretty big." He was not far off. This pub has been serving half-pound burgers since 1970, and a lot of them. Artie Kardaras, head chef at Donovan's for over 35 years, told me they hand patty 400 pounds of quality ground shell steak (New York strip) a day for their burgers. "I make every day fresh," he proudly explained with his thick Greek accent.

The Donovan's burger is a lesson in how a large burger should be prepared. It's cooked in a way that few burgers are in America—in a broiler used for cooking steaks. The loose-pattied burger is broiled to the temperature of your choice with little attention paid to it by the chef. "Too many people press them too much," Artie explained with big hand gestures and twisted facial expressions. Artie believes, and is correct, that the best burgers are left alone and touched the least.

When you bite into the inch-thick Donovan's burger, the first thing you notice is how loose the meat is. The delicate exterior char can barely contain the tender, steamy beef inside. A half-pound burger may sound tough to tackle, but the meat-to-bun ratio is nearly perfect, making the entire experience incredibly satisfying.

Other than a bar, burgers, and regulars, Donovan's also has an impressive dining room and a great menu loaded with comfort food. Go during the colder months and enjoy your burgers by the cozy fireplace in the dark-

paneled dining room with Tiffany lamps hanging overhead.

The most obvious landmark you'll notice outside Donovan's Pub is the undeniably old–New York elevated subway rumbling overhead every few minutes. What you may not pick out is the tavern's odd proximity to a church only a few feet away, directly across the street. "This place was here before the church so they were allowed to stay," regular Don Moran told me from his spot at the bar. According to New York City zoning law, no drinking establishment may be operated within 500 feet of a place of worship. So this may be the closest you'll get to a church to drink and eat great burgers in New York City—in fact, the stained glass windows do give the place a churchlike feel.

The magazine *Time Out NY* recently called the burger at Donovan's the best in New York City. That's quite a claim in this town of diverse food possibilities and unlimited types of burger joints. Did the recent press increase sales at the sleepy neighborhood tavern? "Sure," bartender Robert admitted, "but we've been selling a lot of burgers forever."

THE "MOTZ BURGER" WITH SCHNACK SAUCE

In the Summer of 2006, New York chef Harry Hawk asked me to design a burger for his new concession at Water Taxi Beach in Long Island City, Queens. Harry and the NY Water Taxi had created a beach utopia on the bank of the East River with stunning views of midtown Manhattan. The burger on the menu needed to be great but not gourmet. It needed to be served with the freshest ingredients, on a paper plate. Harry wanted a burger that would involve my collective knowledge of the great burgers of America and I was up to the task. I kept things simple (as most great chefs do) and we created a quarter-pound burger made from Angus chuck steaks ground in a walk-in cooler at the beach. The ground beef is measured in a scoop, balled, and placed on a flattop griddle set at 420 degrees. The ball of beef is pressed flat, cooked for only a minute or two per side, and slipped onto a toasted white squishy bun. That's it. No cheese, no lettuce, and nothing getting in the way of a great tasting burger. The only condiment that graces the Motz Burger is a special spicy, creamy sauce created for the burgers at Harry's Brooklyn burger and hot dog outpost, Schnack. Here are the recipes for both burger. Serve with "Schnack Sauce".

MAKES 4 QUARTER-POUND BURGERS
1 pound fresh ground 80 percent lean chuck
4 white squishy buns
Salt
Butter

Divide meat into quarters and form into loose balls. Place a heavy cast-iron skillet over medium heat to warm for 10 minutes. Turn heat to high, wait a minute, then place the balls of beef into pan. Sprinkle some salt on the meat and press as little as possible into patty shapes using a strong spatula. Cover the pan. Cook on one side for about two minutes (no more!), flip and cook for another minute and a half (do not press again). Remove from heat and place on toasted white buns (to best toast buns, butter and place in pan over medium heat).

SCHNACK SAUCE

Harry Hawk wouldn't give me the exact recipe for his famous sauce so I've recreated something based on a list of his ingredients. It's not that he didn't want to give up secrets, he told me, "People should experiment and come up with their own sauces." So the Hamburger America Test Kitchen got right to work:

MAKES ENOUGH FOR 8 QUARTER-POUND BURGERS
¼ **cup mayonnaise**
2 **tablespoons grainy mustard**
2 **teaspoons canned Mexican chipotle**
(a pinch of chipotle powder and can be substituted,
but the canned chipotles work best)

Combine the ingredients in a food processor and blend well (mix in bowl if not using whole, canned chipotle). Serve on a Motz Burger. Note: this sauce is HOT. If you like creamy hot things, this sauce is for you.

HILDEBRANDT'S

84 HILLSIDE AVENUE
WILLISTON PARK, NY 11596
516-741-0608
WWW.HILDEBRANDTS.KPSEARCH.COM
TUES–SAT 11 AM–8:30 PM
CLOSED SUNDAY AND MONDAY

Densely packed suburban Long Island, New York, is a place where new malls and homes are constantly springing up and, unless protected, the past is unceremoniously swept away. In a part of the country where it's getting harder to find genuine nostalgia, locals embrace Hildebrandt's Luncheonette.

This early-twentieth-century landmark soda counter, confectionery, and ice cream parlor offers a glimpse into the past. The counter, though, is not a washed-up has-been. It's as vibrant as ever and happens to serve some of tastiest burgers this side of Manhattan.

Hildebrandt's opened in 1927 and was the only business in the newly developing dirt road suburb of Williston Park, 20 miles from New York City. Today, Hildebrandt's is owned by Joanne Strano and her son-in-law Bryan Acosta. Joanne and her late husband Al bought the vintage luncheonette in 1974 when longtime owner and chocolate maker Henry Shreiver was

looking to retire. The Acostas learned the chocolate-making trade from Shreiver and made a major improvement to the existing burger on the menu—fresh ground beef.

This classic luncheonette, with its checker-tiled floor and long marble counter with 13 stools, maintains a vintage look by making use of the soda fountain trappings of a bygone era. The seltzer and syrup dispensers are not vintage props. They all function daily, as does the long bank of ice cream chests behind the counter. Ice cream is a big draw at Hildebrandt's because it's made right at the restaurant.

But according to Bryan, most come for the food, which is a mix of classic diner fare and Italian specialties added by the Acosta family in the 1970s. Surprisingly, this amazing burger has been exiled to the bottom of the menu. Look for your cheeseburger in a section marked "sandwiches" at the bottom of the list, just after the meatball hero.

"We have the greatest burger," Bryan told me without pause, and added, "I've never really had a better burger. I really haven't." He can boast all he wants. It really is a great burger. The burgers at Hildebrandt's start as fresh-ground sirloin the restaurant receives from the butcher down the street. Bryan himself hand patties the four-ounce burgers just before the lunch crowd shows up. The burgers are offered at the four-ounce size, or ask for the eight-ounce and get twice the meat. "We just take two four-ounce

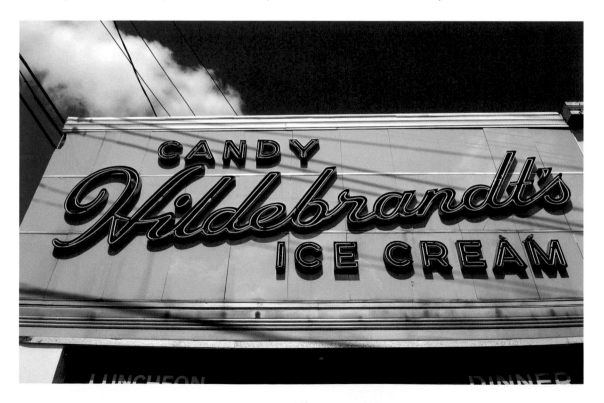

patties and smoosh them together on the grill," Bryan explained. On the flattop griddle, Alfredo presses the burger flat and places a bacon weight on top. It's served on a classic white bun with tomato, sliced onion, and a wedge of iceberg lettuce. Bacon is available, but not necessary (this meat is so good you won't want anything to hide the flavor). Ketchup is king at Hildebrandt's (there's a bottle every few feet on the counter) but mustard has to be culled from the countermen in small pouches.

Hildebrandt's fries are a great addition to your hamburger lunch. They are large, hand-cut, deep-fried slices of potato that, if ordered well done, resemble homemade potato chips. Order a milkshake, listed on the menu in Long Island vernacular as a "frosted," and you'll get a tall glass and the obligatory metal cup the shake was made in. Since the ice cream is homemade, the shakes are superb.

The clientele at Hildebrandt's ranges from little old ladies to large families with kids. Bryan, waiting tables in the back, makes jokes as he takes orders. "These are the best seats in the house," he tells two older ladies looking for a table, "unless of course I'm waiting on you!"

In the vicinity of New York City, Hildebrandt's is not alone. The long-gone business model for this type of soda fountain survives at places like Hinsch's in Bayridge, Brooklyn, and Bischoff's in Teaneck, New Jersey. They too make their own chocolates, and in the case of Bischoff's, countermen still wear white paper caps and striped shirts. At all of these vintage soda fountains of German descent, you can take home hand-packed ice cream by the pint or quart, but the similarities end there. Only Hildebrandt's makes a top-quality burger. That, and the mocha frosted, will keep me coming back.

P.J. CLARKE'S

915 THIRD AVENUE
NEW YORK, NY 10022
212-317-1616
WWW.PJCLARKES.COM
OPEN 7 DAYS A WEEK 11:30 AM–3 AM
BAR CLOSES AT 4 AM

There are few taverns in America as steeped in history as P.J. Clarke's. All at once a neighborhood bar, broken-in dive, and a celebrity hang for decades, it's also a great place to find high-quality pub fare. Among that fare is the world famous P.J. Clarke's hamburger. P.J.'s has not been affected by its own celebrity status. It remains a comfortable place in the heart of a sometimes cold city—a friendly pub with a welcoming staff and a remarkably unpretentious hamburger on the menu.

The iconic corner saloon, in a two-story brick tenement-style structure, looks totally out of place surrounded by the tall glass and steel office buildings of midtown Manhattan. Irish immigrant Patrick J. Clarke started working at the corner bar in 1902, and in 1912 he pur-

The Béarnaise Burger

chased the business and changed the name to his own.

Before the skyscrapers, the neighborhood surrounding P.J.'s was mostly breweries and slaughterhouses. And those who are old enough will remember that the Third Avenue subway was elevated, giving the area a radically different feel. By 1960, the elevated tracks were down and the slaughterhouses were long gone. P.J.'s neighborhood has undergone a profound transformation in the last century but the tiny saloon remains, dwarfed by its neighbors.

The tin ceilings, faded mirrors behind the bar, and stained-glass windows in front remind the casual observer of the saloon's rich past. Sinatra made P.J.'s his last stop on nights out and even had his own table (#20). Affable young general manager Patrick Walsh told me, through his Irish brogue, "If there was anyone sitting there when Sinatra came in they'd get the boot." Buddy Holly proposed to his wife here and Nat King Cole once called the hamburger at P.J.'s "the Cadillac of burgers." Even the famed 1970s sports painter LeRoy Neiman put brush to canvas to create a portrait of the bar in full swing that proudly hangs in the dining room. There are many more stories, but you have to ask Patrick. He told me, "Every single day I learn a new story."

The meat for the burgers comes from cattle that are handpicked for P.J.'s. The energetic head chef Matteo Riccardelli grinds chuck steaks in the kitchen and the fat-to-lean ratio is kept secret. The eight-ounce burgers are hand pressed one by one, cooked on a flattop griddle, and served on a classic white squishy bun. Don't be surprised to find a slice of onion underneath your burger. Today's burgers are served on a porcelain plate, but Patrick told me, "They used to be served on paper plates and the onion was there to soak up the juices"—presumably to prevent the plate from falling apart.

I've been going to P.J.'s for decades and the burger has always been perfect. The bun-to-beef ratio, the slight griddle crunch, and the moist, meaty flavor are what burger dreams are made of. There are a few burger choices at P.J.'s, but I always get the Béarnaise Burger. Imagine the simplicity of the elements—the perfect burger, a soft white bun, and a healthy dose of pure béarnaise sauce.

The dark dining room walls are covered with an amazing collection of New York City ephemera (including P.J.'s death certificate) and old photographs of past patrons. The 100-year-old men's urinals are as famous as the burgers and must be seen to be believed (they're over five feet tall with thick porcelain embellishment). Sinatra once said they were "big enough to take a bath in."

P.J.'s has been part of the collective unconscious of literally millions of former and present New Yorkers. Just like your favorite jacket or an old pair of shoes, the tavern has always been a familiar, unchanging place that many rely on for hearty comfort food, a drink, and good company. The burger at P.J.'s is part of that legacy of comfort and hopefully will be forever.

Four Questions for Chef Daniel Boulud

Celebrated chef, restaurateur, and author of numerous cookbooks, Daniel Boulud kick-started the pricey ultra-gourmet burger phenomenon and fueled a burger resurgence in New York City when he introduced his DB Burger. Here's the description from a DB Bistro press release:

> "The DB Burger is actually a combination of two dishes: on the outside a classic ground sirloin burger, and on the inside a stuffing of tender red wine braised short ribs (off the bone), foie gras, a mirepoix of root vegetables and preserved black truffle. The homemade toasted parmesan and poppy seed bun is spread with a touch of fresh horseradish, oven roasted tomato confit, fresh tomato, red onions and frisée lettuce."

As you can see, attention to detail is of paramount importance and the taste of this burger is off the charts (as is the price). Add fresh black truffles (wintertime only) and the price doubles. The famous burger was born after rioting French farmers dismantled a McDonald's restaurant in Southern France in 1999. When a reporter asked Daniel for a quote, he replied, "The French are just jealous they did not invent the hamburger themselves." He introduced the DB Burger at his new venture DB Bistro in 2001.

GM: Do you think we are in the midst of a hamburger renaissance in America?

DB: I would like to think I may have been at the forefront of the burger renaissance, a movement that has certainly picked up plenty of momentum recently.

GM: What are the key elements to a great hamburger?

DB: 1.Great bun, well toasted, 2.Great, juicy meat well seasoned and cooked just right, 3. Fresh garnishes; the lettuce and tomato should be top quality.

GM: What are burgers like in France?

DB: Traditionally we call it "steak haché" and we don't put it on a bun. The most prevalent is the fast-food kind; hopefully higher-quality versions will make it over there eventually.

GM: Would you eat a butter burger? (see page 296)

DB: If ever I make it all the way to Wisconsin, I won't leave without trying a butter burger. If it's that good I'll have a second one to make sure the trip was worthwhile.

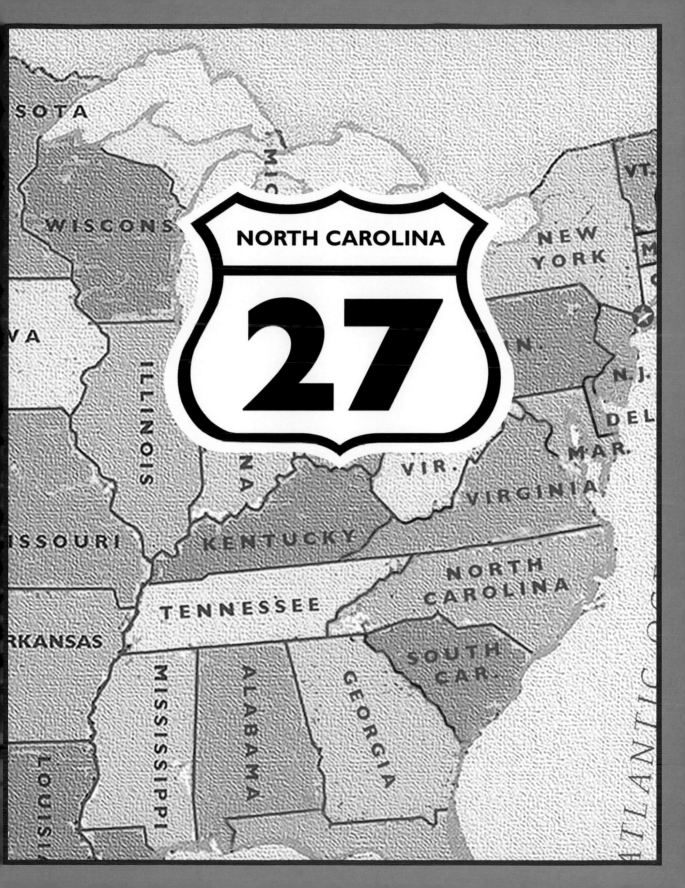

CHAR-GRILL

618 HILLSBOROUGH STREET
(AND THREE OTHER LOCATIONS
IN RALEIGH-DURHAM)
RALEIGH, NC 27603
919-821-7636
WWW.CHARGRILLUSA.COM

Racing to catch a flight I was sure to miss out on Raleigh, North Carolina's own burger mini-chain, the Char-Grill. Fortunately, I did stop, but would have missed the flight had the service not been super-fast.

The set up is pure 1950s drive-in, but the ordering process is peculiar. No honking for service here. You park your car, walk up to the window, and fill out a cryptic order form. Once you have marked your choices, you shove the slim piece of paper into a thin slot in one of the large plate glass windows. Your order form slides down a stainless chute to the waiting grill cook. The lack of indoor seating and a glass-enclosed kitchen creates a sort of public hamburger laboratory—as you wait, you can peer inside and watch your burger being constructed according to the condiments you checked off on your order. Within minutes, your number is called and you are rewarded with a white paper bag full of hot food by a smiling employee.

The burgers are grilled over a flame and come in three sizes, the largest being the half-pound hamburger steak sandwich. Any combination of mayo, lettuce, tomato, onion, pickle, cheese, and bacon can be created. The staff all wear white paper caps and aprons and work at stations to keep this model of efficiency chugging along. The beef comes in fresh daily, as square preformed Angus chuck patties. The manager at the original Hillsborough stand, Scott Hobby, told me "All of the lettuce, tomato, and onion come from a local farmer's market."

Bruce Garner opened Char-Grill in 1959. In 1975, two fraternity brothers, Mahlon Aycock and Ryon Wilder, assumed ownership and over three decades later are still partners in the business. They have expanded from the one location they purchased in 1975 to four locations with a fifth planned. All of the locations are in the Raleigh-Durham area but Mahlon plans to expand throughout North Carolina— and as he put it, "probably beyond."

By design, not much has changed at Char-Grill. The Hillsborough location is a piece of American architecture stuck in time. The deliberately oversized, overdesigned structure is almost sculpture—the enormous white wavy roof looks as if it could crush the floor-to-ceiling windows supporting it. The other Raleigh locations also serve their well-known Charburgers, but it's the original location that has that great drive-in feel. And for almost 50 years Char-Grill has continued to serve the same tasty, flame-grilled burgers and creamy shakes.

All walks of life visit Char-Grill for a dose of nostalgia. Mahlon told me, "We get everybody from the governor of North Carolina to construction folk and anybody in between." And me. I'll be back. I hope my flight gets delayed.

SNAPPY LUNCH

125 NORTH MAIN STREET
MOUNT AIRY, NC 27030
336-786-4931
WWW.THESNAPPYLUNCH.COM
MON–WED & FRI 5:45 AM–1:45 PM
THU & SAT 5:45 AM–1:15 PM
CLOSED SUNDAY

The Snappy Lunch sells one of the best pork chop sandwiches in America and it is "World Famous" according to the menu. But this is a hamburger book, and the restaurant does its part to offer a bit of hamburger history as well. Popular with the locals, the Snappy Lunch sells a curiosity called the Breaded Hamburger. Sometimes referred to as the "No-Burger" or the "old fashioned," this throwback to the Depression was invented when meat was scarce. At the Snappy Lunch, the breaded burger still outsells the regular burger on the menu three to one.

"I don't even get into it with out-of-towners," said Mary Dowell, wife of longtime owner and local food celebrity Charles Dowell. "I don't even like them!" she told me with a smile. I tried my first Depression-era burger at the Snappy Lunch and really liked it. It kind of resembled a

bland crab cake with ground beef inside. "What do ya think?" Mary asked. I told her it tasted like a biscuit and she informed me that I had named the main ingredient.

The breaded burger, referred to as just a "hamburger" by the staff (a nonbreaded burger is a "burger with meat") starts as a blend of ground beef, crumbled cooked biscuits, and day-old bread. The blend, which leans mostly toward bread, is then formed into patties and cooked on the flattop griddle. A finished burger "all the way" has on it coleslaw, mustard, onion, tomato, and chili.

The chili, a tasty, sweet, and chunky concoction, is ladled onto both the pork chop sandwich and the burgers. It was created by Charles in the 1950s by accident. "I was trying to make up something to put on the pork chops—the recipe has not changed since then and everyone wants it."

Charles has been a fixture at the Snappy Lunch since 1943 when, at age 15, he was paid $10 a week. Eight years later his father, a local grocer, helped Charles negotiate the purchase of a share in the restaurant and in 1960 he became the sole owner.

The name Snappy is fitting for the turn-of-the-century post office turned lunch counter because the doors close most days at 1:45 p.m. oddly on Thursday closing time is 1:15 p.m. "As part of the war effort," Charles told me, "restaurants were asked to choose a day to close early."

Mary and Charles met over twenty years

ago when someone tried to set her up with Charles' son at the restaurant. Charles, in his late 70s, still comes to work every day at 4:30 a.m, makes the pork chops at the window griddle, and shuffles around the Snappy Lunch talking to patrons table by table wearing his white paper cap. When I visited, I watched Charles take a break and visit a table of "Redhatters" who were enjoying his famous pork chop. For the unitiated, Redhatters are women over 50 who plan outings donning their best red hat.

In the recently renovated, gleaming kitchen at the rear of the restaurant, I met 16-year veteran cook, Diane. "I never thought a breaded burger could out sell the regular burger, but they do, every day."

Mount Airy, North Carolina, exists in the minds of *The Andy Griffith Show* fans as the inspiration for Mayberry, the setting of the popular 1960s TV show. Not only did Andy grow up in Mount Airy, he also ate at the Snappy Lunch frequently as a child. Because of this, and his massive fan base, avoid the restaurant in late September when thousands descend on the small country town for Mayberry Days. Diane told me "We'll actually stay open late those days just to make sure all those people are fed."

Charles and Mary Dowell take a break in front of the Snappy Lunch

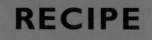
DEEP-FRIED DEPRESSION-ERA BURGER

There was a time in America when ground beef was not readily available. In order to stay in business, many burger counters started mixing day-old bread into their burgers. At the Snappy Lunch in North Carolina, a burger with breading is called a "burger" by the old timers, and a burger without breading is called a "burger with meat." But they are not alone. The breaded burger, sometimes referred to as a "slug burger," is still being served at burger spots throughout the South, cooked to perfection on ancient griddles and skillets. Of course, recipes for these burgers are proprietary and highly secret. The recipe below is my version from the Hamburger America Test Kitchen, prepared the way it might have been 70 years ago.

MAKES 8 BURGERS
REQUIRES 1 HOUR PREP/REFRIGERATOR TIME!
1 cup finely crumbled, stale white bread
1 pound fresh ground 80 percent lean chuck
2 teaspoons salt
Corn or vegetable oil for frying
8 white squishy buns
Pickle
Yellow mustard

Place the bread, salt, and meat in a large mixing bowl and blend well with hands. Form the patties by pressing a golf ball–sized wad of beef flat on a square of waxed paper with the heel of your palm—the flat patties should be a bit larger than the bun. Refrigerate patties for at least an hour (cooling the burger mix helps to keep the patties moist in the center when you deep fry). Heat ½ inch of oil in a cast-iron skillet over medium heat. The oil needs to be HOT. To test it, toss in a small crumb of fresh bread. If the bread immediately bubbles, the oil is ready. Place one patty at a time into the oil; it should float freely. After roughly 30 seconds, flip the patty and cook for another 30 seconds. The patty's edges will crisp to brown and resemble fried chicken. Remove from the oil, drain on paper towels, and serve on buns with pickle and mustard.

SOUTH 21

3101 EAST INDEPENDENCE BOULEVARD
CHARLOTTE, NC 28205
704-377-4509
WWW.SOUTH21DRIVEIN.COM
TUE 11 AM–3 PM
WED & THU 11 AM–9 PM
FRI & SAT 11 AM–10 PM
CLOSED SUNDAY & MONDAY

Traveling along Independence Boulevard just east of downtown Charlotte, NC, you'll notice a vintage red neon sign that blinks with the words "curb service" and beckons you to pull in and float back in time. Slip into one of the many stalls, check out the menu, and push the order button. You are on your way to a classic South 21 drive-in experience.

Since 1959, very little has changed at this Charlotte institution. Owned by the same family of Greek immigrants since the beginning, South 21 serves the same fresh, thin-patty burger that has come from the same local meat supplier for over 45 years. In 1955, George Copsis and his two brothers decided to open a drive-in on South Boulevard in Charlotte. The business boomed and the brothers opened another nearby in 1959. They leased the original location and made the Independence location their flagship. Over the years, the family would open and sell off other drive-ins across town, but offspring Maria and her husband George Housiadas have held on to the flagship icon.

You've heard the story before but it bears repeating—Greeks in the hamburger business.

The Housiadas family is not alone. Many proud Greek families still own classic burger stands across America, namely the famous mini-chains of the Billy Goat of Chicago, Burger House of Dallas, and Crown Burger of Salt Lake City. Or the one-offs like Helvetia Tavern near Portland, Oregon, and Western Steakburger in San Diego. All of these restaurants were the result of hard-working Greeks finding their way in America.

Not surprisingly, most stories of Greek burger entrepreneurism in this country start the same way. "They came here with nothing," Maria told me. "They didn't know what else to do so they started flipping burgers and didn't stop!" She told me that in the beginning the brothers would sell a few burgers, take the cash, run down the street to the Winn-Dixie supermarket, and buy another few pounds of ground beef. "Can you imagine if we did that today?" Maria pondered.

South 21 is the real deal. Expect carhops, window trays, and tasty, classic burgers. The burgers start as preformed fresh-ground four-ounce patties and can be ordered as singles or doubles. Make it a "Super Boy" and you will get two patties on a toasted white bun with chopped lettuce, onion, mustard, and tomato. If you want cheese, you'll need to order the "Jumbo." The burgers show up on your window tray with a large pickle speared to the top bun.

The fries at South 21 are great, but it's the

onion rings that have received decades of accolades. The kitchen at South 21 slices and breads fresh onion rings daily, tasty circles of deep fried goodness.

You'll also notice an item on the menu that sounds almost cartoonish but is anything but— the "Fish-O-Burger." Imagine two pieces of fresh (not frozen) lightly breaded and deep-fried trout served with tartar sauce on a toasted white bun. It's a heavenly sandwich, especially for those who want to partake of the drive-in culture without the red meat.

One thing you may find odd about South 21 is the black fedora your carhop will be wearing as he clips the tray to your car window. It was part of a uniform that was retired about 20 years ago according to Maria. "The uniforms used to be absolutely ridiculous." For years, carhops were required to wear what looked like a period carriage driver's getup—a long red coat with two gold buttons and heavy black pants.

"They looked nice," Maria remembered, "but the carhops hated to wear them. The heavy material was really only comfortable in the three colder months of the year."

South 21 still employs a hard-working staff of four; some have been at the drive-in for over 40 years. One of those is Nick, the Greek griddle master who has been flipping perfect patties at South 21 since 1971.

Late-night cruising is a thing of the past, as the last burgers are sold at 10 p.m. on weekends. Check the drive-in's hours before you head out to South 21 to show off your '66 Corvette Stingray.

Maria is at the drive-in every day to take orders and manage the staff. She seems confident in the quality of their fare and understands why people continue to patronize South 21. "Diehard fans tell people, 'If you haven't eaten there, you haven't eaten.'"

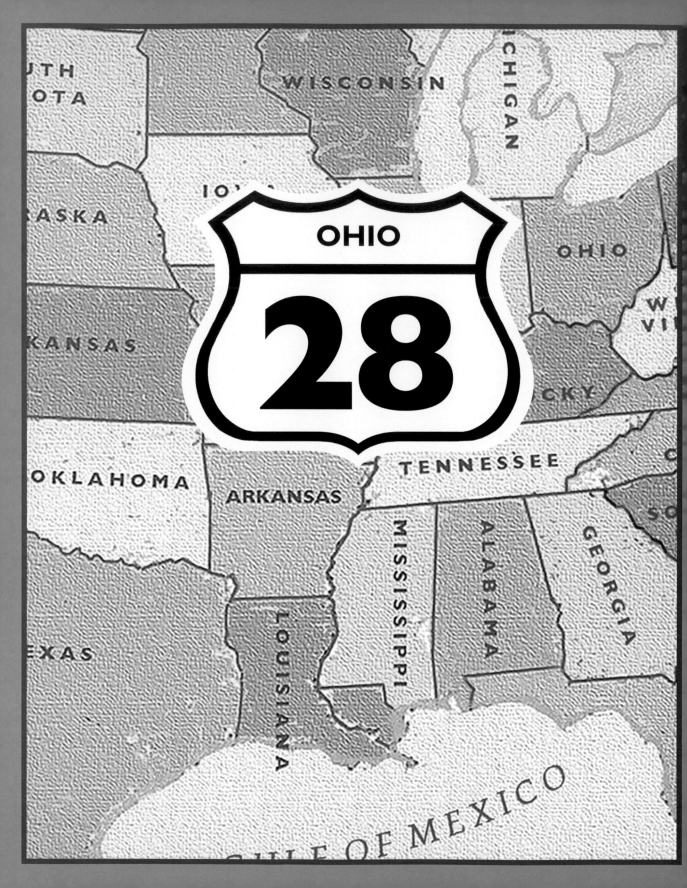

CRABILL'S HAMBURGERS

727 MIAMI STREET
URBANA, OH 43078
937-653-5133
MON–FRI 10 AM–6:30 PM
SAT 10 AM–5 PM
CLOSED SUNDAY

Crabill's is very, very small. What's amazing is that the original Crabill's was much smaller. Eight stools sit bolted to the floor at a small counter and there is barely enough room to pass behind them. "The old place was five times smaller," grill cook Andy Hiltibran told me. Andy is married to third-generation owner Marsha Crabill, the granddaughter of Forest Crabill, who opened this heartland burger stand nearly 100 years ago.

Crabill's started as a hamburger counter in picturesque downtown Urbana. It's the sort of town that Norman Rockwell would have painted in his depiction of everyday life in mid-twentieth century America. Two men, Crabill and Carpenter, opened the minuscule six-stool counter in 1927. After only three days, Crabill bought out Carpenter for $75. The counter remained in operation, run by Forest's son and daughter-in-law, David and Joyce, until it closed in 1988.

Marsha and Andy decided to restart the family business soon after with the help of Marsha's parents. They were eager to leave their factory jobs (she worked at Honda, he worked at Bristol-Meyers) so they purchased a small motor home and dubbed it "Crabill's on Wheels." They made the rounds of county fairs and horse shows, and after three years on wheels the couple decided to go brick-and-mortar. Crabill's was reborn on the west side of town, just a few blocks from, and not much larger than, the original location.

The first time I visited the reincarnation of the burger counter, I sat next to a white-bearded regular named Will Yoder who for decades has played the annual town Santa. Will had recently had his teeth removed and was on a soft food diet. Personally, I couldn't think of a better spot to dine on tasty, soft food. The tiny burgers at Crabill's, with their pillowy Wonder buns and healthy dose of burger grease, actually do melt in your mouth.

The burgers at Crabill's are cooked in a wide, shallow griddle. The griddle is filled with about a half inch of grease. "The griddle in the old place was much smaller," Andy told me, and showed me with his hands only a foot apart. "It was also much deeper." Small balls of fresh ground beef are tossed into the grease, then pressed once with specially made spatulas. The grillperson uses two of these spatulas at a time to systematically press and flip the dozens of patties floating in the grease with a sort of Benihana-like speed and dexterity. As your burger nears doneness, it gets a splash of grease from a spatula and is transferred to a waiting tiny Wonder bun.

Chopped raw onion, spicy mustard, and relish are standard, but cheese and ketchup are also available. There is a sign on the wall menu that explains that ketchup was introduced in 1990. That's right, it took ketchup 63 years to be accepted at Crabill's.

With their pillowy Wonder buns and healthy dose of burger grease, the burgers actually melt in your mouth.

On a busy Saturday Crabill's can move up to 300 burgers in ten minutes. When someone walks in with an order for 20 doubles, the griddle is quickly filled with the balls of meat and the spatulas start whacking at lighting speed.

Don't waste your time with singles; go for doubles. Twice the beef, twice the grease, and half the bread. If you are feeling brave, do what some regulars do—ask for yours *dipped* and you'll get the top of your bun dipped in the grease. "Some people even like theirs double-dipped," Andy told me. "That's where we dip the top *and* bottom of the bun." A double, double-dipped anyone?

GAHANNA GRILL

82 GRANVILLE STREET
GAHANNA, OH 43230
614-476-9017
MON–SAT 11 AM–10:30 PM
SUN NOON–8:30 PM

"This used to be all farm fields out here," owner of the Gahanna Grill Jimmy Staravecka told me, waving his arm. He pointed to a photo that shows the bar in 1900, not surrounded by much of anything. Looking at the restaurant today in this busy suburb of Columbus, it's hard to imagine its former surroundings. No one seems to know the age of the building, but supposedly the business dates back to the days of mud streets and horse-drawn carriages. This means the tavern has been pouring drinks for well over a century and makes the Gahanna Grill one of the oldest restaurants in the area.

The nondescript exterior of the tavern yields to a comfortable interior. The wood-paneled walls are covered with photos of the tavern's past (one depicting the former Gahanna Lanes, a bowling alley on the premises) and the large bar is surrounded by televisions. The surface of the bar is a potpourri of advertisements for local services—from real estate to a hair salon—laminated directly into the finish. One corner of the bar is dedicated to the Beanie Burger Hall of Fame. Floor-to-ceiling photographs show the brave souls who have ingested the burger that has made the Gahanna famous—the Double Beanie Burger.

The regular Beanie Burger itself is a monster, with its patty of fresh ground beef weighing in at about half a pound. The Double gives you two half-pound patties, a photo on the wall, and a free T-shirt for your efforts. But the Beanie Burger, named after the cook who invented it decades ago, does not just contain a perfectly griddled patty. The burger is also piled high with lettuce, tomato, grilled onions, bacon, cheese, and a hearty scoop of homemade coleslaw. The burger is a sloppy, tasty mess that is barely contained by its toasted, soft kaiser roll. For that reason, the kitchen staff takes great pride in stabbing the vertical burger with a large steak knife. I know of no frilly toothpick that could keep this beast together.

Beanie Vesner still mans the grill and turns out hundreds of burgers for the lunchtime crowd consisting mostly of construction workers and faithful regulars. Jim Ellison, a friend who alerted me to this hamburger destination, calls the Beanie Burger "A good, manly lunch," referring to the nearly 100 percent male population at noon. "Dinnertime is different, mostly families," Jimmy, the newest owner of the restaurant, told me. "This used to be mainly a lunch crowd with the bar busy at night." Since he purchased Gahanna in 2005 he has updated the kitchen and added steaks and pastas to the menu.

I asked Beanie how long he had been making burgers at Gahanna and he refused to give me a straight answer. Smiling, with a toothpick in his mouth, he told me, "Maybe 20 years, maybe?" But by other accounts, the figure is more like 30 years.

To make the burger, Beanie grabs a half-pound wad of ground beef measured by hand and presses it flat, also by hand, onto the hot griddle. The burger is flipped once and a bacon weight is placed on top. I asked him how he knew the burger was a half pound and his deadpan response was, "Because I've made up probably about three million of them."

I ordered my Beanie Burger cooked to the chef's specs and ended up with a medium-well, but moist, burger. Beanie told me later, with a shrug, "Most people around here like their burgers well done."

Jimmy is far from the typical Midwesterner or Ohio native. That's because he was born in Albania and lived in Brooklyn, NY, for 17 years. He attended cooking school in New York City, owned a pizza parlor, and for a few years was Mayor Rudolph Giuliani's chef at Gracie Mansion. He came to Columbus for opportunity and the quality of life it promised. "In Bensonhurst, we lived in a studio apartment on the sixteenth floor. Here, I live in a mansion, wife, two kids, two-car garage, backyard, and a pool." All that, and he owns a restaurant that makes one of the best burgers in America.

HAMBURGER WAGON

12 EAST CENTRAL AVENUE
MIAMISBURG, OH 45342
937-847-2442
MON–SAT 10:30 AM–7 PM
SUN 11 AM–7 PM

Every day of the year two dedicated employees of the Hamburger Wagon open a small garage door and drag a tiny spoked-wheel lunch cart 50 feet to a spot across the street. "It's pretty awkward to pull," said longtime employee Jessi, "but if you get a running start it's OK." The wagon has been selling burgers in roughly the same spot for almost 100 years to faithful regulars from the center of this picturesque town south of Dayton. I asked current owner Michelle Lyons if the Hamburger Wagon would be around for a while and she told me, "I think there would be civil unrest if they tried to get rid of the wagon."

Born of necessity, the Hamburger Wagon was started by Sherman "Cocky" Porter just after the devastating Dayton Flood of 1913. Miamisburg was evacuated and in shambles, left without power or water. Cocky served burgers from a cart to relief workers and locals who were put to the task of rebuilding the town.

Today, the wagon still sells the one thing it has sold for almost a century—hamburgers. It's as basic as you can get. The burger comes one way only, on a bun with pickle and onion, no cheese. "We always know when someone

on line is new when they ask for cheese," Jessi explained. Michelle told me that before she and her husband Chad bought the wagon, "various cranky old men worked here" through the decades. "If you asked for cheese, they'd tell you, 'If you want cheese, get yer ass over to the Mc Donald's!'"

The small patties, around three ounces apiece, come as singles or doubles on tiny Wonder buns. Chips and pop are offered, but that's about it. If you were looking for variety you came to the wrong place. If you were looking for one of the tastiest burgers in America, dig in.

The burgers at the wagon are unique. The first thing you'll notice upon first bite is the extraordinarily crunchy exterior and the pleasantly moist interior. Think chicken-fried burger. You also probably watched your burger being deep-fried in the enormous skillet through one of the wagon's windows. The reason for the super-crunch of the burgers is kept secret by Michelle, but I'd venture to guess that one of the ingredients is some sort of breading. Adding bread to ground beef was a government-sanctioned method for stretching food during the Depression. It's a method that a few old-time burger stands in America still operate

Hamburger Wagon (which on weekends can be 30 deep) tells me that most people have given up trying to guess.

An average order at the wagon is four burgers. A customer of close to 60 years named Glenn makes the 40-mile round trip twice a week for four of the tasty deep-fried burgers. The day I was there he added a Diet Coke to his order. Rubbing his belly, he told me, laughing, "I'm watching my figure!"

Two employees work at lightning speed to prep, cook, and bag over 200 burgers an hour. One stands at the skillet managing the tiny bobbing and bubbling patties while the other preps buns and makes change. This sounds entirely ordinary except that it is accomplished in a space that is no more than four by five feet wide. The illusion of the small cart is perpetuated though by a large commercial kitchen across the street where the meat, onions, and buns are prepped and stored.

Michelle and Chad try to close for around two weeks in the dead of winter for a vacation every year. Predictably, a few locals protest the absence of the cart in downtown and ache for their burger fix. Michelle told me that one year a regular left a message on her answering machine while she was on vacation that said simply, "Cocky Porter is flipping in his grave!" People really love this place.

HAMBURGER WAGON®

ESTABLISHED IN 1913 BY SHERMAN PORTER™

Open pretty much all year long for lunch & dinner. Doesn't matter what the weather conditions are!

Call for specific hours (937) 847-2442

successfully with. "Everyone has been trying to guess the recipe for years," Michelle told me, "and think they can make them at home." One glance at the line in front of the

KEWPEE

111 NORTH ELIZABETH STREET
LIMA, OH 45801
419-228-1778
MON–THU 5 AM–10 PM
FRI & SAT 5 AM–MIDNIGHT
SUN 3 PM-10 PM

In the center of Lima, Ohio, sits a slice of Americana that is impossible to ignore. A well preserved Art-Deco restaurant with a big history, this 1920s hamburger tradition once existed throughout the Upper Midwest with over 200 locations that competed with White Castle and outlived White Tower. Today there are only six Kewpees remaining, and of those, three are in Lima.

Owner Harry Shutt hasn't done much to his enameled-brick burger restaurant that was built in 1938 (and replaced a version built in 1928). "We have tried to maintain our image and not change much." That's a good thing because this Kewpee has been turning out tasty square-patty burgers for close to 80 years.

Yes, the burgers at Kewpee are square, not round. Sound familiar? In 1969, Dave Thomas, the founder of the ubiquitous Wendy's chain, introduced a square burger to America. It may have been a new concept to some, but both Kewpee and White Castle have been serving square burgers since the 1920s. Dave was clearly influenced by the local Kewpee in his hometown of Kalamazoo, Michigan. But unlike both White Castle and Wendy's, the burgers at Kewpee are made from fresh ground beef, not frozen.

Step into the Kewpee of downtown Lima and instantly step back in time. Very little has changed from the food to the 1930s fast-food décor. The restaurant's original curved white enamel steel wall and ceiling panels look as clean as if it were opening day. Newish orange plastic booths, a low counter with stools, and random tables fill the small terrazzo-floored restaurant. In the dining area two large Kewpee dolls stand watch over customers enjoying their burgers and thick shakes. Fortunately, Harry has held on to these icons of a forgotten age and has even had the priceless dolls refurbished recently. The Kewpee name comes from the popular early twentieth-century doll of the same name (but different spelling), the Kewpie doll.

The burgers are fresh. "I buy boneless carcass beef and grind it here," Harry told me. The beef comes from a Lima slaughterhouse that uses local cows only. Harry said it best when he explained, "The worst thing you can do to meat is haul it. These animals have never been more than 40 miles from Lima." This makes Harry and Kewpee an anomaly in fast-food America. The hamburger über-chains today, with their cross-country shipments and city-sized warehouses, could not even begin to imagine this sort of localized business plan.

Two separate griddles work full time during the lunch rush; one services the drive-thru and the other walk-up customers inside. All of

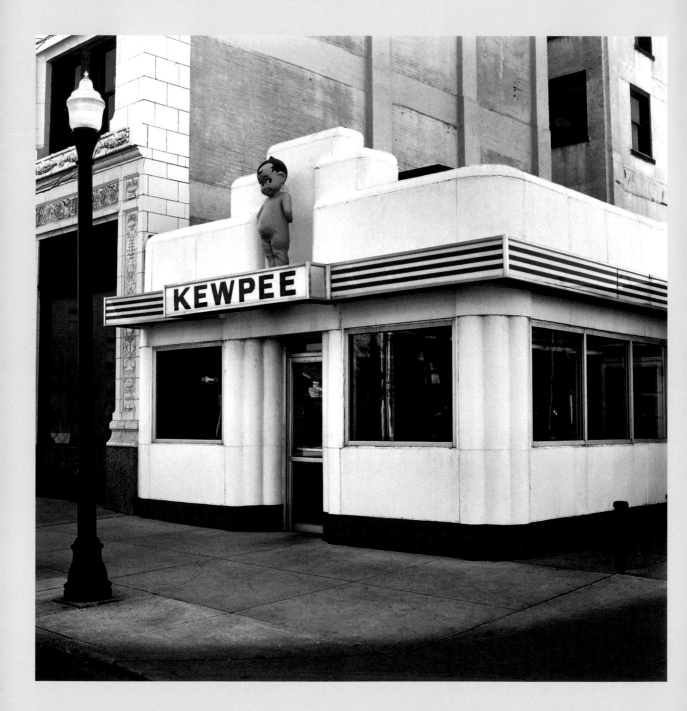

the women working behind the counter slinging patties and dressing burgers have been at the Kewpee for over 30 years. Amazingly, grill cook Nancy has been employed at Kewpee since the Kennedy administration.

The burgers are superthin and so fresh they are almost falling apart. The usual condiments like mustard, ketchup, and pickle are available, but most order "The Special," which is a burger with mayonnaise, lettuce, and tomato. The produce for Kewpee comes from a local farmer and is hydroponically grown. One menu item, the vegetable sandwich, appears to be a late addition for a health-conscious America, but this is not the case. On the menu for decades, the sandwich was probably added during World War II to make up for the lack of available burger meat. "We've had a vegetable sandwich for over 70 years," Harry pointed out. Harry has been at Kewpee for over 50 years and owns the rights to the franchise as well as two other "contemporary" Kewpees in Lima. He started flipping burgers at the downtown Kewpee when he was 25 and became the owner in 1980. Harry has a lot to say about the "Wal Marting" of America. He feels the crush of commercial fast food and the lack of support for small business in America. Coincidentally, one of his Kewpees is threatened by highway expansion designed to accommodate . . . a new Wal-Mart! Regardless, Kewpee does a brisk business and is hardly fazed by the seven McDonald's restaurants in Lima.

You owe it to yourself to visit Kewpee. It's a part of American hamburger tradition that remains vital in the face of a homogenizing fast-food culture. Pay homage to a burger chain that preceded Burger King and Wendy's by almost 40 years. Look for the wide-eyed smiling Kewpee doll over the front door and remember the Kewpee slogan, "Hamburg pickle on top makes your heart go flippity-flop."

THURMAN CAFE
183 THURMAN AVENUE
COLUMBUS, OH 43206
614-443-1570
WWW.THETHURMANCAFE.COM
OPEN DAILY 11 AM–12 AM

The quaint, historic German Village in Columbus, Ohio, with its low, ancient buildings and streets paved with red brick, is the perfect setting for this broken-in, dark and cozy tavern. The menu at Thurman Café is loaded with great food from decades-old family recipes like the Coney sauce for the hot dogs and terrific French fries. But it's the burger you came to eat, so settle into one of the odd-shaped booths and prepare to feast on one of the tallest burgers in the land—the Thurman Burger.

Thurman Café has all the trappings of a typical time-tested favorite local hang—walls covered with the obligatory license plates, beer ads, and old photos. But look a little closer and discover the amazing ceiling covered in vintage Budweiser wallpaper and the thousands of signed dollar bills dangling over the bar area like party decorations. Chances are, while you are waiting for your Thurman Burger to arrive, one will pass by on its way to another customer. Your first glance at the famed burger will result in an audible gulp that signals either fear or hunger. This is because the Thurman Burger is enormous.

Macedonian immigrants Nancho and Dena Suclescy opened the Thurman Café in 1937. Today, more than 70 years later, the café is still in the Suclescy family, run by third-generation siblings Mike, Paul, and Donna.

The "Johnnie" burger is drizzled with a shot of top-shelf 1800 tequila.

There are many different burgers on the menu but it's the Thurman Burger that outsells them all. The creation starts with a three-quarter-pound patty of griddled fresh ground beef that is topped with (follow me here) grilled onions, lettuce, tomato, sliced sautéed mushrooms, pickle, jalapeño slices, mayonnaise, and a half-pound mound of sliced ham. The pile of ingredients is then covered with both mozzarella and American cheese, capped with a toasted bun, and speared with extra-long toothpicks. When I say tall, I'm guessing this burger stands no less than seven inches high. Get your

mouth ready.

"The best way to eat this thing," local burger expert and friend Jim Ellison told me, "is to press it down and flip it over. The juices have already destroyed the bottom bun." He was right, and flipping worked, but after the first few bites something went wrong and my burger imploded. The combination of ingredients and sheer size beg for your patience. Take your time and enjoy this pile of goodness. It's a sloppy burger.

On a busy Saturday at Thurman, the kitchen will prepare and serve up to 500 of the famed burgers. "We go through over 1,500 pounds of beef a week," Mike Suclescy told me. Good meat too. Mike buys only top-quality 85/15 ground chuck and told me, "We ran out once and went over to the Kroger Supermarket for ground beef. The taste just wasn't the same."

The Blue Cheeseburger (for which the Suclescys go through over eight gallons of blue cheese dressing a week) is also a big seller as is the Macedonian, served on Texas toast with sweet red peppers. A regular cheeseburger has been banished to the bottom of the menu, clearly a lightweight choice at this tavern. My favorite-sounding concoction was the Johnnie Burger (not on the menu). Invented by a chronic tequila-quaffing regular, the Johnnie is a three-quarter-pound burger with bacon and blue cheese that's drizzled with a shot of top-shelf 1800 tequila. No lettuce, tomato, or mayo is offered because, as Johnnie once explained, "If I wanted a salad, I'd order one!"

The very large Thurman Burger

WILSON'S SANDWICH SHOP

600 S. MAIN ST.
FINDLAY, OH 45840
419-422-5051
MON–THU 7AM–10PM
FRI–SAT 7AM–MIDNIGHT
SUN 2PM–10PM

It's hard to miss Wilson's as you roll through downtown Findlay, Ohio. The restaurant is on a busy crossroads in the center of town with the word "WILSON" spelled above the front door in large black letters. Across the street sits the impressive former Marathon Oil world headquarters: a beautiful glass, steel, and concrete monument to the automobile age.

Wilson's has walls of windows on three sides. From inside, the sun-drenched space makes you feel like you're in a huge fishbowl.

Grab a stool at one of the long counters lining the windows, watch small town America unfold, and enjoy a fresh-ground hamburger and a chocolate malt.

The building is the second constructed in the restaurant's long history. The first, built in 1936, was a stunning example of enamel steel road food culture. It was replaced with a greatly expanded Wilson's in the mid 1960s.

"They moved the tiny old restaurant to the back of the lot while they built the new one," Michael Fenbert told me. Michael is Wilson's manager and son of owner Wilbur Fenbert. "It was tiny, and yellow," Michael told me. "It only held 32 people and it was like a subway car. It was that small." Today's newer building seats over 130 hungry patrons in a wide dining room filled with a combination of booths, tables,

and counters. Expect to find a line at lunch and dinner.

Stub Wilson opened Wilson's Sandwich Shop in 1936. A few years earlier, Stub had opened two Kewpee restaurants in nearby Lima, Ohio and decided to open another in Findlay. Finding another Kewpee already in Findlay (the restaurants were independently owned) he chose to name the new restaurant after himself. When Stub Wilson died, he passed all three restaurants onto his managers—the Kewpees in Lima went to Harrison Shutt and Wilson's went to three managers, one of them Wilbur Fenbert. Today, octogenarian Wilbur is still involved with day-to-day operations at the restaurant. "He still does the payroll every week and stamps the checks." Mike told me.

There's no question that the burgers at Wilson's are fresh. Three times a week the restaurant receives a delivery of 600 pounds of beef from a slaughterhouse in Lima. Every morning the staff grinds and patties enough for the day's burgers. "People think we put something special in the burgers," Mike chuckled, "but it's just fresh ground beef." A patty machine attached to the grinder forms them into square patties, a shape that Wendy's popularized in the late 1960 but actually hails from the original Kewpee restaurants.

The basic, three-and-a-half -ounce griddled burger comes with mustard, pickle, and onion. Make it a "Special" and you'll also get lettuce,

tomato, and mayo (for only 20 cents more). Just think; it only takes 20 cents to make your burger special.

Similarities between the Kewpees of Lima and Wilson's still exist, but the most notable is the historically significant vegetable sandwich. Listed on the menu as the "Veggie," this meatless sandwich (a Special without the patty) is a product of the WWII years when meat rationing forced many burger stands to adapt or shut down. White Castle temporarily embraced the grilled cheese sandwich, many others went to fish sandwiches, and Wilson's (and the Kewpees of Lima) introduced the vegetable sandwich.

Wilson's is the type of happy place that you remember from your youth. People come from all over to eat the burgers they ate growing up in Findley. Mark Metcalf, an actor from Findley best know for his role as the R.O.T.C. commander Neidermeyer in the film Animal House, recalls Wilson's burgers fondly. He told me by phone, "My grandfather used to go down to Wilson's and bring back bagfuls of hamburgers." Mike Fenbert is aware of the restaurant's popularity and its place in the memory of anyone who was raised on Wilson's burgers. "We've shipped burgers all over the country." He told me, "In fact, a guy came in today, bought 18 burgers, ate three, and took the rest back to Dayton with him!" That's a long drive. Do you think all 18 made it to Dayton?

FOLGER'S DRIVE-INN

406 EAST MAIN STREET
ADA, OK 74820
580-332-9808
MON–FRI 10:30 AM–7 PM
CLOSED SATURDAY & SUNDAY

If you didn't know what you were looking for, you could drive right by Folger's. The unassuming little 50s prefab on the east end of downtown Ada has only two neon signs in the window—one that reads "Folger's," the other "Open." A short flight of red concrete steps leads directly into hamburger heaven.

Inside you'll find a bright, sunny, clean restaurant filled with the friendliest people. I'm not kidding. Within 15 minutes of my visit to Folger's I knew everyone in the place.

Folger's is definitely a family-run business. In October 1935, G.G. and Christine Folger opened a hamburger concession in the local movie theater just up Main Street. They opened the current location in 1950 and eventually turned over operations and ownership to their two sons, Jim and Jerry Folger. Today, Jim and Jerry spend the better part of their day behind the large flattop griddle and Jerry's wife Wanda works the tiny 12-stool counter. Orders to-go

come in on the pay phone by the front door and Jim makes change at the register between burger flips.

"We have a few other things on the menu but hamburger baskets are 90 percent of our business," a very busy lunchtime Jim told me. I stood and watched him methodically flip and manage 12 quarter-pound burgers on the griddle at the same time. The Folger brothers engage in a sort of silent culinary dance in their open, narrow kitchen—Jim flips burgers, Jerry dresses them, and Wanda delivers. The dance is repeated over and over again for hours at lunch until hundreds of burgers have been dispensed to happy customers.

A regular customer named Mike told me, smiling and rubbing his belly, "You can tell I've had a bunch of them." The burger at Folger's comes with mustard, onion, lettuce, and tomato. Ask for an Educated Burger (not on the menu) and you'll get a burger that replaces the onion with mayo. Make it a "basket" and you'll get to experience the other reason you came to Ada–for their outstanding fries. Every day, Folger's manages to go through over 200 pounds of potatoes for their fresh-cut fries.

"The produce and meat are fresh, every day," Jim told me as he flattened another hand-formed patty on the griddle with a long spatula. Jim uses large Wonder buns that are perfectly toasted on the griddle. The finished product is a wide, flat burger that is bursting with greasy goodness and flavor.

"The grill used to be right behind the counter, and was smaller," Bill Peterson, the district attorney in Ada, told me. If it had not been for Bill and mutual friend Tom Palmore, I may never have found Folger's. Both Bill and Tom grew up in Ada and were classmates of Jerry Folger's. They agreed that Folger's was not to be missed on the hunt for great burgers in America—they were right.

HAMBURGER KING

322 E. MAIN STREET
SHAWNEE, OK 74801
405-878-0488
WWW.HAMBURGERKING.COM
MON–SAT 11 AM–8 PM
CLOSED SUNDAY

Legend has it that there used to be two Hamburger Kings in Oklahoma, one in Shawnee and one in Ada, and the Ada location was lost in a craps game. The owners of both were George "The Hamburger King" Macsas and his brother Joe. The Macsas brothers emigrated from Beirut to Oklahoma and opened the successful hamburger venture in 1927. Today, more than 80 years later, the Hamburger King still stands in Shawnee and proudly remains in the Macsas family.

Dusty downtown Shawnee, Oklahoma, feels proudly American. A restaurant named Hamburger King is almost required in this

setting, along with the Rexall Drug store, the furniture store (with layaway plans), and the enormous grain elevators on the edge of town. The Hamburger King exists in its third location in Shawnee; the other two were only steps away and the previous one burned down in a grease fire in 1965.

Soon after the fire, the Macsas family rebuilt a much larger version of their burger restaurant a block up Main Street. Today's Hamburger King is a large, airy diner awash in pastels. The walls are pink-and-white striped Masonite panels. Two long rows of booths and a small counter in the rear service customers and there are the constant sounds of sizzling burgers and the whir of the milkshake machine. Since 1965, at least, nothing has changed. "We switched to Pepsi once and the people rebelled," Colleen Macsas told me. Colleen is the restaurant's manager and met her husband, owner Michael Macsas, at the Hamburger King in 1975.

The burgers at Hamburger King are fantastic. Fresh 80/20 patties are delivered to the restaurant daily and cooked on a large, well-seasoned flattop griddle. Quarter-pound singles and doubles are offered. Order a double and you'll get double the cheese as well. Waitress Beverly pointed out, "Most men order the double meat burger." I was not about to let my manhood be challenged and naturally ordered a double, a half-pound burger loaded with lettuce, tomato, onions, pickles, and mustard on a toasted white squishy bun. This burger is not small. Order a "basket" and you'll get deep-fried potato wedges or tater tots, not fries.

The method for ordering your burger at Hamburger King is one of the most unique in America. If you sit at the counter, expect normal interaction with a counterperson. Sit at one of the many booths and you'll need to place your order by *phone*. That's right, each table is equipped with a red phone and a single button— your lifeline to the kitchen. On the other end of the red food phone is a switchboard operator who relays your order to the grill cook. The funny thing is, the restaurant is not so large

that you can't just call out your order, but the quirkiness of the phone system can't be beat.

Regulars in a place like Hamburger King are as expected as good burgers. "See those guys over there," Colleen said to me pointing to a group of older men at a booth in trucker hats, overalls, and plaid shirts, "they come in here every day and they bring in their wives on Saturday." Naturally, I had to approach and ask them the obvious, "Do you guys phone in your order?" One guy, smiling, told me, "Naw, they know what we want."

J&W GRILL

501 WEST CHOCTAW AVE.
CHICKASHA, OK 73018
405-224-9912
MON–WED 6 AM–2 PM
THU–SAT 6 AM–9 PM
CLOSED SUNDAY

"Just down from the courthouse in Chickasha there's a little place that makes a *great* burger," was the advice Bill Peterson gave me. Bill is the district attorney for the area, and a man to be trusted with hamburger knowledge. It was Bill who had led me to the amazing burger at Folger's in Ada, so hopes were high. Not only was the burger at J&W first-rate, but unbeknownst to Bill, I had stumbled upon one of the most historically important burger joints of the Oklahoma

onion-fried burger phenomenon.

Onion-fried burgers are to this part of Oklahoma what cheesesteaks are to Philadelphia. The epicenter of the onion-fried burger world is 35 miles north from Chickasha in El Reno. This small town near Oklahoma City boasts three of the best burgers in America, served at counters that are only a few hundred feet from each other. The onion-fried burger craze, started in the 1920s, was created in an effort to stretch meat and feed laid-off railroad workers cheaply. Restaurants serving the tasty local burger popped up all over town and competition was fierce. But in 1957 a man named

Richard Want moved down to Chickasha to open the J&W Grill. He was not alone in his venture though. Johnnie Siler, already successful with Johnnie's Grill in El Reno, helped to finance the new onion-burger counter.

In an effort to avoid confusion when attempting to figure out the rich histories of these Oklahoma burger joints, let's just say that they are all connected in some way. Many owners and employees of the remaining burger stands have all worked at each other's stands, though most worked for and learned from Johnnie Siler. Current owner Darren Cook seems to be the only burger man in this part of

Oklahoma who did not work in El Reno. "I started at J&W when I was 12 years old washing dishes," Darren told me, "I had to use a milk crate to reach the sink." When he was 19 he purchased a share in the restaurant, and in 1981, when he was only 23, bought the restaurant outright. Understandably, J&W is his life and he has been at the burger counter for over 35 years. A restaurant in El Reno made a few offers to buy J&W from Darren, but he told me, "I'm only in my forties, what would I do?"

The "J" in J&W stands for Johnnie, the "W" for Want. "I think it was supposed to be 'S&W' for their last names but the sign people

made a mistake," Maryann Davis, wife of past owner Jim Davis, told me.

J&W has everything you'd want in a burger joint—meat ground fresh on premises, onions hand sliced in back, a basic menu, and fast service. The concept is simple. Order a "hamburger" and it comes with onions. A quarter-pound wad of fresh ground beef is pressed onto a hot flattop griddle and sprinkled with a large amount of sliced (not diced) onions. The stringy onions go limp, and the burger is flipped and pressed again, forcing the onions into the cooking beef. The result is a mess of beef and caramelized onions that create a moist burger with an intense onion flavor. At J&W, if you want a double, two wads of beef are pressed together and twice the amount of onion is dispensed.

The restaurant sits on the busy thoroughfare of Choctaw Avenue near downtown Chickasha. It's a very visible red and white cinder block structure with a large American flag painted on one side. The long, low, wood-grain Formica counter has 16 swivel stools that are never empty at lunchtime. "It gets crowded in here at lunch. The line goes out the door," counterperson Brandi told me. The good news is that the average time at a stool is 10 minutes and, Brandi said with a smile, "We can move them in and out of here in 15."

Brandi knows just about everyone who walks in the door and calls out their order to the grill cook before they even take a seat. Biscuits and gravy are a big seller in the morning, but she told me some customers order burgers first thing. "We'll start making burgers at 6 a.m. if someone wants one."

When I visited J&W there was no music playing, just the sounds of the exhaust fan, regulars talking about just getting off a night shift, and the sizzle of burgers on the griddle. It was refreshing to enjoy my burger without music for once, just the mesmerizing sounds of America.

JOHNNIE'S GRILL

301 SOUTH ROCK ISLAND
EL RENO, OK 73036
405-262-4721
MON–SAT 6 AM–9 PM
SUN 11 AM–8 PM

Steve Galway is a dedicated man. The first time I visited Johnnie's to taste an onion-fried burger, the pride of El Reno, Oklahoma, Steve was not there. "He comes in every day at two," a counterperson told me. But it was 3 PM and he was nowhere to be found. That's because Steve comes in every day at 2 AM to prep the restaurant for the day and is gone by 11 AM. Now that's dedication to burgers. When I finally caught up with him we had a long talk about what it takes to keep a restaurant successful. "Give the best you've got and the people will come back," are the words he lives by. He must be doing something right because every time I've been there the place has been packed—the people most definitely come back.

Don't be fooled by the fairly nondescript exterior of Johnnie's Grill. Located on one of the main drags in downtown El Reno, the simple, brick-faced restaurant is set back from the street by a small parking lot. The only windows are the glass in the front door and a small drive-up on one side of the building. The inside is bright and clean with a sea of tables and booths, a fact you could not imagine from a parking lot assessment. There's also a short counter with seven stools and a clear view of the large flattop griddle that's usually loaded with onion-fried burgers.

This version of Johnnie's is new as of 2005. Prior to that, Johnnie's was a narrow burger joint at the same location with a counter on the left and four booths on the right. Prior to that, the original location was across the street, but, collapsed under the weight of snow in 1986. Today's Johnnie's could easily seat up to a hundred. There's even a "party table" in the new Johnnie's that seats 20.

But for all its newness, Johnnie's remains one of the most historically important purveyors of the El Reno onion-fried burger, important because it seems all that roads lead back there. Sid and Marty Hall from the popular Sid's (only two blocks away) both worked at the counter and Johnnie himself brought the onion-fried burger south when he opened the J&W Grill of Chickasha in 1957.

Order a hamburger at Johnnie's and it comes standard with onions smashed in. In the old days, onion was used in a burger to stretch the day's meat and to add flavor, but Steve told me, "Back then it was a lot of onion and a little meat."

The grillman takes a ball of fresh-ground chuck, slaps it on the grill, covers it with thin-sliced onions, and starts pressing the patty until the onion and red meat are one. The thin patty cooks on the hot griddle until the beef has a crunchy char and the onions are caramelized. As it nears doneness, a white squishy bun is placed on the burger, softened by onion steam. The burger is served with pickles on the side only. All other condiments are self-serve.

Steve started working at Johnnie's for then owner Bruce Otis at age 12, almost 40 years ago. He and Marty (from Sid's Diner) worked at the grill at the same time and have remained friends. "It's not like it used to be," Steve said, referring to the cutthroat competition in the early days between rival burger stands in El Reno. "If I need some sacks (paper bags) I'll call Marty. We try to help each other."

If you really want to experience El Reno at its peak, show up in town on the first Saturday in May. That's when this proud town just west of Oklahoma City celebrates Burger Day. Thirty-thousand people descend on El Reno for live music, a car show, and a public construction of the "World's Largest Onion-Fried Burger." The three main burger outposts, Sid's, Robert's, and Johnnie's, all within a block of each other, operate at beyond capacity. "That day we'll have a six-block line for burgers and 40 employees," Steve told me.

Steve has three sons and plans to bring them up in the business if they are interested, but makes a point to tell them his secret to success. "I tell them if you are going to own one of these you have to come down and talk to the people." But he doesn't plan on ceding control to anyone just yet. "If I'm going to do something the rest of my life, I want it to be here." Like I said, Steve is a dedicated man.

My Favorite Sides

On my seven-year journey to the best hamburgers in the nation, I came across a few regional treats that I just could not pass up. Here's a short list of the not-to-be-missed sides you'll find while burgering your way through America. I didn't include fries because most burgers come with them anyway. These are the sides, drinks, and desserts you would likely miss out on if I didn't alert you to their greatness.

Fried Donut—The Yankee Doodle, New Haven, CT

A treat that has to be tasted to be enjoyed. The grillperson at the Doodle takes a donut, slices it lengthwise, and places both halves face down on the griddle. Don't think for a minute that this local favorite is not enhanced by residual burger grease.

Barbeque Brisket–Meers Store, Meers, OK

When Joe Maranto sends his Texas Longhorns to slaughter for the burgers at his restaurant, he saves the enormous tenderloins for barbeque....

Banana Cream Pie–The Apple Pan, Los Angeles, CA

The king of all banana cream pies. Reserve your slice with one of the countermen *before* you bite into your burger.

Cheese Curds–Dotty Dumplings Dowry, Madison, WI

These are a must-have on a burger tour of Madison. Skip the fries and get some curds, a treat whose distant cousin is the overprocessed mozzarella stick. You'll never look at hot cheese the same way again.

Cherry Smash–Northgate Soda Shop, Greenville, SC

Made from homemade cherry syrup, this is the perfect accompaniment to their pimiento cheeseburger.

Onion Rings–Crown Burger, Salt Lake City, UT

Made by hand in a private, windowless basement room. Amazing dipped in Utah's favorite fry sauce.

Fried Pies–Phillip's Grocery, Holly Springs, MS

Basically a skillet-fried, fruit-stuffed popover. Owner Larry Davis is tired of making these tasty Southern treats—so get them soon before he gives up.

Peanut Butter Chocolate Shake–Sid's, El Reno, OK

After inhaling two of Marty Hall's beautiful onion-fried burgers, this was the last thing I needed. I managed to finish it though, knowing that it would be a while before I'd taste something this great again.

Deep-Fried Vegetables–Krazy Jim's Blimpy Burger, Ann Arbor, MI

My vegetarian wife, Casey, joined me on the burger trail a few times, only to find that food options for her were slim. And then she discovered Blimpy's deep-fried goodies like mushrooms, cauliflower, and broccoli. Wow.

Raspberry Lime Rickey–Mr. Bartley's Burger Cottage, Cambridge, MA

A mix of seltzer, sugar, raspberry, and lime syrup. Refreshing, crisp, and cool, it's the perfect accompaniment to Bartley's large, flavor-packed burgers.

Onion Rings–Bobo's, Topeka, KS

Lightly greasy oniony goodness. In a word—sublime.

THE MEERS STORE & RESTAURANT

HIGHWAY 115
MEERS, OK 73501
580-429-8051
WWW.MEERSSTORE.COM
MON, WED, THURS, SUN 10:30 AM–8 PM
FRI–SAT 10:30AM–8:30PM
CLOSED TUESDAY

The Meers Store is way out in the country. About two hours from Oklahoma City and four from Dallas, the Meersburger had better be good because it's the only reason you got in the car this morning. The burgers are better than good, they are excellent, and the drive is beautiful. Joe Maranto, the latest owner of the 95-year-old burger mecca, put it best when he told me, "We're out in the middle of nowhere, but the good thing is we're the only thing in nowhere." Meers is not as desolate as it sounds. The restaurant is a short drive from the entrance to the Wichita Mountain Wildlife Preserve and the next town over is Medicine Park, former hideout of Bonnie and Clyde and

turn-of-the-century resort for Oklahomans.

The restaurant is made up of a bunch of cobbled-together old buildings and newer ones, the older left behind when Meers did not produce the copious amounts of gold it promised. Remnants of the tiny post office have been incorporated into the newer buildings, all of them strung together like a pile of shoeboxes. Joe is responsible for the larger additions. The expansion is a result of the popularity of his Meersburger and the need to accommodate the 500 plus daily burger seekers, bike tours, and other backcountry tourists.

It's no secret what goes into a Meersburger. Joe proudly displays, inside and out, the key ingredient to his success—the lean Texas longhorn cattle. What's better, Joe raises the longhorns himself (with the help of his son Peterhood) at a ranch nearby, and they are free of antibiotics and hormones. During the summer, Peterhood and Joe send at least 2,500 pounds of longhorn to slaughter every six days. "We sell A LOT of Meersburgers. They wait in line for the burgers," one of the grill cooks told me. On a busy day, Joe can sell over 400 burgers. That's quite a feat, considering the burger is a half pound of lean Texas longhorn beef served on a specially made seven-inch bun. Joe claims, and is correct, that longhorn beef is lower in cholesterol than chicken or turkey, especially since he is raising them the old-fashioned way—on grass, not grain.

Recently, Joe decided that the Meersburger

was not large enough to feed his hungry patrons. The Seismic Burger was created to fill this need. The Seismic is a gut-busting one pound of ground longhorn beef on the same seven-inch bun, topped with cheese, onions, lettuce, tomato, sweet relish, pickles, jalapeño slices, and bacon. Whoa. I finished one without trouble, just some sweat and a full belly. The grease was in the bacon, not the burger.

The store's proximity to the Wichita Mountains Wildlife Preserve, where the Texas longhorn was saved from extinction in the 1920s, is a little odd. But the cattle in the preserve and on Joe's ranch have quite the life. Joe said it best when he told me once "These are happy cows. Happy cows taste better."

ROBERT'S GRILL
300 SOUTH BICKFORD
EL RENO, OK 73036
405-262-1262
MON–SAT 6 AM–9 PM
CLOSED SUNDAY

Step into Robert's and step back in time. Much like the Texas Tavern in Roanoke, Virginia, or the Cozy Inn of Salina, Kansas, very little has changed at Robert's Grill in the last 80 years. Maybe the stools and the red Formica counter are new, or the front door was moved about a half century ago, but Robert's is a perfect example of what all hamburger stands looked, felt, and smelled like in the 1920s. Robert's is, historically speaking, one of America's most important treasures.

Don't expect warm hellos, pictures on the walls, or a large menu. Robert's is a tiny, clean, utilitarian place—a counter with 14 stools facing a flattop griddle surrounded by a wall of stainless steel. It's the kind of counter where you don't linger long, and the burgers come fast and go down even faster. The exterior is sparse as well. The building is a bright-white box with small windows and red trim—the visual effect may be off-putting to the untrained gourmand but believe me, you have come to the right place.

Robert's menu is limited to Coneys (chili dogs), grilled cheese, fries, tater tots, and the burger that made El Reno famous, the onion-fried burger.

Located in the burger belt of El Reno, Robert's is only a few hundred feet from Johnnie's and Sid's, and across the street from the spot where the onion-fried burger was born. "The Hamburger Inn was right where that bank is now," owner of almost two decades, Edward Graham, told me. It was at the eight-stool Hamburger Inn that a man named Ross Davis tried to stretch his burger meat by pressing in sliced onions, appealing to cash-strapped, out-of-work railroad men. The Hamburger Inn was

situated on old Route 66, an outpost at the onset of the auto age, so you can imagine the brisk business. Imitators were born and a legendary burger was embraced.

The hamburger at Robert's, as it is all over town, is an onion burger. Edward smashes a ball of fresh-ground chuck on the hot griddle with a sawed-off mason's trowel, and a pile of shredded onions is placed on top. The onions are pressed hard into the patty. The contents fuse, creating a beautiful, caramelized, onion-beef mess. Edward places a white squishy bun on the patty as it finishes so that the bun soaks up the onion steam. The result is a flat, odd-looking burger that tastes incredible.

When Robert's opened in 1926 it was called Bob's White Rock. The front door was on the Route 66 side only steps from a trolley stop. Edward told me, "People could get off the trolley here, get burgers at the window, and jump back on again. The grill used to be in the front window." Edward started working at Robert's in 1979 and purchased the counter in 1989.

After 20 years of ownership Robert has decided he needs to expand. "I lose a lot of the family traffic here by not having booths," he told me. "Only a block away, Johnnie's Grill can seat almost a hundred."

For locals, there is an abundance of great onion-fried burger options in El Reno. When I asked a regular named Troy at the counter why he chose to patronize Robert's, he seemed to fall back on brand loyalty. "I've been coming here

for 50 years. I remember when they were eight for a dollar." Now that's a good customer.

SID'S DINER

300 SOUTH CHOCTAW
EL RENO, OK 73036
405-262-7757
MON–SAT 7 AM–8:30 PM
CLOSED SUNDAY

"Do you know what the definition of a diner is?" Marty Hall, part owner of this El Reno burger destination asked me. "It's a place where the grill is in view and I can turn around and talk to the people." And he does, making Sid's one of the friendliest places I have ever set foot in. But it doesn't stop there—Sid's also makes one of the best onion-fried burgers anywhere.

Sid's is named after Marty's father, who passed away just before the restaurant opened in 1989. Marty had planned to work side by side with Sid, a retired highway employee. When he died, Sid's brother Bob asked if he could take his spot. This sounds like a customary role for a family member to play, except that Bob left a six-figure job at Exxon in Houston to flip burgers.

El Reno, Oklahoma, is famous for one thing—onion-fried burgers. Invented just across the street from Sid's at the long-gone Hamburger Inn.

Sid's is not alone in El Reno. At one point there were over nine onion fried burger joints within five blocks of downtown. Today, Sid's, Johnnie's, and Robert's, the three remaining diners, are just a few hundred feet from one another.

If you choose a seat at the counter you'll have a great view of the construction of an onion-fried burger. Sid or Bob grab a ball of fresh-ground chuck from a beautiful pyramid of beef balls at the side of the griddle. Gobs of thinly sliced onions are piled onto the ball of beef on the large flattop griddle. The ball is pressed thin and the onions are worked into the soft meat. The burger is flipped after a few minutes, once the carmelized onions have fused to the griddle-charred beef. Prepare your mouth for a taste explosion.

Their decoupage countertop features the history of El Reno. "I wanted people . . . to know something about my town," Marty told me.

The burger is served on a white squishy bun with the meat and gnarled onions hanging out of it. Nothing is served with a regular burger except pickles (on the side) but you may find condiments unnecessary. If you require lettuce and tomato, ask for a Deluxe. Make yours a King Size and the meat and onions are doubled. The King is the most popular burger and makes for a perfect meal, especially if enjoyed with Sid's excellent hand-cut, homemade fries. "I learned how to make fries down at J&W," Marty told me, referring to another not-to-be-missed onion-fried burger further south in Chickasha.

One of the more unique features of Sid's is their impressive decoupage countertop, sealed in poured resin. "The history of El Reno starts on that end," Marty told me, pointing to the far left side of the counter. The patchwork of vintage El Reno photography includes everything from early shots of downtown to color photos of local baseball teams. "I wanted people who came in who weren't from here to know something about my town."

Even though Sid's is technically a newcomer to the onion-fried burger phenomenon, Marty has been involved just about his entire life. "I used to work at Johnnie's and my father helped out there as well." Sid's, he told me, was modeled after the old Johnnie's.

Bob and Marty take turns flipping and pressing a lot of onions into their burgers. When the pyramid of beef balls next to the griddle gets low, a new, perfect pyramid miraculously appears. Every once in a while Marty will turn and dispense life lessons with a smile to anyone at the counter. "Be good to your daddy," he says to some teenaged girls picking at their fries, "I should know. I have three daughters."

Bob and Marty Hall—truly dedicated burger men.

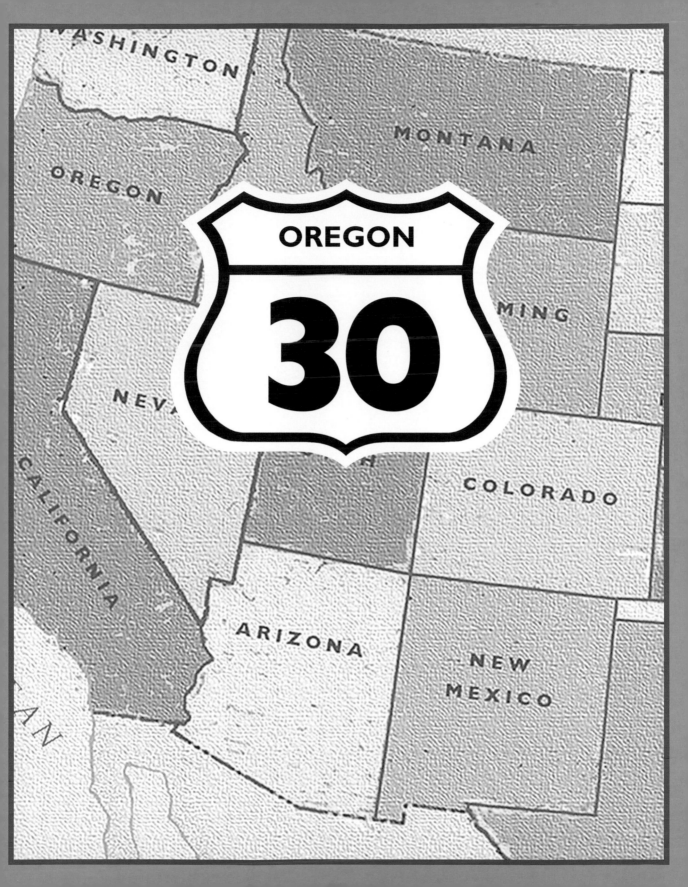

GIANT DRIVE-IN

15840 BOONES FERRY ROAD
LAKE OSWEGO, OR 97035
503-636-0255
SUN–THU 10 AM–9 PM
FRI & SAT 10 AM–10 PM

Hooray for the mom-and-pop hamburger stand. Giant Drive-In is quite literally a mom-and-pop—owned and operated by a husband and wife team that is dedicated to bringing quality comfort food to the neighborhood and have done so for almost 30 years.

Bill Kreger and his wife, Gail, bought Giant in 1981 after Bill had burned out on a mechanical engineering career. "We had planned to fix it up and flip it, but here we are!" Bill told me enthusiastically. The odd looking A-frame ski chalet structure was originally part of a failed '60s chain called Mr. Swiss. In 1970 it became Giant and was open for 10 years until a Burger King opened across the street. "The previous owner just gave up, locked the doors, and walked away," Bill told me. But today, the Burger King is gone. When I asked Bill what happened, he just smiled and shrugged. I gathered there's only room for one burger stand in this stretch of suburban Portland.

Starting the business was not easy for the Kregers. "You have to keep your hand in it or you are not going to have it," Bill explained. "We spent seventeen hours a day seven days a week for the first seven years to get this place up and running." The time invested shows—the burgers are excellent.

The Burger King across the street is gone. When I asked Bill what happened, he just smiled and shrugged.

The list of hamburger concoctions is vast. You can order a standard quarter-pound burger or choose from an eclectic selection of burgers like the Teriyaki, the Hawaiian, or an Avocado Burger. But the burger that gets its own neon sign is the enormous "Filler." The Filler is almost too big to put in your mouth, but I managed. Its contents are similar to nearby Stanich's signature burger, but the Filler contains two quarter-pound patties instead of one. The burger also contains a slice of ham, cheese, a fried egg, bacon, lettuce, onion, pickles, tomato, and mayo. All this piled neatly on a locally baked seeded sourdough roll. I was speechless (and dazed) for hours after I consumed this thing. Amazingly, Gail told me it was her burger of choice, but said, "Believe it or not, I actually put an extra patty on it."

The fresh hamburger patties are delivered daily and come from local grass-fed Angus sirloin. The Kregers request a 90 percent lean grind. "Any less fat and the burger breaks up on the griddle. Any more and the burger shrinks to nothing." The cheese is also local Tillamook, purchased in 40-pound blocks and sliced on premises. Bill explained, "We try to only use local, fresh ingredients," and added, "In the summertime Oregon tomatoes can get to be this big," making a shape with his hands the size of an invisible grapefruit.

The interior of the Giant is a classic retro burger drive-in. Bright, clean, and inviting, the Giant has floor-to-ceiling windows on three sides, booths for seating, and a yellow-and-brown checkered linoleum floor. Hanging over the cash register is a photo of a half dozen UPS trucks lined up in the Giant parking lot. "Once a week the local UPS guys converge on Giant," Bill explained. "Sometimes there are over 15 trucks out there."

I watched the Kregers greet familiar faces, pleasantly take orders, and flip burgers. They make the business of selling hamburgers look easy. But as I left, Gail gave me some sage advice, "Keep your sanity and stay out of the restaurant business!"

HELVETIA TAVERN

10275 NW HELVETIA ROAD
HILLSBORO, OR 97124
503-647-5286
SUN–THURS 11 AM–10 PM
FRI & SAT 11 AM–11 PM

Nestled in the rolling farm country of western Oregon, a short distance from Portland but a world away, sits a restaurant and bar that amazingly turns out over a thousand burgers on a busy Saturday. The restaurant is the comfortable Helvetia Tavern (pronounced Hel-VAY-sha) and is way out in the country. Regardless of how far it is from anything, burger lovers gladly make the trek to the Helvetia for their signature Jumbo Burger and great selection of microbrews on tap.

"It's a pretty simple menu and nothing has changed since we opened," part owner Mike Lampros told me. "We did add salads, though, two years ago." There are a few sandwiches on the menu and a grilled cheese, but I looked around and saw mostly burgers being consumed. A lot of them too—the grill stayed full the entire time I was at Helvetia. They easily served over 200 burgers in the hour that I sat at the counter.

The Jumbo is just that—two thin quarter-pound patties of fresh ground beef are cooked on a large flattop griddle and served on a toasted six-inch bun with bacon, cheese, lettuce, onion, tomato, and the ubiquitous and tasty Pacific Northwest condiment, "Goop" (see sidebar pg. 287). The bun is larger than the patties, which are arranged slightly overlapping so the burger is presented wider, not taller. "That's the way we've always done it," Mike explained. "The single patty is served on a smaller bun." As a finishing touch, the Jumbo is stabbed in the center and delivered with a plastic knife, as Mike explained, "to keep the contents from sliding around." The burgers are moist and exploding with flavor, thanks to the mustardy-mayo Goop holding the large burger together. Wash your burger down with the tasty and hard-to-find RC Cola, on tap at Helvetia.

The building that houses the Helvetia first opened in 1914 as a general store. In 1946 a bar was added to one side and burgers were served. Mike's father, Nick Lampros, bought the tavern in 1978 and changed nothing until the late 1990s when he and his son turned the old general store into a dining room. "Up until then it was a 21- and-over bar crowd," Mike told me, taking a break from the grill. "The dining room allowed us to start attracting families." And they do, and those families have the benefit of dining at Helvetia with a picture-perfect view of the sheep grazing across the street. The dining room tables are actually enormous foot-thick blocks of timber with a high-gloss finish. Mike pointed out, "They came from a tree that fell in a neighbor's yard."

The tavern side of Helvetia is a comfortably dark, broken-in bar with a 1950 Brunswick pool table that still costs only a quarter to play. A strange collection of baseball caps hangs from the ceiling, some signed by pro athletes. Mike explained that the thousand of caps were up there to hide the ugly ceiling. "We take them down twice a year to clean them."

If there was any doubt as to how accommodating this place was to regulars, just take a counter seat at the last stool in the back of the restaurant. That's Cliff's seat. Then look over the food prep area directly in front of you. Hanging on an air duct is a mirror positioned perfectly to read the TV *behind* you in reverse. "He comes in here at 3:00 everyday, like clockwork," the grillman told me. Then Mike explained, "We blocked his view of the TV across the room with a new sign. This was his solution."

★ ★ ★ ★ ★

STANICH'S TAVERN

4915 NE FREMONT STREET
PORTLAND, OR 97213
503-281-2322
MON–THURS 11 AM–10 PM
FRI & SAT 11 AM–11 PM

Once upon a time in America, the "sports bar" was merely a neighborhood bar where you could guarantee that the game you wanted to watch would be on the TV hanging in the corner over the bottles of booze.

If there were two games on at the same time, the TV at the other end of the bar would be tuned in. At some point, the sports bar concept went corporate and today it is not uncommon to find many with stadium seating and games on up to 30 screens, some of them full-sized movie screens. The sports bar became a soulless, unfamiliar place where the only reason to go was to ensure you'd see your game. Stanich's is a real sports bar, one that is oozing soul. One where there are only two TVs at the bar, and the day I was there, one was broken. It's an unquestionably comfortable, welcoming place that also happens to make one of the tastiest burgers I've ever eaten.

"Sometimes the wait for a burger can be an hour, but we have a great jukebox," Debbie Stanich told me as she sang along to Sonny and Cher. Debbie manages Stanich's and is married to Steve Stanich, the owner and son of the couple who opened the tavern in 1949. Serbian immigrants Gladys and George Stanich opened this Portland tavern and put a burger on the menu. "Gladys cooked and George was out back playing pinochle," Debbie says. It was Gladys who invented what the menu still today bills as the "World's Greatest Hamburger," the sloppy two-fister Special.

The Special is large. Gladys must have had the very hungry in mind when she dreamed up this burger. Grill master Josiah swiftly assembles the impressively diverse ingredients that go onto the Special, which include a quarter-pound patty of fresh chuck, an egg, bacon, ham slice, cheese, lettuce, red onion, and tomato. All of this is piled high on a large five-inch toasted bun with the obligatory mustard, mayo, and "burger relish" that seems to adorn all burgers in the Northwest. "There's no 'special sauce' here at Stanich's, just mayo, mustard, and relish," Debbie explained.

There's a two-napkin limit per burger, so use them wisely. The moment the juices, hot cheese, and mayo start running down your arms (and they will) resist the urge to reach for a napkin. "We don't like to hand out napkins," Debbie told me, "but if you really need one, OK."

When you first walk into Stanich's you'll be shocked by the décor. Every inch of the walls at this decades-old tavern is covered in those felt triangular pennants and pretty much nothing else. There could be a thousand, and all were donated by regulars. The bar is one of the deep-est I've ever seen, lined with cozy leather swivel stools that take practice getting into. There is no way to look cool getting into one of these seats, Debbie pointed out laughing, "It's kind of a 'slide'n twirl' move," and as she demonstrated, she looked like she was dancing with an invisible partner.

Steve Stanich, an ex-pro football player for the 49ers, believes in giving back. Among the sea of pennants that lines the walls of his tavern are more than a few accolades of his philanthropic efforts. On the fiftieth anniversary of Stanich's, Steve brought the price of his family's signature burger back to its original 25 cents. The proceeds built a gymnasium for a local school. He also sponsors numerous local teams and every year gives out scholarships to college-bound kids.

"It's a bar, but people don't come in here to drink. They come in here to eat," Debbie pointed out. Or maybe for a burger and a scholarship? They both sound good to me.

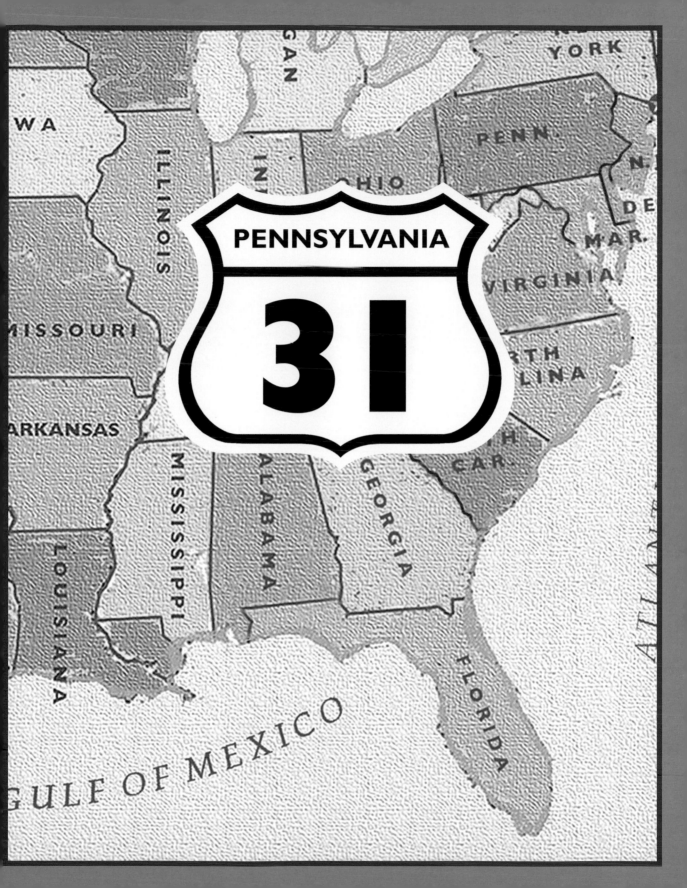

CHARLIE'S HAMBURGERS

ACADEMY AVE. AT KEDRON
(ROUTE 420)
FOLSOM, PA 19033
610-461-4228
MON, WED, THU, FRI, SAT
11 AM–10 PM
SUN 1–9PM
CLOSED TUESDAY

If you prefer your burgers with ketchup, Charlie's is the place to go. A "loaded" burger at this decade-old hamburger spot comes with onions, ketchup, pickles, sweet relish, and cheese, creating a sweet burger experience that is hard to find among the more staid and traditional burger stands of America. "Pretty much everyone orders them that way," a teenaged prep girl told me. She wasn't kidding—just about every person who walked in during the hour I spent at Charlie's ordered burgers with ketchup. Of course the burgers can also be ordered with mustard and tomato, but not lettuce.

Charlie's is a real place with real food. A menu of hamburgers, hot dogs, and milkshakes keeps things simple. Some may see a greasy spoon. Others see a haven for grease lovers. You get the point—this is not health food. Fortunately, the burgers are made from fresh-ground chuck (pattied in the kitchen with a small patty former) and the shakes are made with great ice cream and real milk. In fact, people frequent Charlie's more for its shakes then for its burgers. The milk for the shakes still comes out of a large vintage aluminum milk dispenser.

The crowd is a mix of airport employees from nearby Philadelphia International, kids from the local schools, and a blend of salty regulars. When I visited, the better part of a girls volleyball team had landed in search of nourishment.

Charlie's location is relatively new, though the business dates back to 1935. Charlie Convery operated the restaurant nearby at an intersection of the Baltimore Pike until 1984, when an expansion of the road spelled the end of Charlie's. Through a confusing set of purchases and sales, the restaurant relocated a mile away to a former fruit stand next to a defunct miniature golf course (the concrete skeleton of the weeded-over course is still visible behind the restaurant).

Colorful character and part-time manger of 11 years Mike Goodwin explained, "After they moved, changed owners, and reopened, they still went back to Charlie's original butcher." The small burgers are cooked on a very seasoned flattop griddle, smashed thin, and cooked in the bubbling grease of previous burgers. They are served on a toasted white squishy bun. "No lettuce, no bacon, no tofu, no pineapple," Mike jokes, emphasizing the simplicity of the burgers at Charlie's.

One important note: Charlie's is closed on Tuesdays. In a vestige of wartime America, the restaurant still observes "meatless Tuesdays," a day that most burger joints closed during World War II for meat rationing. "Are you familiar with Wimpy?" Mike asked me. "I'll pay you TUESDAY for a hamburger today?" A light-bulb went off in my head—Wimpy was a lot smarter than I thought.

TESSARO'S

4601 LIBERTY AVENUE
PITTSBURGH, PA 15224
412-682-6809
MON–SAT 11 AM–MIDNIGHT
CLOSED SUNDAY

For years, the incredible ground beef that Tessaro's used for its burgers came from a butcher shop directly across the street called House of Meats. When the shop closed one day, Kelly Harrington, part owner of this Pittsburgh burger destination, did what seemed the most sensible—he hired the butcher.

Dominic Piccola, a retired Pittsburgh fire-man, is now employed by Tessaro's as their in-house butcher. He has become their link to hamburger perfection. Six days a week, at 7 a.m., Dominic grinds hundreds of pounds of chuck shoulder for the day's burgers. "Since I'm the only one grinding, the consistency is always the same," Dominic told me through his classic fireman's bushy handlebar moustache.

I was interested in Tessaro's because of its stellar reputation among hamburger cognoscen-ti, but it was the method of cooking the burgers that put me on an airplane to Pittsburgh. I had to see for myself the fabled hardwood grill that many had talked about. Unique to the burger world, the hamburgers at Tessaro's are grilled over a fire made from west Pennsylvania hard-woods, not the charcoal or the blue propane flames that seem standard for indoor flame grilling. Tessaro's uses a mixture of yellow maple, red oak, and walnut, all indigenous to the area. "We stay away from hickory because it's too strong," Kelly pointed out, "and no fruit trees because they are loaded with pesticides." Hardwoods produce a flame that is far hotter than gas or charcoal. Grillman of 20 years Courtney McFarlane told me, "The fire can get up to 600 degrees in there."

Courtney invited me into the grill area, a section of the restaurant adjacent to the bar that was once the dance floor and is now a small room with a big picture window. I stood about three feet from the grill and the heat was so intense it felt like my eyebrows were burning right off my face. Every few minutes, Courtney tossed a small cup of water onto the flames and told me, "That's just to slow the heat down a bit."

The burgers at Tessaro's are unmeasured but somewhere near a half pound. Courtney grabs a wad of Dominic's fresh ground beef and tells me, "After a while it's easy to guess the size." He then swiftly forms the ball into a patty, slaps the beef onto a stainless steel surface

next to the grill, and does this move where he spins the patty to form an edge. The entire process takes seconds. He is a master burger maker and the finished product strangely resembles a large, machined-pressed patty.

The burgers are served with many cheese options and just about any condiment you can think of from barbecue sauce to three types of mustard. To be honest, this burger is so amazing it'd be foolish to cover it with anything. Served on a soft, Portuguese-type roll from a bakery down the street, the hefty burger is a sight to behold. It's perfectly charred on the outside and juicy and moist on the inside. And thanks to the

hardwood, the burger has a taste like no other—a woodsy, barbeque essence that manages not to overpower the flavor of the high-quality beef.

In 1984, Kelly, his sister Ena, and their mother Tee bought the bar and restaurant from Richard Tessaro. It was Richard who began the tradition of flame grilling burgers that the Harringtons perfected. He started by grilling on the street in front of the bar on a makeshift barbeque made from halved 55-gallon drums. He eventually moved the operation to the backyard, once starting a fire that burned part of the building and finally moved the grill indoors.

The restaurant is dark and cozy with a long

vintage bar running along one side. The walls are wood paneled and the aroma of the burning hardwoods is arresting. The building has been a bar for 75 years, but previously housed a dry goods store and a nickelodeon as far back as the turn of the century.

Kelly's sister Ena told me that if they run out of ground beef on a busy night, they'll call Dominic the butcher back in to grind some more. I asked her why the burgers were so good and she told me bluntly, "Not everybody can afford a butcher."

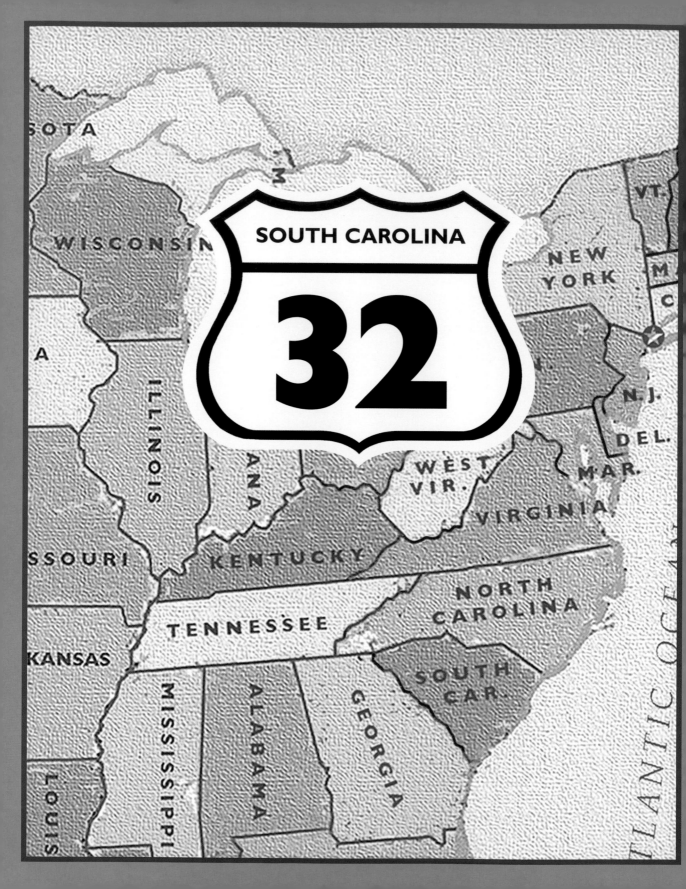

NORTHGATE SODA SHOP

918 NORTH MAIN STREET
GREENVILLE, SC 29609
864-235-6770
WWW.NORTHGATESODASHOP.COM
MON–FRI 9 AM–8 PM
SAT 9 AM–3 PM
CLOSED SUNDAYS

Just up the hill on Main Street in Greenville, SC, where the high-rises give way to trees and homes, I discovered an excellent spot to enjoy a Southern favorite—the Pimiento Cheeseburger.

Upon arriving I met the new owner, Catherine Christophillis. Longtime owner of 41 years Jim DeYoung was looking to retire, and had sold the shop to a lawyer with an office just 20 feet away. I was sitting at the round table Catherine had purchased at Jim's request (for daily visits with his friends) when Jim told me, "I wanted to sell the shop to someone who would keep everything almost the same." That sounds like a simple request, except that just about every square inch of the Northgate is covered in four decades of collectibles. It resembles an antique shop that happens to have a soda fountain, with signed 8 x 10s, extensive bottle, can, and cigar box collections, beer and soda

neon, a vintage Ex-Lax sign, and an impressive church fan collection. This is the real deal—no fake Applebee's crap here. When Catherine bought the shop, she bought the stuff too. "Where was I going to put it?" Jim said of his antiques. "It belongs here anyway."

The menu at the Northgate is classic soda shop diner fare—tuna, peanut butter and jelly, hot dogs, grilled cheese, and egg sandwiches, but the big seller is their fantastic Pimiento Cheeseburger.

"You'll either love it or hate it," waitress Brenda warned me before I bit into my burger. I have to admit I had never had one, even though my mother is from South Carolina. Fortunately, I fall into the "love it" category.

The pimiento cheese for the Northgate's sandwiches and burgers is a tangy mix of mayo, cheddar, and diced pimientos. "We make it right here, fresh every day," veteran waitress Maudie told me of the over 40-year-old recipe. Both Maudie and Brenda were inherited in the sale of the shop as well. The beef is also fresh, picked up daily from a butcher just up Main Street (this fact is also proudly announced on the menu, complete with the butcher's name and address).

The burger starts as fresh ground beef that is pressed in a vintage burger press. The press produces a three and one-half ounce patty that is cooked on a flattop griddle. The burger comes to you on a toasted bun with tomato, lettuce, and a large dollop of pimento cheese. I also had a cherry smash, a drink made from cherry syrup and soda water, dispensed from the Northgate's venerable soda fountain. A few years ago, Jim's cherry syrup supplier stopped making the syrup, so he started making it himself. "I found some extract so we started making it in-house."

Catherine couldn't be a more perfect fit as owner of this South Carolina time warp. She is active in community theater (she had just starred as the witch in *The Wizard of Oz*), she served on the city council, and her husband grew up just down the street. "He has been coming here forever. Now my kids do too."

HAMBURGER INN

111 1/2 EAST 10TH STREET
SIOUX FALLS, SD 57104
605-332-5412
MON–SAT 8 AM–3:30 PM
CLOSED SUNDAY

On a corner in the heart of downtown Sioux Falls (which is in the midst of a revitalization) sits the tiny Hamburger Inn. It is a classic '30s burger joint specimen—11 stools, a single counter, minimal menu, and a griddle in the front window. When I visited, the small TV on the wall was tuned to *The Price Is Right* and the first customer of the day was a blind regular who found his stool without help. This is my kind of place.

The Sioux Falls favorite "eggburger" is served here—a fried egg is placed on top of a finished burger, the yoke popped and cooked through thanks to health department rules. "Can't decide on breakfast or lunch? Have an eggburger!" Maria Poulsen, the current owner, exclaimed when I asked about the origins of the strange pairing of chicken and cow. If you've never had one, fear not—the combination works well. It's basically steak and eggs on a bun.

Many past patrons have fond memories of

Mel Nelson, the longtime proprietor of the Hamburger Inn. Sadly, Mel is no longer pressing balls of ground beef into a puddle of grease, cooking burgers the "old-fashioned way." But the good news is that three months before he died, local chef Maria offered to buy the place. This is always great for the burger world, especially when the plan is to keep a similar menu and scrape up some of the caked-on grease. Maria said, "It was a mess when I took over. Grease up to here!" and she made a gesture about two feet from the floor.

The burgers are no longer cooked in a tray of grease like Mel did for 32 years and previous owners did for close to 75 years. Now, one-third pound balls of fresh ground beef hit the hot griddle, are flattened with a spatula, and cooked until the fresh meat has an exterior crunch.

The small TV was tuned to The Price is Right and the first customer of the day was a blind regular who found his stool without help. I knew this was my kind of place.

The menu at Hamburger Inn is sparse but focused. Burgers are the star attraction here and can be ordered with cheese, bacon, or the afore-mentioned fried egg. Standards such as onion rings and fries are also on the menu, as is a curiosity called "cheeseballs." This Midwestern treat is also known as the deep-fried cheese curd, one of my all-time favorite side dishes.

Look for Ron, the full-time grillman at the Hamburger Inn. He works the griddle six days a week and still finds time to moonlight as an ice sculptor. He told me, "I carve ice sculpture for banquets and weddings every few weeks."

For those old-timers who may miss Mel's tasty sliders, there is no need to fret about the state of burgers here. The Hamburger Inn is still turning out great burgers and your clothes will still smell of grease all day. Maria also refurbished the decades-old neon-and-glass sign that hangs over the front door, using all of the original lettering. "It was falling apart but I didn't want to change much," she told me. In keeping with the integrity of the old place, the Hamburger Inn still looks like a shoebox with a door, a burger bunker whose only window faces 10th Street.

Maria understands good food, service, and simplicity. She runs a catering business in the Sioux Falls area and this is the second restaurant she currently owns. "I'm looking for an old stainless steel diner to buy and fix up," she said as I was leaving. "Got any ideas?"

NICK'S HAMBURGER SHOP

427 MAIN AVENUE
BROOKINGS, SD 57006
605-692-4324
WWW.NICKSHAMBURGERS.COM
MON–FRI 11 AM–7 PM
SAT 11 AM–4 PM
CLOSED SUNDAY

Dick Fergen is my kind of guy. He left a job in farm management in Texas to return to his home town of Brookings, SD. Upon his arrival, he inquired about the landmark burger joint, Nick's, and soon after purchased it from the notorious and sometimes volatile third owner, Duane Larson. In his nearly three decades at the grill, Duane was known to close early because he ran out of buns, and refused to sell the business to just anyone, saying that he'd burn the place down before he sold it to the wrong person. Duane was also involved in a spat between the Coca-Cola Company and Nick's that led to a dramatic photo in *Time* magazine of Duane pouring Coke into the street.

The good news is that, Dick Fergen is now

in charge and he will never run out of buns or Coke. I watched Dick at the grill for one and a half hours, waiting patiently to speak to him. He was in a zone, pressing small balls of ground round into a puddle of bubbling grease, transferring them to buns, and serving them at a rate of about 700 per hour. When I finally got his attention, he was taking a break and eating, not surprisingly, a burger. "I eat mine dry," he said. This meant he had squeezed some of the grease out, "Makes it a little bit healthier." Amazingly, Dick creates his own "solution" for the deep-frying of his burgers. This is not just any old grease. He starts with solids and adds seasoning according to a recipe that has been handed down for decades.

Dick doesn't really look like your typical hamburger stand owner. He is a 60-something, impossibly fit, tanned, and a self-described Harley nut. What brought him to and keeps him at Nick's is pure nostalgia. Nick's was started by Harold and Gladys Nickalson in 1929 and was later passed on to their son Harold Jr. in 1947. When Duane Larson bought Nick's in 1972, much to the dismay of the old timers, he

added the cheeseburger to the menu. The small burgers come with a secret relish whose recipe goes back to the beginning. It's a mustard based pickle-and-onion relish that has "other seasonings," waitress Laurie told me.

Orders are not taken, they are yelled. "We just holler at Dick what we need," Laurie said. First, you tell the counterperson what you want. When your burgers are ready you tell them what you want *on* them. They arrive at your counter spot on a square of waxed paper and can be consumed at a rate of roughly one every 20 seconds, which is good, because you will need to make room for the 30 people waiting for your stool.

A man named Stewart sitting to my left told me that he had been coming back to Nick's every time he visited his alma mater, South Dakota State University. "I've been coming ever since I graduated in '52." Old-timers refer to their visits as getting their "Nick's fix."

"If you are not from South Dakota, then you wouldn't understand." Dick pondered seriously while gazing at the ceiling. "There's something about these people. I wouldn't trade them for anyone in the world."

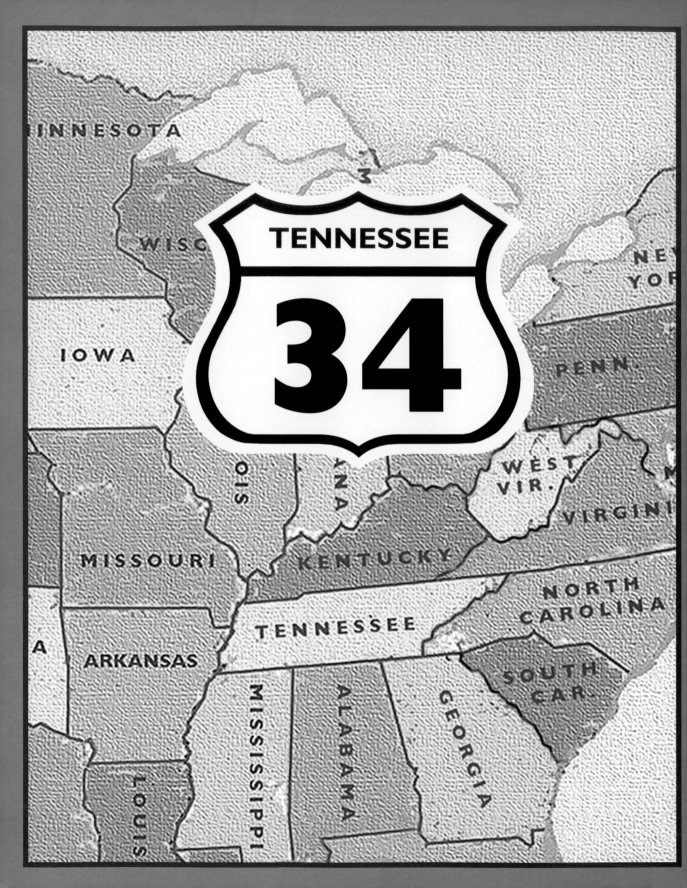

BROWN'S DINER

2102 BLAIR BOULEVARD
NASHVILLE, TN 37212
615-269-5509
MON–SAT 10:45AM–11 PM
SUN 11AM–10PM

It may not look like much, but Brown's may be one of the most historically significant burger joints in this book. The fact that it survives is a miracle, and a testament to the power of hamburger culture in this country. It has lived through more than one fire and withstood many facelifts.

To the untrained eye, Brown's appears to be a dump—an unimpressive double-wide with a drab grey/beige exterior. But to American cultural historians it is a treasure. There was a time in this country when hamburgers were not king. They were considered dirty food for wage earners, and were served in establishments much like Brown's. The only difference is that places like this, which once dotted the America landscape in the thousands, and were mostly found in close proximity to factories and urban areas, are just about gone.

What makes Brown's Diner special is that its core is made up of two retired trolley cars, mule-drawn cars that were left at the end of the line in the early 1920s as the automobile became ubiquitous in city life. The trolleys are

Photo courtesy of Brown's diner

Charlie Brown demonstrates the new "electric" coffeemaker, mid 1930's

arranged in a T shape, one making up the bar, the other serving as the kitchen. Terry Young, the bartender and manager, told me, "The wooden wheels are still on it, though I wouldn't suggest going down there." The practice of converting trolleys and diner cars into eating establishments was so popular in the early part of the twentieth century that companies emerged to fabricate the restaurants without the wheels—and the modern diner was born.

Today, Brown's is a beloved spot in Nashville and has numerous regulars, famous and not. Vince Gill loves the burgers, as do Marty Stuart and Faith Hill, among other members of Nashville's country elite. Johnny Cash dedicated an album to the place and John Prine was as comfortable there as you will be. According to a regular, Prine was at the bar one night when someone recognized him and put one of his songs on the jukebox. Apparently, Prine stood up and mimicked himself continuing to sing along to his own music and giving the bar patrons a twisted, impromptu karaoke performance.

Randy, a 25-year veteran of Brown's, told me "This is a good anti-anorexia place." I'm assuming he was referring to the gloriously unhealthy menu that includes, beyond burgers, grilled cheese, Frito pie, hush puppies, and a catfish dinner. The only salad on the menu is coleslaw. The burger at Brown's has been on the menu since it opened in 1927. It's made from a daily delivery of fresh chuck, hand

pattied to around five ounces. A cheeseburger comes with mayo, tomato, lettuce, and onion on a squishy white bun with pickles speared to the top. If you ask for a cheeseburger, you don't get mustard. If you ask for a hamburger, you do. I'm confused too—just read the menu and have another Budweiser.

DYER'S BURGER'S

205 BEALE STREET
MEMPHIS, TN 38103
901-527-3937

FALL/WINTER HOURS
MON–THURS & SUN 11 AM–9 PM
FRI & SAT 11 AM–5 AM
SPRING/SUMMER HOURS
MON–THU & SUN 11 AM–1 AM
FRI & SAT 11AM–5AM

No hamburger restaurant in America flaunts the method of deep-frying a burger like Dyer's in Memphis, Tennessee. There are other burgers out there that are cooked in skillets of bubbling proprietary, blended grease, but Dyer's goes to the extreme and employs a two-foot-wide skillet that I'm guessing holds more than three gallons of grease. But that's not all. Dyer's claims the grease has never been changed since the restaurant opened almost a hundred years ago.

I know this sounds nuts, but according to previous owner Tom Robertson, the grease has never been changed, just added to. "We'll top off the grease but never throw it out and start over," he told me as I interviewed him for my film, *Hamburger America*. As I sat there in disbelief, he produced one photograph after another documenting the momentous, police escorted moving of the grease from the old location to the new. On some news footage I obtained for the film, you can hear someone say, "As soon as the mayor gets here we'll go inside and make some lunch!" Now I've really seen it all.

The burgers are not deep-fried in just any old grease. Dyer's uses beef tallow, or rendered beef fat to add to the decades-old skillet. You'd think your burger would emerge from the grease a sludgy disaster, but quite the opposite occurs. The grease of course adds flavor, but the burger turns out being no greasier than a regular, griddled burger. It's probably because of this that some regulars ask to have their bun *dipped*, which is where the top half of the bun is returned to the skillet for a dip in the grease.

The method for cooking a burger at Dyer's is the most peculiar of any burger counter in America. A quarter-pound wad of fresh ground beef is placed on a marble surface. A large spatula rests atop the meat as the cook pounds the beef into a paper-thin patty nearly eight inches wide. The flat beef is then scraped off the surface and slid into the nearby skillet of bubbling, brown grease. Within a minute, the patty floats to the top and it's done. Ask for cheese and watch what happens. The cook lifts the patty out of the grease with the spatula, places an orange square of cheese on it, and the patty is quickly dipped back *into the grease to melt the cheese.*

If you want to broaden your horizons, order their most popular sandwich—the deep-fried bologna sandwich.

Mississippi native Elmer Dyer opened Dyer's Restaurant in 1912 in the midtown section of Memphis. The burger shack proudly served both blacks and whites, though in the Southern tradition before the civil rights movement, they had to enter though separate doors. At some point, Dyer's moved around the corner to Poplar and North Cleveland, and from there made its historic move to Beale Street. The North Cleveland location became a Vietnamese restaurant that curiously continued to sell deep-fried burgers among a selection of traditional Vietnamese dishes.

The Dyer's of Beale Street comes off as a tourist trap, but maintains the fabled grease and uses only fresh ground beef for the burgers. If you want to broaden your horizons, order the second most popular sandwich at Dyer's—the deep-fried bologna sandwich. Previous owner Tom once told me bluntly, "If you are watching your health, I recommend going next door."

ROTIER'S RESTAURANT

2412 ELLISTON PLACE
NASHVILLE, TN 37203
615-327-9892
MON–FRI 10 AM–10:30 PM
SAT 9 AM–10 PM
CLOSED SUNDAY

Nashvillians are proud of Rotier's and the burger that is served there on French bread. At first glance, the burger looks impossible to eat, a tower of edible elements that defy gravity, thanks, only to those, feathery sandwich toothpicks. And that bread—why the big loaf of French bread? "My father ordered some loaves of French bread from Sunbeam one day in the '40s to serve with our spaghetti," owner Margaret Crouse told me. One thing led to another and the famous Rotier's cheeseburger on French bread was born. Despite how tall the burger looks, it's a breeze to eat and the supersoft bread cradles the burger patty and condiments perfectly.

It should be a good burger. It has been on

the top of every best burger list in Nashville for decades. Loretta Lynn, Tim McGraw, and Faith Hill are all fans of the cozy dive. Jimmy Buffett used to sit at the bar and write songs and eat burgers regularly back in the late '60s when he lived in Nashville, prompting many to assume that he penned the famous "Cheeseburger In Paradise" at Rotier's. Alas, he did not.

Evelyn and John Rotier opened their tavern and restaurant in 1945 just steps from the esteemed Vanderbilt University. Today, the giggly, effervescent Margaret Crouse, daughter of the Rotiers, owns the dark, comfortably broken-in tavern with her brother Charlie Rotier. "I've worked here for 34 years," she told me, but many of her employees can boast similar claims. Grill cook Pamela has been flipping hand-pattied burgers for almost two decades. Her mother gave her the job after she had flipped burgers there for over 30 years, starting in 1951.

There are three burgers on the menu at Rotier's and the descriptions can be somewhat confusing. The well-known "cheeseburger on French bread" is self-explanatory, but order a grilled cheeseburger and it comes on white or wheat toast. Order just a cheeseburger and you'll get the same patty on a white squishy bun. The six-ounce burgers are hand pattied every morning from over 200 pounds of fresh-ground chuck. A burger with everything comes with lettuce, onion, and tomato. Order a "half & half" and you'll get a plate with both fries and onion rings.

Other than hamburgers and the surprisingly good spicy fried pickles, Rotier's is also known for its plate dinners that come with Southern sides like lima beans, broccoli casserole, and fried okra. And don't miss Eddie Cartwright's Lemon Ice Box Pie, a tangy, creamy dessert similar to key lime pie with a buttery graham cracker crust. Jack-of-all-trades Eddie and his pie recipe have been at Rotier's for over twenty years.

My good friend from Nashville, Vadis Turner, told me once, "My dad took me here for my first burger. It is the kind of place where you bring your kid to get them their first real hamburger."

Pamela the grill cook was taking a break near the bar, smoking a cigarette, waiting for the next rush. "This place is a home away from home for a lot of people," she mused. "Once you sit down, you don't want to get up."

ZARZOUR'S CAFE

1627 ROSSVILLE AVENUE
CHATTANOOGA, TN 37408
423-266-0424
MON–FRI 11 AM–2 PM
CLOSED SATURDAY & SUNDAY

Zarzour's is one of the places I visited where I had wished this book wasn't just about hamburgers. In addition to serving up one of the best burgers I've ever had,

Zarzour's also provides a meat-and-threes menu that the locals love. But even if burgers were the only draw, it's worth a trip to this South Chattanooga food gem.

Zarzour's burgers are not on the menu. Local lunch patron Blythe Bailey told me, "I came here a few times before I realized they even made burgers." I asked Shannon Fuller, a Zarzours family member, grill chef, and master of ceremonies, why the burgers were not advertised. "Because I hate making them!" she said laughing hard, "Just kidding! But in the summertime it gets real hot in here because of the burgers."

It couldn't be a friendlier place. Everyone knows one another and some descendant of Zarzour is always in the restaurant either eating or working. "They come here to eat and I put every damn one of them to work—go clear that table," Shirley Fuller told me.

Shirley is the matriarch of the family, owner, and third-generation Zarzour. Her grandfather, Charles Zarzour, a Lebanese immigrant, opened the café in 1918. Shirley is in charge of the desserts for the three hours a day the restaurant is open. If a pie is running low, she'll spot a regular with a favorite and tell them so.

The burgers are large. How large? Shannon made an air patty with her hands "about this big" and burst out laughing. "And the large burger is this big!"and she made a bigger air patty. Each burger is pattied to order. Shannon scoops ground chuck out of a Tupperware dish next to the grill, hand forms a patty and places it on the small, flattop griddle in the front part of the restaurant, surrounded by customers. No burger is the same, though she gets pretty close. If you ask for grilled onion, a thick slice is cooked like a burger patty on the griddle. A cheeseburger with everything comes with pickles, lettuce, tomato, onion, mayo, and mustard on a seeded, toasted bun.

From the outside, Zarzour's doesn't look like much. Look for the small painted-brick structure with heavily fortified windows. The only warmth on the exterior is the red-checked curtain hanging in the window of the front door. Inside you'll find just the opposite—a warm country café with tables of all sizes covered with the same red-checked fabric and a capacity crowd happy to be there.

Besides burgers, I watched plates of great Southern food be dispatched to tables. Butter beans, collard greens, and skillet corn bread are on the menu, as is the local favorite, lemon ice box pie.

The tables all have clear bottles filled with odd science experiments: things like homemade chow chow relish and pickled okra. One bottle's contents even the waitress could not identify, but I'm sure it was tasty.

It would be easy to miss out on a lunch at Zarzour's if you showed up, for example, after 2 p.m., or on a weekend. I asked Shirley why they are only opened for 15 hours a week and she explained succinctly with a smile, "That's all I want."

BURGER HOUSE

6913 HILLCREST AVENUE
DALLAS, TX 75205
214-361-0370
WWW.BURGERHOUSE.COM
OTHER LOCATIONS AROUND DALLAS
AND ONE IN AUSTIN, TX
OPEN DAILY 11 AM–9 PM

Any visit to Dallas, Texas, warrants a stop at this tiny, beloved burger stand. Impossibly small and showing its age, Burger House (aka Jack's from a previous owner) serves excellent, fresh-meat burgers to hungry college students and locals in this wealthy Dallas suburb. Constantly topping best-of lists, Burger House, opened in 1951, has been a favorite of Dallas natives for generations.

Jack Koustoubardis built Burger House and worked at the Hillcrest location flipping burgers for over 30 years. Even though there is no mention of his name anywhere in the restaurant's signage, dedicated regulars still refer to the restaurant as Jack's Burger House. In 1982, friends of Jack's, Angelo Chantilis and Steve Canellos, bought the burger stand and the recipe for its now famous "seasoned salt." The salt goes onto all of the burgers and fries and creates the taste that regulars crave.

The restaurant is split in two—one part a tiny, fluorescent-lit diner (no more than two hundred square feet) with a few stools and a narrow counter, the other an alleyway dining room with a sloped concrete floor and carved-up picnic tables. Of curious note, the stand closes every night at 9 p.m., but the dining room side stays open all night. Manager Nicholas told me, "That's just the way it was. Jack kept it open all night." Angelo, aware of the extremely low crime rate in this suburb, confirmed the policy, but said of would-be thieves, with a chuckle "Let 'em walk in instead of breaking the damn glass."

The most popular burger at Burger House is the double cheeseburger. Every morning Burger House gets a delivery of large, flat quarter-pound patties of 80/20 chuck. Angelo told me, "We buy from a local purveyor of meat and they only give us the best." The burgers have been cooked on the well-seasoned, original griddle from opening day at Burger House, a griddle that's over 50 years old. A wide, toasted sesame-seed bun is standard, as are shredded lettuce, tomato, onion, pickles, and mustard. The double with cheese is a large, two-fisted wad of greasy goodness that will fill you up and have you dreaming about your next visit even before you take your last bite.

The seasoned salt, a garlicky secret recipe invented by Jack's brother Jerry, is so popular that in the 1990s Angelo and Steve decided to bottle and sell the stuff. "People would walk off with the shakers of the salt that we put out," Angelo told me, "so we figured we should just start selling it." Now you can attempt to re-create Jack's burger at home.

Today, Burger House is a mini-chain with

five locations around Dallas and more to come. The enormous Mockingbird location (with its large dining room and drive-thru) does the most business, but it's the original Hillcrest location with its red, white, and blue neon sign that burger lovers visit to get their dose of Americana. I asked Angelo if there were plans to keep expanding, and he responded with an emphatic. "Hell yeah." Angelo's confidence in the franchise led me to believe that there might just be one near you in the future.

CASINO EL CAMINO

517 EAST 6TH STREET
AUSTIN, TX 78701
512-469-9330
WWW.CASINOELCAMINO.NET
OPEN DAILY 4 PM–2 AM

Casino El Camino is not a burger joint. It's a dark punkabilly rock bar with tattooed and pierced patrons that maintains one of the best jukeboxes just about anywhere. People go to Casino to drink and listen to great tunes at this bar on the Sixth Street party strip in downtown Austin, Texas. I was in a rock band for 10 years so I feel at home in a place like Casino. But it wasn't until my third visit that I realized they offered amazing burgers to the buzzed clientele.

I was informed of Casino's burger prowess by a film crew member of mine in Austin, John Spath, who begged me to give it a shot. In a town whose burger culture is dominated by Hut's and Dirty Martin's, and in a state enormously burger-proud, I was skeptical. Even John commented, "It's not the kind of place you'd expect to find good food."

I approached the tiny opening in a dark back corner of the bar to place my order. The small kitchen is manned by a staff of one. A solitary chef takes orders, preps buns, and grills the burgers. When the chef on duty that night, Orestes, was through tending to burgers on the grill, he reluctantly sauntered over to take my order. I waited over half an hour, but for my patience I was rewarded with a heavenly burger.

The burgers at Casino el Camino start as fresh-ground 90 percent lean chuck that's hand formed into 3 quarter-pound patties. They are cooked on an open-flame grill, placed on a bun, halved, then the two halves are placed back on the grill again, cut side down, to achieve a decorative *grill brand* on the cross section of your burger. It should be noted that cooking over a flame and achieving decent results don't often go together. Most grill cooks, especially those working from a Weber in their backyards, manage to overcook and ruin burgers. Every time I've been to Casino, the burger has been cooked perfectly. Casino el Camino cooks their burgers to temperature. If you ask for rare, get out the napkins and listen for that mooing sound. The cooks know what they are doing. Even a medium-well comes out juicy.

Don't be alarmed when your burger shows up on a wheat bun. In this dark punk rock hang, a wheat bun was probably the last thing you'd expect. It's quite the opposite—the kitchen's attention to quality, from the toppings to the beef, follows through to the bun.

The menu lists burger concoctions that use the three-quarter-pound burger model and add condiments. There's the Buffalo Burger, which is not actually buffalo beef, but a regular burger topped with hot wing sauce and blue cheese. Or try the Amarillo burger with roasted serrano chiles, jalapeno cheese, and cilantro mayo. My favorite is the standard bacon cheeseburger with cheddar, listed as the Chicago Burger.

Casino el Camino is both a bar and a person. Casino el Camino, the stage name for this rocker and bar owner, came to Austin for the famed South by Southwest Music Festival in 1990. He was impressed with the forward-thinking Texas town and told a friend back in Buffalo, NY, that it would make a great spot for a bar. "Before I went I thought Texas was all tumbleweeds and fucking cowboys," the Long Island, NY, native admitted. Casino el Camino, the bar, became a joint venture between Casino and the Buffalo restaurateur, Mark Supples.

Expect to wait for your burger, sometimes forever. Casino told me, "The grill only holds 15 burgers at a time so we are limited in what can come out of that small kitchen." On busy nights the wait can be over an hour. But so what? Enjoy the music, gawk at the crazy piercings, and get a drink. If you complain, you may make it worse. Just remember, this is not fast food. It's slow food at its best.

CHRISTIAN'S TAILGATE BAR & GRILL

7340 WASHINGTON AVENUE
HOUSTON, TX 77007
713-864-9744
MON–FRI 10 AM–9 PM
SAT 11 AM–9 PM
BAR OPEN TO MIDNIGHT

Imagine walking into an open mike night at a Texas roadhouse and finding Billy Gibbons, front man of ZZ Top, on stage. At Christian's this is entirely possible because Billy's good friend Steve Christian owns the place.

Manager Kim told me, "He'll come in and put his name on the list for open mike." When the Texas rocker comes to town, Christian's is his first stop for drinks and one of the best burgers in Houston. "Billy thinks Steve is all that and a bag of chips."

Steve Christian is the third-generation owner of this roadhouse burger joint just off I-10 west of downtown Houston. Steve's grandfather opened Christian's Totem in the early '40s as a convenience store and icehouse. Before refrigeration and air conditioning, icehouses were integral to daily life in warm climes. Steve told me, "Guys would come down here to get ice for their wives and end up staying and drinking beer for a while." The beer fridge used to sit in the parking lot with a padlock on it. "My grandfather would leave for the night and toss the guys the key. Eventually, Christian's became a bar."

Steve's grandfather and father ran Christian's as a convenience store and a roadside bar for over 50 years. Steve told me, "In the '40s this was a dirt road out here," pointing to the impossibly busy Washington Avenue, large trucks rumbling in every direction. After a stint as a DJ in a topless club and a job as a crane operator, Steve told his dad he wanted to be the third-generation owner of Christian's. When he took over the business he had plans for expansion. Part of his plan was to put a great burger on the menu, and that burger wins "Best of Houston" awards annually.

The burger to get is the jalapeno cheeseburger—a fresh-ground, half-pound, griddled two-fister that comes in a green plastic basket on a toasted white bun with lettuce, onion, tomato, pickle, mustard, and mayo. The jalapenos are snappy and hot and complement the large portion of meat well. Halfway through my burger I had a good sweat going and a slight buzz from the heat. "I only buy cold-packed jalapenos. They are the only ones that have a crunch," Steve explained. "I've spent years getting the ingredients just right."

The crowd at Christian's is mixed. It's common to see construction workers, businessmen in suits, and tourists all enjoying their burgers. Kim, the bar's infamous "burger Nazi," told me, "There's such a variety you'd be amazed. See those guys over there? Undercover cops." Kim is both loved and feared at Christian's. She gives everyone crap as they walk in the door, including me. Her warning to all—"Come in here messin' around and I'll chew you up!"

In 2004, Steve changed the longtime name of the bar from Christian's Totem to Tailgate Bar & Grill for purely logistical reasons. "We were not really a 'totem' any longer (Texas vernacular for the convenience store) and we were getting too many calls from people thinking we sold religious books." The Tailgate in the new name conjures up images of face-painted football fans in parking lots eating buffalo wings. Not so here. Steve has modified and welded actual pickup truck tailgates that serve as wall sculpture, and one supports a large plasma TV over the bar. *Guy Art* to the extreme.

This burger joint will be around for a while. Steve plans to turn the business over to his son eventually. "We'll see. He's only five years old now!"

DIRTY MARTIN'S PLACE

2808 GUADALUPE STREET
AUSTIN, TX 78705
512-477-3173
WWW.DIRTYMARTINS.COM
OPEN DAILY 11 AM–11 PM

Dirty Martin's does not serve thick, gourmet burgers. Dirty Martin's serves excellent, greasy, thin-patty burgers to Austin locals and students from the nearby University of Texas. Alongside these famed grease bombs, Dirty's also serves a guilty pleasure of yours and mine—the deep-fried tater tot.

Opened in 1926 as Martin's Kum-Bak Place by John Martin, the burger counter earned the nickname "Dirty's" for the dirt floor that remained until 1951. The original counter had just eight stools inside and most of the business was conducted in the parking lot with carhops. Today, the carhops are gone and the dirt floor has been covered for half a century, but Dirty's is still cranking out great burgers over 80 years from opening day.

The menu at Dirty Martin's is loaded with great bar food geared to pre and post-party revelers in search of nourishment. The lunch crowd looks to be on the other end of the spectrum,

nursing hangovers. There are many choices on the menu, but the burgers are king at Dirty's.

The burgers start as fresh ground, thin patties. They are cooked on a flattop griddle and slid onto waiting toasted sesame seed buns. It seems that the thinness of the patty allows the grillman to cook burgers faster.

Have fun trying to interpret the somewhat cryptic burger options on the menu. Ask for a hamburger and you'll get a single patty with mustard, onion, pickle, and tomato. Ask for a large hamburger and get the same but twice the meat (two patties). Then there's the infamous "Sissy Burger," which replaces the mustard and onion with mayonnaise. I asked the grill team about the definition of a Sissy Burger and was directed to a man named Wesley sitting at the end of the counter. Wesley Hughes, retired from the grill, flipped burgers at Dirty's for 45 years. He bluntly explained to me, "Mustard is strong and not for sissies." I deduced that mayo *is* for sissies and left it at that. If you need a double-patty burger with mayo, be prepared to tell your waiter you need a "Big Sissy."

Few restaurants in America have the guts to put tater tots on their menus. This trashy little potato treat somehow has the ability to get crispier than fries and retains more grease (or flavor). You can go to the freezer aisle of your supermarket, buy a bag of tots, and cook them in your oven, but we all know how that tastes. Tater tots are best enjoyed deep-fried at places like Dirty Martin's. And what could be

better than tater tots? How about the ultimate guilty pleasure—cheese tots.

If you find yourself hungry and near the University of Texas, don't hesitate to stop at the oldest burger stand in Austin. Order some cheese tots and a double burger and look for Wesley at the end of the counter during lunch. He's Dirty Martin's unofficial Head of Public Relations and knows how to spot a sissy, so order yours with mustard.

HUT'S HAMBURGERS

807 WEST 6TH STREET
AUSTIN, TX 78703
512-472-0693
MON–SAT 11 AM–10 PM
SUNDAY 11:30 AM–10 PM

Hut's Hamburgers is not on the party drag in downtown Austin, Texas, where the crowds migrate to East 6th street. This out-of-the-way burger restaurant is on the quiet west end of 6th street, identifiable from blocks away by its vintage green and red neon sign. Follow the arrow on the sign to the odd-shaped 1930s red, white, and blue building.

The history of Hut's is so convoluted that I'll spare you the details and give you the skinny version. Basically, Homer "Hut" Hutson opened Hut's Hamburgers on South Congress in 1939. Across town the same year, Sammie Joseph opened Sammie's Drive-In on West 6th street. In 1969, after numerous owners, Sammie's became Hut's.

The Memorial Day Flood of 1981 devastated downtown Austin. A witness to the aftermath described it as looking like a week of hurricanes had rambled through town. The west side of town, particularly where Hut's is situated, was destroyed. A local newspaper noted that through all the death and destruction, Hut's remained standing, prompting the phrase "God Bless Hut's."

Since 1981 Hut's has been owned and run by two families, the Hutchinsons and the Gists. Kim Hutchinson told me, "Since we bought Hut's very little has changed. We make everything from scratch." The Hut's they purchased was still selling burgers and chicken-fried steak, but the Hutchinsons updated the menu. The restaurant now offers salads and daily blue-plate specials like fried catfish on Fridays, but every time I've been to Hut's, I'm there to consume one of their award-winning burgers.

If you are looking for variety, you have come to the right place. Hut's serves high-quality, fresh-meat burgers with just about any topping you can think of. The menu is loaded with cute names for the burgers like the Alan Freed (with hickory sauce) and the Beachboy (with pineapple). Stick to the basics like the Hut's Favorite, a bacon cheeseburger, and be rewarded with an unforgettable burger experience.

A rarity in the burger world, Hut's gives you the option to choose the type of meat for your burger. Hut's offers traditional fresh ground beef, buffalo, or Texas longhorn. "We added buffalo and longhorn to the menu for health reasons," Kim told me. Both Texas Longhorn beef and buffalo meat are superlean, and in the case of Longhorn beef, low in the type of fat that causes bad cholesterol. The one-third-pound patties are cooked on a well-seasoned flattop griddle. The longhorn beef and buffalo meat come from a nearby ranch, and the traditional cow beef comes to Hut's as 90 percent lean ground chuck.

By noon most days, the restaurant is packed. On game days (the University of Texas is nearby) expect to be waiting on line or at the bar surrounded by fans decked out in UT orange. Use the time you'll spend waiting for a table to browse the flood photos on the wall. By the time you bite into your burger, you'll be glad Hut's was saved too.

KINCAID'S HAMBURGERS

4901 CAMP BOWIE BOULEVARD
FORT WORTH, TX 76107
(VARIOUS OTHER LOCATIONS
AROUND FORT WORTH)
817-732-2881
MON–SAT 11 AM–8 PM
CLOSED SUNDAY

A visit to Kincaid's is a must on the burger trail in America. The restaurant is a revamped corner grocery that today is profoundly dedicated to the American hamburger. Most burgers found in Texas fall into the half-pound category and a hamburger at Kincaid's is no exception. The good word spread in the early 1970s that Kincaid's was serving up a stellar burger in the rear of the store. It was only a matter of time before burger sales eclipsed grocery sales and the rest is history. Today, Kincaid's grinds and patties up to 800 pounds of fresh beef daily (you read that correctly). For groceries, you'll have to go elsewhere.

Kincaid's is located on a corner on the edge of a quiet residential neighborhood in Fort Worth and the atmosphere inside and out is laid-back and comfortable. Inside, the long, original stock shelves remain in place, their tops sawed off to act as surfaces to stand at, unwrap your burger, and dig in. It was O.R. Gentry, a meat cutter and manager at the grocery store, who bought the business from the ailing Charles Kincaid in 1967. It was O.R. who cut down those shelves and created countertops out of old doors he found for $1. And it was O.R. who created one the greatest burgers in America, a burger whose fame is so widespread that it can claim fans from every corner of the globe.

"He started with a $25 grill," Lynn Gentry said of her father-in-law. "O.R. would take the prime meats that didn't sell and grind them to make hamburgers the next day," Lynn explained. As the need for the corner grocery faded in America in the 1970s (spurred by the proliferation of the supermarket), O.R. began to focus more on burgers and less on groceries. When his son Ronald took over the business in 1991, he and wife Lynn did away with the remaining groceries for good. "We pulled out all of the produce bins and refrigeration in the front and replaced them with picnic tables," Lynn told me. "We needed the space."

Kincaid's is a gigantic place. Today it's a clean, functional, bright restaurant where the integrity of the old grocery has been preserved. The concrete floors are polished to a high shine, and the original neon grocer's sign continues to glow red over the front door. The interior walls are still painted sea-foam green and Lynn told me, "The local hardware store calls this color Kincaid's Green." The restaurant can accommodate up to 280 burger enthusiasts, either standing or sitting, in over 3,500 square feet of space.

Every day Kincaid's grinds on premises the

meat for their half-pound burgers. They use only chuck steaks from organic Texas beef that is free from hormones and steroids. The burgers are cooked on two six-foot flattop griddles. You can cook a lot of burgers with 12 linear feet of griddle space.

The burger is served on a white, seeded, toasted bun with tomato, shredded lettuce, pickles, yellow mustard, and thinly sliced onions. The elements of this burger are so well balanced that, taken as a whole, they create a nearly perfect burger experience and in turn a euphoric first bite. Curiously, the burger's condiments are placed underneath the burger instead of the standard above-the-patty placement. "We do that for speed," Lynn explained, pointing out that the buns are prepped before the burgers come off the grill. The inverted burger actually allows the juices from the meat to drip into the condiments and Lynn told me, "We think it makes the burger taste better."

Kincaid's is a family business. The Gentrys two sons work at the restaurant and Lynn's father retired from American Airlines and has been the manager of Kincaid's for over a decade. In the last few years, the Gentrys have opened a few new locations around Fort Worth including a 5,000 square foot replica of the original complete with sawed-off grocery shelves and "Kincaid's green" painted walls.

Many refer to the burger at Kincaid's as the best in Texas. That's a mighty claim in this burg-er-proud state. It is a claim that the Kincaid's burger lives up to and a challenge the Gentry family takes in stride.

LANKFORD GROCERY

88 DENNIS STREET
HOUSTON, TX 77006
713-522-9555
MON–SAT 7 AM–3 PM
CLOSED SUNDAY

"There's nothing better than a good burger," was the first thing out of Edie Prior's mouth when I told her about the book I was working on. Edie is the owner of Lankford Grocery, a breakfast-and-burger destination opened by her parents, Nona and Aubrey Lankford, in 1939. From 1939 to 1977 the Lankfords operated the business as a grocery store before turning it into the café it is today. The only visible evidence of the store's past are the original Coca-Cola grocer's sign out front and the large enameled steel meat case separating the kitchen from the dining area. "I don't have the heart to pull it out," Edie said of the case. "We use it for storage now."

Lankford's is a funky place with a lot of heart and soul. There's a wall with pegs where locals hang their personal coffee mugs, the floor is impossibly slanted and creaky, the ceiling is low, and each table has a roll of paper towels in lieu of napkins. Edie heavily decorates the restaurant depending on the season. My first visit was just before Halloween so you can imagine the décor. "We just took down our summer theme," Edie's brother Jimmy told me, "We had beach balls and stuff hanging from the ceiling."

Jimmy also works at Lankford making change and small talk at the end of the counter. He said to me, referring to the much-debated *GQ* magazine hamburger list, "What do these swanky men know about good hamburgers anyway?" True. A real man would do well to put one of these burgers down—a Texas-sized, fresh meat, two-fister.

Burgers at Lankford's are cooked to perfection on a flattop griddle, juicy on the inside and crisp on the outside. They start as hand-pattied fresh ground meat and are roughly eight ounces. Order a double and you are getting a pound of meat. The burger to order is the Bacon Double Cheeseburger (the bacon single works just fine, especially if you plan on eating again that day). The burgers come with shredded lettuce, red onion, pickles, tomato, cheese, mayo, mustard, and copious amounts of crisp bacon. All of this is served on a large toasted bun with a single toothpick straining to keep the contents vertical. I'm a hamburger professional and can deftly maneuver the sloppiest of burgers with ease, but this one got the better of me. "Uh, would you like a fork?" Jimmy said, sensing my struggle with the unruly pile of ingredients.

There are other burgers on the menu that sound excellent, like the Soldier Burger, explained best by waitress Robin. "A man walked in one day and asked for a burger with an egg on it, so I did it!" Or try the Fire House Burger that contains a homemade habanero paste. "It is REALLY hot!" Edie warned me as she approached with a mason jar containing an orange paste. "Just try a little . . . do you have water?" The paste contained radishes, onion, mustard, and habanero peppers and was hot as hell. It was a deep-down hurt though, not a sharp pain, with lasting heat. Would I spread this on a burger? Absolutely.

Lankford's is only open for breakfast and lunch, so don't plan on having dinner there. Burgers are served all day though, starting when they open at 7 a.m. "People order burgers for breakfast, right when we open," Edie told me.

The small, sleepy café looks slightly out of place in this neighborhood very close to downtown Houston. "We used to be able to see the buildings downtown. These were all vacant lots," Edie pointed out. Those lots are being quickly transformed into condos and other large construction projects. Edie plans to be around for a while though. She wants to leave the business to family one day but told me, "I plan on being here as long as I can flip that burger."

TOOKIE'S

1202 BAYPORT BOULEVARD
SEABROOK, TX 77586
281-474-3444
SUN–THU 11 AM–9 PM
FRI & SAT 11 AM–10 PM

Tookie's is not in Houston. A burger friend once told me it was "near Houston" and I'm guessing that by Texas standards a 60-mile round trip for lunch is nothing. Regardless, I'd drive a hundred miles to eat a burger at this Texas roadhouse, the home of the Squealer.

Food writer and burger savant John T. Edge informed me that no trip to the Houston area would be complete without a Squealer in my belly. Houston food critic Robb Walsh backed up the claim and I was off.

Seabrook, Texas, is sort of midway between Houston and Galveston and is home to astronauts and scientists employed by the nearby Johnson Space Center. Tookie's sits near a crossroads of the main drag in Seabrook and a road awkwardly named NASA 1 Road. For those working at the Space Center, Tookie's is only a short drive down this road. For everyone else, it's a destination.

Tookie's serves a few unique burgers, but it's the Squealer that'll have you planning your next trip back to Seabrook. Imagine fresh ground beef mixed with fresh ground bacon, pattied, griddled, and placed on a bun. The taste is expectedly sublime and ups the ante on the traditional bacon cheeseburger. John T. described this unique burger creation best when he told me, "If a mule is the result of a donkey mating with a horse, then Tookie's Squealer is a kissing cousin from a similar marriage of a pig to a cow. The resulting beast is better for it." The Squealer is basically a wad of beefy bacon with a crispy, salty exterior. The bacon gives the burger a blush-red color and there's even a warning on the menu to prepare for this color shift. At a quarter pound, the Squealer is small compared to most Texas burgers. If you are feeling hungry, order the Piggyback and you'll get a burger with two Squealer patties.

Other burger creations include the Bean Burger, which includes refried beans and crushed Fritos. Or try the super-hot Stomp's Ice House Special, which includes jalapenos, hot sauce, and grilled onions. A regular "hamburger" has been banished to the bottom of the list, understandably, because you came here to eat the Squealer.

Chuck steaks and hickory-smoked bacon are ground by a local butcher. The elements are combined in top-secret proportions, balled, and flattened on the griddle. The bacon-to-beef ratio for the Squealer is so classified that a neighboring restaurant sent their son to work at Tookie's with the mission to steal the recipe. "It didn't work," Jim confided. "The kid was just a dishwasher and didn't really know what was going on."

Before it was a hamburger destination, the structure housed a soft-serve ice cream business, then became a location in the now-defunct local burger chain Bonus Burger. In 1975 Jim Spears opened Tookie's and remains the sole proprietor over three decades later. The name came from a long-gone drugstore in Humboldt, Texas, called "Tooker Brothers." Jim explained, "We wanted the restaurant to feel like an old drugstore."

The interior of Tookie's has a homespun roadhouse feel. "We've added onto the building seven times," Jim told me. The rambling multi-room restaurant is filled with all sorts of authentic bits of road culture and Americana and seems sturdy enough to take some punishment. Everything from a vintage barber pole to a full-sized gas pump surrounds you while you eat. Waitress Kathy told me, "Every time you look up you notice something different."

Another must-eat at Tookie's are the amazing lightly battered and fried onion rings. They are made fresh twice daily at the restaurant and an order consists of a large, perfectly balanced pile of the bracelet-sized rings. On average, the restaurant will make almost 300 orders of onion rings a day.

On your way out, take note of the large painting of a woman behind the register. It's a portrait of Evelyn Walsh McLean, a Galveston grande dame and apparently the last private owner of the Hope diamond. Jim picked it up in an antique store years ago, unaware of its subject or provenance. "A lot of people think it's Mrs. Tookie," Jim told me laughing, "and it's just a name we made up."

CROWN BURGERS

(MULTIPLE LOCATIONS)
118 NORTH 300 WEST
SALT LAKE CITY, UT 84103
801-532-5300
MON–SAT 10 AM–10:30 PM
CLOSED SUNDAY

Behold the Crown Burger. At first you see what appears to be a pastrami sandwich, then, upon closer inspection, realize that your wildest fantasies have just come true—you are gazing at a cheeseburger stuffed to bursting with warm, thinly sliced pastrami.

Unique to Salt Lake City and its neighbors, the pastrami cheeseburger is a beloved Utah burger that, according to some locals, is best represented at the Greek, owned Crown Burger chain.

The Crown I visited was the second built (in 1979) in Salt Lake City. I was assured that the other six Crowns were similar, which is hard to believe given the almost indescribable décor of the interior of this restaurant. "Back in the '70s my family was in the Greek nightclub business," Mike, son of owner Manuel Katsanevas, tried to explain. Gargoyles, stuffed quail in flight, large chandeliers, Greek statuary, lush wallpaper, and a huge working fireplace round out the phantasmagorical setting. "We know we are fast food but we wanted to create an upscale dining experience," Mike told me.

It's true—don't be put off by the large staff in uniform behind the counter working at warp speed, multiple registers, numbers being called over a loudspeaker, and a general feeling of ordering food at one of the superchains. As you wait for your number to be called you stand between an ancient nine-foot-tall ornately carved wooden hutch and a grandfather clock, both salvaged from a hotel in France. "People ask all the time if this stuff is for sale," Mike said, pointing to the clock. "No, it is not."

The genius behind Crown is their business plan, which could only be pulled off by an intensely proud Greek family (they are actually from Crete). Each restaurant in the chain is independently owned by a family member. They share recipes and suppliers to maintain sameness and quality.

Your wildest fantasies have come true: a cheeseburger stuffed to bursting with warm pastrami

The burgers come in fresh as quarter-pound patties "every morning," Manuel explained. The menu is large and eclectic and includes hot dogs, tuna sandwiches, a fish burger, and, you guessed it, some of the best souvla-ki and gyros in town.

The Crown Burger, char-broiled over an open flame, comes wrapped tightly in waxed paper and includes lettuce, tomato, chopped onion, American cheese, and of course, gobs of pastrami. My warning to you—do not remove the waxed paper prior to hoisting this beast to your lips. It will explode and the pastrami will end up in your lap.

The idea for pastrami on a cheeseburger was imported from Anaheim, California, by a relative of the Katsanevas family. "Uncle James had a restaurant called Minos Burgers and served a pastrami burger," Mike explained. When he moved to Salt Lake, he brought the idea to his family.

The burger also includes a Utah curiosity called fry sauce. For those unfamiliar with the fast-food habits of Utahans, fry sauce is basically ketchup and mayo mixed together. Mike told me "We make our own fry sauce in house, made of seven ingredients, most of them secret." The sauce is mainly used as a dip for fries.

The Katsanevases have been approached more than once with offers to franchise but have resisted. Fear that the quality of their product would decline was not their only reason. "We make a comfortable living and we're happy with the way things are," Mike told me. "We have worked very hard for everything we have. Besides, this couldn't be a franchise; everything is made to order!"

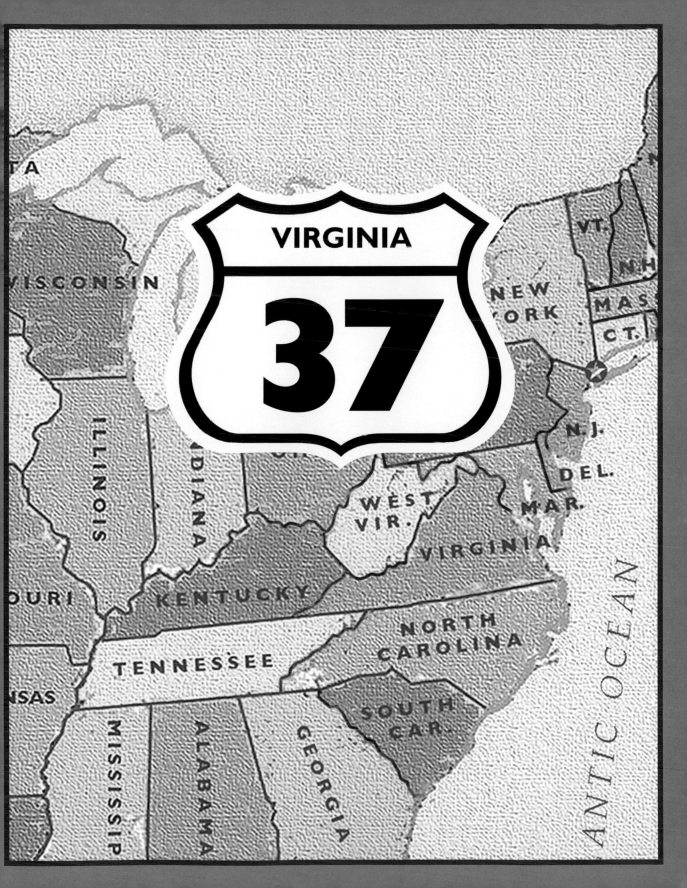

TEXAS TAVERN

114 W. CHURCH AVENUE
ROANOKE, VA 24011
540-342-4825
WWW.TEXASTAVERN-INC.COM
OPEN 24 HOURS A DAY,
7 DAYS A WEEK (EXCEPT CHRISTMAS)

"I hope you plan on having a Cheesy Western" were the first words out of Matt Bullington's mouth after I had introduced myself. I was thrown, because I thought I had come to the Texas Tavern for a straightforward hamburger, possibly a thin patty on a white bun. What Matt was selling me was actually the most popular burger at his over 75-year-old hamburger stand.

The Cheesy Western is a glorious combination of fried egg, thin hamburger patty, cheese, pickle, onion, and relish on a soft white bun. "We sell hundreds of Cheesys a day, especially to the late-night crowd," Matt told me. How late? "We're open all night." In fact, the only time the Texas Tavern closes is for part of Christmas Eve and day.

Matt is the great-grandson of Nick Bullington, the man who opened the tiny hamburger stand in 1930. "My great-grandfather saw Roanoke as a boomtown and decided to build his restaurant here." In the 1920s Roanoke had a vibrant locomotive construction industry. Nick, an advance man for the Ringling Brothers Circus, had collected recipes from his extensive travels around the U.S. He had observed the best ways to make hamburgers (no doubt gleaning what he could from the success of White Castle at the time), had adopted a mustard-based relish from a circus recipe, and most importantly had borrowed a chili recipe from a hotel in Texas.

Curiously, the chili and burgers are sold separately as they have been for over seven decades. A chili burger is absent from the menu, though Matt said "A few people order them, but not many." The chili is so popular at the restaurant that it can be taken away by the gallon if necessary. That may be because the chili is more soup than condiment.

The grill area is just inside the front window, which was typical of burger joints of the era. The cook's station is a testament to efficient food prep. A hot dog steam box sits in front of a deep canister of chili. Next to that is the impossibly small 12-by-18-inch griddle. To the right of the griddle are two small burners for frying eggs and a box containing burger buns, relish, pickles, and onions. The entire complement of ingredients and cooking apparatus to prepare everything on the menu occupies a mere six square feet—absolutely amazing.

The Texas Tavern is a rare specimen of a bygone era because nothing has changed since it opened. "Everything is original," Matt told me. The dented countertop, worn footrest, and 10 lumpy red leather stools all feel so real. Some repairs to the griddle in 1975 are the extent of any "renovations," outside of the frequent paint jobs that keep the place looking as fresh and inviting as it may have in 1930.

A quote posted in the restaurant calls the tiny burger counter "Roanoke's Millionaire's Club". Matt explained, "We get all types in here. Whether you are the governor or a hobo you'll be treated like a millionaire at the Texas Tavern."

EASTSIDE BIG TOM

2023 EAST 4TH AVENUE
OLYMPIA, WA 98506
360-357-4852
WWW.EASTSIDEBIGTOM.COM
OPEN DAILY 10:30 AM–8 PM

Big Tom could easily be the most nondescript burger stand in America. If it were not for the large menu on the street side of the building, you'd think you had arrived at a construction trailer that had been haphazardly dumped in a parking lot. But the long lines of cars on each side of the structure are a hint that something good is happening inside. Indeed there is. Big Tom daily sells over 500 fresh thin-patty wonders to loyal drive-up customers. But that's not all. Big Tom's trademarked "Goop" is dispensed here, a salad-type dressing that, in varying forms, is a Pacific Northwest mainstay for burgers.

"Goop is essentially mayo, mustard, and pickle relish with a secret salad dressing mixed in," longtime owner Chuck Fritsch told me. "What's the saying? 'If I told you I'd have to kill you'?" he said with a laugh. "It's really not a big secret," he admitted, "But if you are not making it in huge batches it doesn't taste the same." I can see why someone might want to copy the recipe—the taste is addictive. Besides adorning the Big Tom special double-double, Goop is also offered as a dip for the tater tots and fries. What could be more appealing or more American than "Tots 'n Goop"?

In 1948 Millie and Russ Eagan opened a burger stand east of downtown Olympia and called it (coincidentally) In and Out. Millie took her inspiration for a drive-thru from a popular motor court across the street. For the original stand the Egans relocated a minuscule barbershop from another part of town. Since then, the stand has been rebuilt and changed names more than once, but has always been on the same spot. Through the decades the Egans expanded to nine stands in and around Olympia, but today only one remains.

Big Tom was the son of Millie and Russ Eagan. Overweight and inventive, he was known to help himself at the griddle and created a large burger that was not on the menu. Today it's a best seller at the burger stand that bears his name, a double meat, double cheese burger with lettuce, tomato, chopped onion, and the famous Goop. Be prepared for the inevitable dripping Goop as you take your first bite. Chuck told me, "We are known for making a sloppy burger." Chuck buys fresh ground 18 percent fat thin patties for the burgers at Big Tom. They are cooked on a flattop griddle that is usually filled to capacity with the sputtering patties.

The interior of Big Tom, which is all kitchen, is a lesson in functionality. An astounding amount of prep and cooking is done in the 288 square feet that is populated by up to seven employees at peak times. Every square inch is utilized—think submarine galley.

Chuck started working at the tiny burger stand in the '50s when he was 15 years old peeling potatoes. "It was warm and dry and sitting in a cubicle did not appeal to me," Chuck said about his longevity in the business. He is a true entrepreneur. The diesel pickup truck that makes the 90-mile round-trip to and from work each day is fueled by fry oil from Big Tom. "I used to have to pay to dispose of it." Now he drives down the road smelling like burning French fries. Chuck, closing in on 50 years at Big Tom, plans eventually to turn the business over to one of his sons, who literally grew up in the stand. Chuck pointed to a small space between the employee bathroom and slop sink. "We had the crib right there."

GOOP SAUCE, MY WAY

Goop is the sauce that adorns just about every burger in the Pacific Northwest. All of the goop sauces I've had taste pretty much the same, yet all contain highly secret ingredients. I've attempted to re-create goop sauce here, but remain fully aware that the best place to try this heavenly condiment is at places like the Eastside Big Tom in Olympia, WA, and Dick's in Seattle.

MAKES ENOUGH FOR 12 BURGERS
½ cup mayonnaise
¼ cup sour cream
4 teaspoons sweet relish
4 teaspoons yellow mustard

Mix contents. Spread on your favorite burger. The color should resemble a stock canary yellow Plymouth Barracuda. Tell your friends it's not the real thing, but pretty damn close. I can hear Chuck from Big Tom laughing as he reads this recipe.

DICK'S DRIVE-IN

111 N.E. 45TH STREET
SEATTLE, WA 98105
206-632-5125
MULTIPLE LOCATIONS AROUND SEATTLE
WWW.DDIR.COM
OPEN DAILY 10:30 AM–2 AM

At first glance Dick's looks like it might be a tired old drive-in serving frozen hockey pucks for burgers. But Dick's is anything but tired, and as the locals know, it's as vibrant as ever, serving excellent fresh-beef burgers, addictive fries, and hand-dipped milkshakes. The '50s have come and gone, but Dick's remains over five decades later, proving that simplicity and good food are the keys to longevity.

Dick's is a drive-in. There are five locations around town and only one has indoor seating. It's the sort of drive-in where you park your car and walk up to the window to order and pay. General manager Ken Frazier told me, "Dick's has always been a walk-up. Originally there were three separate lines, one for shakes and ice cream, one for burgers and soft drinks, and one for fries." In the '60s Dick's streamlined the system selling, all products at all windows. At the 45th Street location there's no seating anywhere and Maria, the longtime manager, told me, "In the summertime people bring picnic tables and chairs and set up in the parking lot. It's really cute."

The first Dick's was built in 1954 in the Wallingford neighborhood of Seattle just west of the University of Washington. On my first visit to the popular burger stand I arrived 15 minutes before opening to find workers inside scurrying to ready the griddle and cook the fries. There was no one in the parking lot. But within five minutes a hungry mob had gathered. When the first window called, "May I take your order?" I counted 45 people waiting to get their "Dick's Fix," a phrase a regular left me with.

The efficiency of Dick's is mind-boggling. Twenty-four employees, all wearing crisp paper caps and clean aprons, are set to repetitive tasks such as weighing the fresh ice cream that goes into the shakes or prepping the buns with their secret sauce.

The menu is simple—hamburgers, cheeseburgers, fries, shakes, and soda. The thin patties of fresh steer beef are delivered to all locations in the chain every morning. The burgers, cooked on a flattop griddle, can be ordered plain or as the preferred Dick's Deluxe. The Deluxe comes with two quarter-pound patties, cheese, lettuce, mayo, and their special chopped pickle and mustard sauce. The sauce, a tangy, sweet, and creamy proprietary blend, should not be missed. All burgers are served on the perfect white squishy bun wrapped in waxed paper.

If you love fries, you'll be in French fry heaven at Dick's. The fries are lightly greasy, thin, and fresh, not frozen. The shakes, also incredible, only come in the three classic flavors of chocolate, vanilla, and strawberry.

If you ask for extra sauce for your burger or ketchup for the fries you'll get a little serving in a small condiment cup, but expect to pay. Ketchup and other condiments are five cents extra and the reason is mostly environmental, not financial. "We feel that the cup is much nicer to use for dipping than some foil pouch," Ken explained, "and by charging a nominal amount we feel we are minimizing waste." Gotta love a burger joint with a conscience.

The people of Seattle *love* Dick's. I was hard-pressed to find a carnivore who didn't frequent the place. Bill Gates visits frequently. "Last week he had a Deluxe, fries, and a shake," Maria told me. Even Sir Mix-A-Lot, Grammy Award winner and Seattle native, immortalized the Broadway location in his first hit song. In the lyrics, his posse skips Taco Bell for Dick's. The truth is, if there were more places like Dick's, serving wholesome, fast food, we'd all be skipping Taco Bell.

DOTTY DUMPLING'S DOWRY

317 NORTH FRANCES ST.
MADISON, WI 53703
608-259-0000
WWW.DOTTYDUMPLINGSDOWRY.COM
OPEN 7 DAYS 11AM–1AM

Dotty's is in its fifth location in over 35 years. "Goddamn eminent domain was the reason for the last move," Jeff Stanley mumbled when I asked him about the moves. Seems the latest incarnation of Dotty's is working for him though. The exterior resembles a working-class Irish pub complete with black paint, small-paned windows, and the bar's name in gold. The interior is impressive—quality-crafted dark wood, large inviting bar, and an astounding collection of model aircraft dangling from the ceiling. There is even an eight-foot scale model of the Hindenburg positioned over the grill area.

Friend and columnist Doug Moe, who

referred to Jeff as "The Hamburger King of Madison" directed me to Dotty's. Jeff's bigger-than-life persona is infectious and he is a well-liked underdog around town. He is damn proud to hold the title of king and knows his burgers. The first time I walked into Dotty's, Jeff announced, "Hey everybody! This is the guy who made that hamburger film!"

"We only use the highest-quality ingredients," Jeff said as I took a big swig from my beer. His burgers are made from six ounces of fresh-ground chuck, pattied in-house. They are grilled on an open flame in plain sight of all customers and placed on specially made local buns that have been warmed and buttered. Grill master David explained, "Jeff requests that the buns are not cooked fully so they remain soft." David is a bit of an anomaly in the burger world. Not that other burger chefs don't have his love of the craft, but none to date have been comfortable quoting celebrity chef Anthony Bourdain. "Have you read his stuff on kitchen cleanliness?"

This attention to detail and Jeff's public persona have put Dotty's on the top of local hamburger polls for decades. Being a stone's throw from the University of Wisconsin's Kohl Center and Camp Randall Stadium doesn't hurt either.

The name Dotty Dumpling's Dowry comes from an Arthur Conan Doyle short story, the same writer who brought us Sherlock Holmes.

Dotty's menu is extensive, including an ostrich dish and the bar has an impressive 24 beers on tap. But please don't leave Dotty's without trying their excellent deep-fried cheese curds—they are indeed a necessary evil.

THE PLAZA TAVERN

319 N. HENRY STREET
MADISON, WI 97213
608-255-6592
WWW.THEPLAZATAVERN.COM
OPEN DAILY 11AM–10:45PM

The sauce is the draw and its ingredients are most definitely kept secret. Only a handful of insiders know the 40-plus-year-old recipe. "A bunch of restaurants claim they serve a Plaza Burger but they don't," grill-man Mick told me with assurance. "Hey, I don't even know the recipe!" Which is a little strange for a guy who probably made over a thousand of the thin patty wonders that week alone. Owner Dean Hetue sequesters himself in a locked room in the kitchen to concoct the creamy white, tangy sauce the Plaza has been putting on their burgers since the mid-1960s. "All I can tell you," Mick went on, "is that it's a sour cream and mayo-based sauce, and the rest is a secret." Whatever it is, this unique topping is good. Very, very good.

The Plaza is a tavern first, so the burgers at this popular watering hole seem like an afterthought. Cooked on a tiny griddle next to the long rows of hard booze, their unique arrangement of elements suggests that this is more than just another bar burger (fresh beef, wheat bun, and salad dressing). And regardless of the Plaza's standard collegiate look and feel, the burger is anything but standard. Fresh, thin quarter-pound patties are grilled in plain sight of bar patrons, placed on incredibly soft wheat buns, and served with a dollop of the secret dressing/sauce. The presence of a wheat bun actually makes it feel like you could have one or two more, guilt-free.

The bar feels like an enormous romper room for adults, complete with endless diversions for the buzz-addled, ranging from darts to pool and with pinball and video games for the solo drinkers. There are TVs everywhere and The Plaza's sheer size suggests that large, boisterous crowds can fill the place (with the University of Wisconsin around the corner that's not difficult to imagine, and it's been rumored that Joan Cusack was once tossed from the bar). But the few times I've been there (during lunch) I pretty much had the place to myself.

The Plaza has been a bar for over a century, with a stint as a speakeasy during Prohibition. In 1963 Mary and Harold Huss bought the bar and introduced their burger. Mary concocted the now-famous sauce and placed her burger on a half-wheat bun that is still used today.

Dean started working at the Plaza in 1980 in hopes that one day he might own the place. "I figured that if I stuck around long enough . . ." His patience paid off, and in 2003 the second generation of the Huss family sold Dean the tavern—and the recipe for the secret sauce. "I have a great photo of me handing Tom Huss the check and he's handing me the recipe," Dean told me laughing. "It almost looks like we are in a tug-of-war." That recipe now rests in a safe deposit box, and in Dean's head. "My wife knew the recipe, but it's been five years since she's made the sauce. I'll bet she forgot."

Owner Dean Hetue sequesters himself in a locked room to concoct the secret tangy sauce that has accompanied the Plaza burgers since the 1960s.

The menu at the Plaza is limited to things you might eat while drinking, i.e. "bar food." Hot dogs and a fishwich are available, but you'd be wise to indulge in a few Plaza Burgers. They also serve one of my favorite sides, a not-to-be-missed treat of the upper Midwest, the fried cheese curd. Imagine a rustic, homespun version of the processed mozzarella stick and you'll get the picture. Impossibly good, these deep-fried, random-sized wads of breaded fresh cheese are worth every calorie.

The Plaza sits on a bizarre little street near the state's capitol building and among the bustling stores catering to Madison's large student population. "There's so little parking out front," Dean mused, "so it's amazing that so many people find their way here." Dean has noticed, in his nearly three decades at the tavern, students turn into alumni and continue to patronize the Plaza. "It's the sauce that brings them back."

PETERSON'S HAMBURGER STAND AND ICE CREAM PARLOR

200 EAST RACINE STREET
JEFFERSON, WI 53549
920-674-3637
MON-SUN 10:30 AM–9:30 PM
FRI & SAT 10:30 AM–10:30 PM

Somewhere south of Route 94 on a lonely stretch of highway between Madison and Milwaukee sits a gem of a burger stand. I was tipped off to Peterson's by good friend and burger icon himself, Glenn Fieber of Solly's Grille in Glendale, WI. He told me, "Ya gotta go out there, he's making a great little burger."

The stand at Peterson's is actually 8½ x 8½ feet, which is 65 square feet—small for a place that can move up to 600 burgers on a busy day.

When I asked Bill Peterson, owner of the nearly century-old stand, the size of his minuscule, he went inside the larger adjacent ice cream parlor and produced a tape measure. The parlor, formerly a grocery store and at one time a hat shop, is over 800 square feet larger than the separate stand that sits proudly on the corner. Longtime Jefferson residents Bill and his wife Janet bought the stand in 2002 from Rick Armstrong, becoming the seventh owners. While under Armstrong's ownership the stand was leveled by a reckless drunk driver, two kids were flipping patties inside. Miraculously, the employees survived with only grease burns but parts of the stand were scattered for blocks. The original griddle, a perfectly seasoned, low-sided, cast-iron skillet was recovered from the debris. A small hole was patched and it was put back into service. After much cajoling the stand was rebuilt on the same spot. I asked Bill why he wouldn't just move the burger operation into the larger ice cream parlor but I knew the answer. "The people of Jefferson won't allow me to change anything. I can't break tradition."

The burger is a classic one-sixth-pound patty griddled and served on a white squishy bun. Bill grinds chuck steaks in the basement of the parlor, throws in some "secret seasonings" (tastes peppery) and rolls the grind into small golf ball–size balls. The balls are smashed thin on the 90-year old griddle and cooked until the edges are crispy.

The grillmen, or boys, are all-American

small-town stock. Tony and Bert are barely 20 but have been flipping burgers at Peterson's all through their teens. I couldn't help but notice that when things got slow behind the grill Bert would step out of the stand and sit on the steps of the ice cream parlor. Do you think he was trying to avoid being the next victim of a hit and run? I do.

SOLLY'S GRILLE

4629 NORTH PORT WASHINGTON ROAD
MILWAUKEE, WI 53212
414-332-8808
MON 10 AM–8 PM
TUE–SAT 6:30 AM–8 PM
SUN 10 AM–8 PM

For the burger purist and lover of the things that make America unique, a visit to Solly's is imperative. Pure and simple, Solly's serves one of the last *real* butter burgers in the nation. When I say "real" I'm referring to the copious amounts of creamy Wisconsin butter that is used on their burgers, as opposed to what their surrounding competition calls a butter burger. To everyone else who peddles this great Wisconsin treat, the burger bun is coated with a thin swipe of butter, much in the way you might butter your toast if you were on a diet. Solly's dramatically bends the rules and treats the butter as a condiment. In other words you actually won't believe how much butter goes on the burger. The first time I visited

Solly's, I stood and watched that which I had only heard about from disbelieving past patrons. Could they really use upwards of two three tablespoons of butter on one smallish cheeseburger? Oh yes, they do, and have been for over 70 years.

I kid you not when I say that a butter burger at Solly's, as gross as it may sound, is an absolutely sublime experience in the gastronomic fabric of America and should be experienced by all. You may also catch yourself doing what I did subconsciously on my first visit—dipping the last bite of your burger *back into the pool of butter on your plate*. You quickly discover that whatever guilt you harbored while taking your first bite has dissolved by your last.

In 1936 Kenneth Solomon bought Bay Lunch in Milwaukee a clean 16-stool diner that served coffee, hamburgers, and bratwurst, and changed the name to his own. In 1971, he relocated Solly's Coffee Shop a few miles north to the Milwaukee suburb of Glendale. He left the restaurant to his second wife, Sylvia, and she in turn sold the business to her son and current owner Glenn Fieber.

The cheery and cherubic Glenn, fresh from a successful construction business, was faced with an unusual dilemma early in his ownership—move or perish. In 2000, the city government actually assisted Glenn in moving the entire restaurant a few hundred yards south to make way for, of all things, an outpatient heart clinic.

The interior of Solly's is a comfortable

blend of yellow Formica horseshoe counters, swivel stools, and wood paneling. As they have been for decades, the burgers, fries, and shakes are all prepared in view of the counter patrons.

The fresh-ground 3-ounce thin patties show up at Solly's daily and are cooked on a large flattop griddle. The toasted buns are standard white squishy but a soft "pillow" bun is also offered. There are many burger combinations and sizes (like the impressive two-patty "Cheese Head" that an ex Navy Seal friend of mine devours with ease), but I suggest doing what my good friend and butter burger devotee Rick Cohler has been doing for over 50 years at Solly's—just order a butter burger.

Rick introduced me to Solly's. On our first visit together he begged me to try a burger "without" which is a burger on a bun with butter only, no onions. I obliged and immediately understood what all the fuss was about. As you bite into a freshly built butter burger you actually have the opportunity to experience the texture of soft butter before it melts into a pool on your plate. Unlike Rick, my "usual" at Solly's is a burger with onions. The stewed onions at Solly's are like none other I have experienced. They are both sweet and salty, and full of flavor. I could eat a bowl of them with a spoon.

Glenn is one of my truest allies in the burger world. He understands his place in American history and his duty to supply hungry burger lovers with a treat as unique as the butter burger.

ACKNOWLEDGMENTS

'm not a writer, I'm a filmmaker. My quest to find America's greatest burgers and the people who make them started with a film I made called *Hamburger America*. As a result of that project and the research for this book I have amassed an absurd amount of hamburger knowledge. I owe a debt of gratitude to dedicated food experts in many parts of the country for pointing me in the right direction and filling my brain and belly with unforgettable burger experiences.

Many thanks to Rick Kogan for being the president of the George Motz Fan Club and smelling success in hamburger reportage far before anyone else could. To columnist Doug Moe who hosted me in Madison, Wisconsin, and food writer Robb Walsh who made sure I was on the right track in Houston, Texas. To Ed Levine from the *New York Times* for giving me tips on writing. To columnist Marshall King, my host in Indiana, and Jim Ellison, who led me through Ohio. To Tom Palmore and Bill Peterson, who introduced me to great burgers in Oklahoma. To friend Greg Ennis, who led me to burger greatness in Montana and protected me from drunken rugby players. And Rick Cohler who will never say no to a Butter Burger (or three) at Solly's Grille. To Kacy Jahanbini for venturing into Ann's Snack Bar before I did, and to Mac Premo for flying all the way to Meers, Oklahoma just to be

nearly killed by a buffalo. And to John T. Edge, the dean of the school of hamburger, a writer, and a man who truly understands the importance of regional food in America. Thanks also to Josh Osersky, Melena Ryzik, Jason Perlow, and Adam Kuban, all food and culture writers of the highest order. And of course to all of the tipsters who gave me advice about their favorite hamburger joint, whether they were driving the airport rental car shuttle, at the hotel bar, or sending me endless amounts of e-mail. And thanks to my food photography mentor, Greg Ramsey, and Ports Bishop, friend, photographic consultant, and expert burger taster.

This book never would have seen the light of day had it not been for my agent, Laura Dail, and my patient editor, Jennifer Kasius, at Running Press. Both women share a love of hamburgers and were unstoppable in making this the best book ever on the subject. Thanks also to everyone else at Running Press, especially designer Matt Goodman and publicity whiz Craig Herman.

The cooperation of the restaurants involved made writing this book a pleasure (with the exception of Ann's Snack Bar). Enormous thanks is due as well to my close friends and family who have supported me and my burger mission from the start. And most importantly, my vegetarian wife, Casey, and children Ruby and Mac, who have endured enough of my meat exploits to last a lifetime